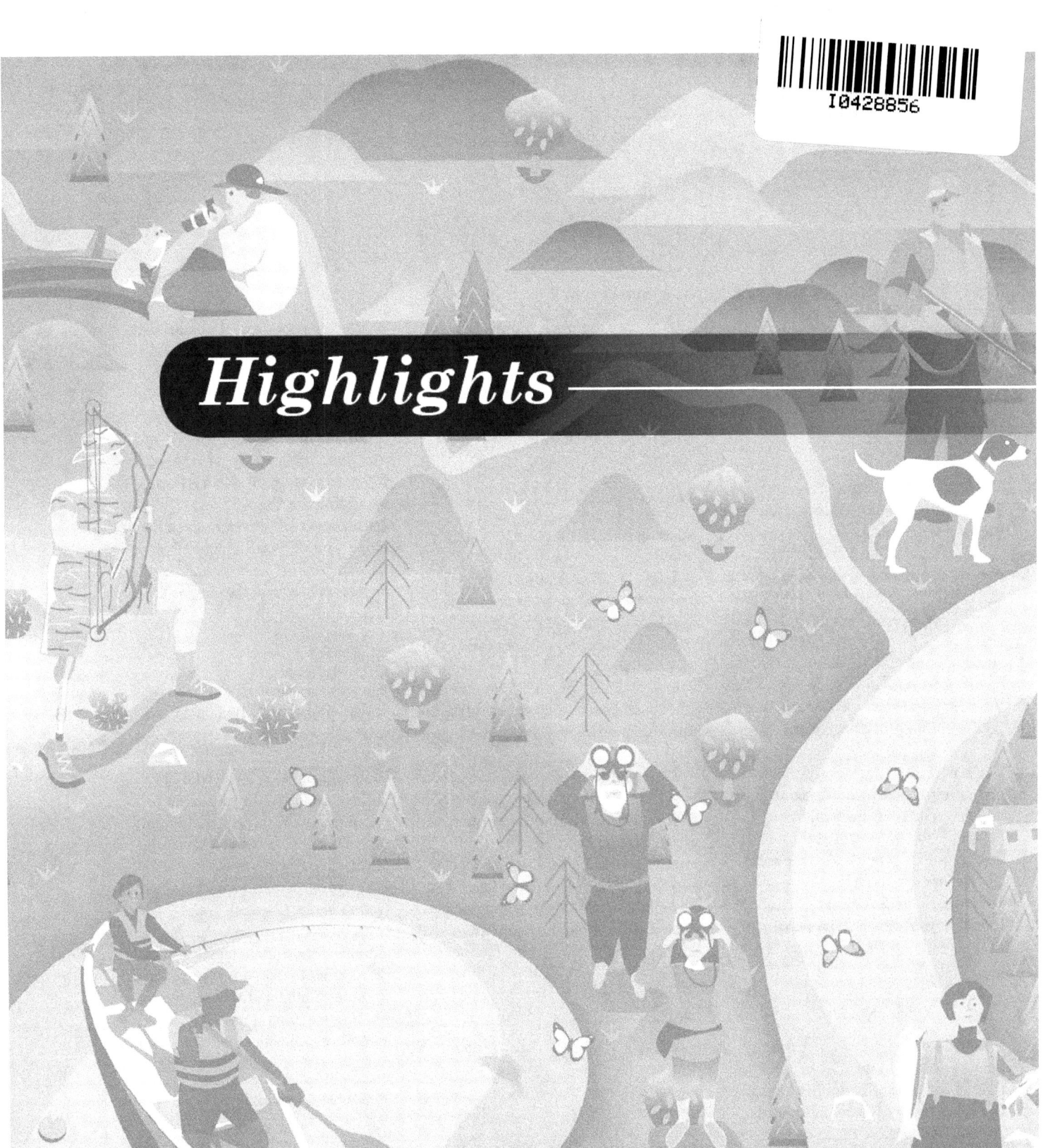

Highlights

Introduction

The National Survey of Fishing, Hunting, and Wildlife-Associated Recreation reports results from interviews with U.S. residents about their fishing, hunting, and wildlife watching. This report focuses on 2011 participation and expenditures of persons 16 years of age and older.

However, in addition to 2011 numbers, we also provide trend information in the Highlights sections and Appendix C of the report. The 2011 numbers reported can be compared with those in the 1991, 1996, 2001, and 2006 Survey reports because they used similar methodologies. However, the 2011 estimates should not be directly compared with results from Surveys conducted earlier than 1991 because of changes in methodology to improve accuracy.

The report also provides information on participation in wildlife-related recreation in 2010, particularly of persons 6 to 15 years of age. The 2010 information is provided in Appendix B. Information about the scope and coverage of the 2011 Survey can be found in Appendix D. The remainder of this section defines important terms used in the Survey.

Wildlife-Related Recreation

Wildlife-related recreation is fishing, hunting, and wildlife-watching activities. These categories are not mutually exclusive because many individuals participated in more than one activity. Wildlife-related recreation is reported in two major categories: (1) fishing and hunting, and (2) wildlife watching, which includes observing, photographing, and feeding fish or wildlife.

Fishing and Hunting

This Survey reports information about residents of the United States who fished or hunted in 2011, regardless of whether they were licensed. The fishing and hunting sections report information for three groups: (1) sportspersons, (2) anglers, and (3) hunters.

Sportspersons

Sportspersons are those who fished or hunted. Individuals who fished or hunted commercially in 2011 are reported as sportspersons *only* if they also fished or hunted for recreation. The sportspersons group is composed of the three subgroups shown in the diagram below: (1) those that fished and hunted, (2) those that only fished, and (3) those that only hunted.

The total number of sportspersons is equal to the sum of people who only fished, only hunted, and both hunted and fished. It is not the sum of all anglers and all hunters because those people who both fished and hunted are included in both the angler and hunter population and would be incorrectly counted twice.

Sportspersons

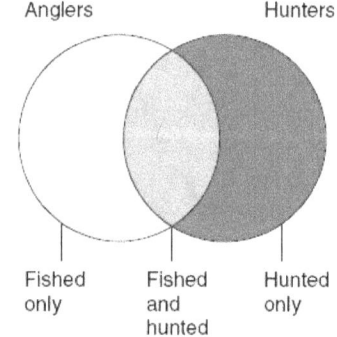

Anglers   Hunters

Fished only   Fished and hunted   Hunted only

Anglers

Anglers are sportspersons who only fished plus those who fished and hunted. Anglers include not only licensed hook and line anglers, but also those who have no license and those who use special methods such as fishing with spears. Three types of fishing are reported: (1) freshwater, excluding the Great Lakes, (2) Great Lakes, and (3) saltwater. Since many anglers participated in more than one type of fishing, the total number of anglers is less than the sum of the three types of fishing.

Hunters

Hunters are sportspersons who only hunted plus those who hunted and fished. Hunters include not only licensed hunters using rifles and shotguns, but also those who have no license and those who engage in hunting with archery equipment, muzzleloaders, other primitive firearms, or pistols or handguns.
Four types of hunting are reported: (1) big game, (2) small game, (3) migratory bird, and (4) other animals. Since many hunters participated in more than one type of hunting, the sum of hunters for big game, small game, migratory bird, and other animals exceeds the total number of hunters.

Wildlife Watchers

Since 1980, the National Survey has included information on wildlife-watching activities in addition to fishing and hunting. However, unlike the 1980 and 1985 Surveys, the National Surveys since 1991 have collected data only for those activities where the *primary* purpose was wildlife watching (observing, photographing, or feeding wildlife).

The 2011 Survey uses a strict definition of wildlife watching. Participants must either take a "special interest" in wildlife around their homes or take a trip for the "primary purpose" of wildlife watching. Secondary wildlife watching, such as incidentally observing wildlife while pleasure driving, is not included.

Two types of wildlife-watching activity are reported: (1) away-from-home (formerly nonresidential) activities and (2) around-the-home (formerly residential) activities. Because some people participated in more than one type of wildlife watching, the sum of participants in each type will be greater than the total number of wildlife watchers. Only those engaged in activities whose *primary* purpose was wildlife watching are included in the Survey. The two types of wildlife-watching activity are defined below.

Away-From-Home

This group includes persons who took trips or outings of at least 1 mile from home for the primary purpose of observing, feeding, or photographing fish and wildlife. Trips to fish or hunt or scout and trips to zoos, circuses, aquariums, and museums are not considered wildlife-watching activities.

Around-The-Home

This group includes those who participated within 1 mile of home and involves one or more of the following: (1) closely observing or trying to identify birds or other wildlife; (2) photo- graphing wildlife; (3) feeding birds or other wildlife; (4) maintaining natural areas of at least 1/4 acre where benefit to wildlife is the primary concern; (5) maintaining plantings (shrubs, agricultural crops, etc.) where benefit to wildlife is the primary concern; or (6) visiting parks and natural areas within 1 mile of home for the primary purpose of observing, feeding, or photographing wildlife.

Summary

The 2011 Survey revealed that over 90 million U.S. residents 16 years old and older participated in wildlife-related recreation. During that year, 33.1 million people fished, 13.7 million hunted, and 71.8 million participated in at least one type of wildlife-watching activity including observing, feeding, or photographing fish and other wildlife in the United States.

The focus of the National Survey is to estimate participation and expenditures of persons 16 years old and older in a single year. These estimates are based on data collected in the detailed phase of the 2011 Survey. They are comparable to the estimates of the 1991, 1996, 2001, and 2006 Surveys but not to earlier Surveys because of changes in methodology. A complete explanation is in Appendix C.

While the focus of the Survey is to estimate wildlife-related recreationists 16 years and older and their associated expenditures in a single year, information collected in the Survey screen can be used to estimate the number of anglers and hunters who were active over a five-year window of time. Because many do not participate every year, the following estimates may be more representative of the number of individuals considered to be anglers and hunters in the United States: 49.5 million individuals fished and 19.7 million hunted over the five-year period from 2007 to 2011.

The Survey screen also provides some information about 6- to 15-year olds' participation which was calculated by using data from the Survey screen. Assuming their proportions of participation were the same in 2011 as in 2010, the following estimates were calculated: Of the 6- to 15-year-olds in the U.S., 1.8 million hunted, 8.5 million fished, and 11.7 million wildlife watched in 2011. More information about this age group is provided in Appendix B. For the rest of this report all information pertains to participants 16 years old and older, unless otherwise indicated.

There was a considerable overlap in activities among anglers, hunters, and wildlife watchers. In 2011, 69 percent of hunters also fished, and 28 percent of anglers hunted. In addition, 51 percent of anglers and 57 percent of hunters wildlife watched, while 29 percent of all wildlife watchers reported hunting and/or fishing during the year. Wildlife recreationists' avidity also is reflected in the $144.7 billion they spent in 2011 on their activities, which equated to 1 percent of the Gross Domestic Product. Of the total amount spent, $49.5 billion was trip-related, $70.4 billion was spent on equipment, and $25.1 billion was spent on other items such as licenses and land leasing and ownership.

Sportspersons spent a total of $89.8 billion in 2011—$41.8 billion on fishing, $33.7 billion on hunting, and $14.3 billion on items used for both hunting and fishing. Wildlife watchers spent $54.9 billion on their activities around the home and on trips away from home.

Total Wildlife-Related Recreation

Participants	90.1 million
Expenditures	$144.7 billion

Sportspersons

Total participants*	37.4 million
Anglers	33.1 million
Hunters	13.7 million
Total days	836 million
Fishing	554 million
Hunting	282 million
Total expenditures	$89.8 billion
Fishing	41.8 billion
Hunting	33.7 billion
Unspecified	14.3 billion

Wildlife-watchers

Total participants**	71.8 million
Around the home	68.6 million
Away from home	22.5 million
Total expenditures	$54.9 billion

* 9.4 million both fished and hunted.

** 19.3 million wildlife watched both around the home and away from home.

Expenditures for Wildlife-Related Recreation
(Total expenditures: $144.7 billion)

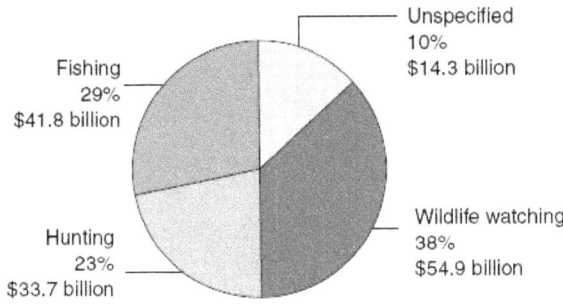

Fishing
29%
$41.8 billion

Unspecified
10%
$14.3 billion

Wildlife watching
38%
$54.9 billion

Hunting
23%
$33.7 billion

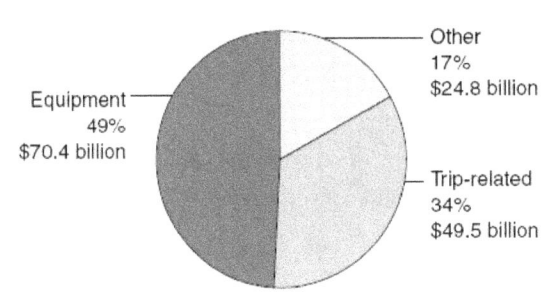

Other
17%
$24.8 billion

Equipment
49%
$70.4 billion

Trip-related
34%
$49.5 billion

Expenditures by Sportspersons
(Total expenditures: $89.8 billion)

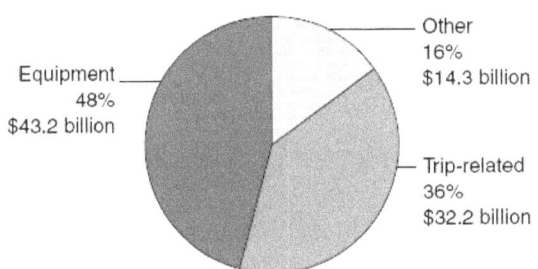

Equipment
48%
$43.2 billion

Other
16%
$14.3 billion

Trip-related
36%
$32.2 billion

Expenditures by Wildlife-Watching Participants
(Total expenditures: $54.9 billion)

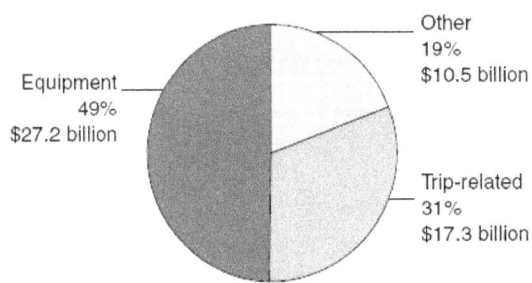

Equipment
49%
$27.2 billion

Other
19%
$10.5 billion

Trip-related
31%
$17.3 billion

Fishing and Hunting

In 2011, 37.4 million U.S. residents 16 years old and older went fishing and/or hunting. This includes 33.1 million who fished and 13.7 million who hunted— 9.4 million both fished and hunted.

In 2011, expenditures by sportspersons totaled $89.8 billion. Trip-related expenditures, including those for food, lodging, and transportation, were $32.2 billion—36 percent of all fishing and hunting expenditures. Total equipment expenditures amounted to $43.2 billion, 48 percent of the total. Other expenditures—magazines, membership dues, contributions, land leasing and ownership, and licenses, stamps, tags, and permits—accounted for $14.3 billion, or 16 percent of all sportspersons' expenditures.

Wildlife-Watching Recreation

Observing, feeding, or photographing wildlife was enjoyed by 71.8 million people 16 years old and older in 2011. Of this group, 22.5 million people took trips away from home for the purpose of enjoying wildlife, while 68.6 million stayed within a mile of home to participate in wildlife-watching activities.

In 2011, wildlife watchers spent $54.9 billion. Trip-related expenses, including food, lodging, and transportation, totaled $17.3 billion, 31 percent of all expenditures. A total of $27.2 billion was spent on equipment, 49 percent of all wildlife-watching expenses. The remaining $10.5 billion, 19 percent of the total, was spent on magazines, membership dues and contributions made to conservation or wildlife-related organizations, land leasing and owning, and plantings.

2006 and 2011 Comparison

A five-year comparison of estimates from 2006 to 2011 shows a 3 percent increase in the total number of people, 16 years of age and older, participating in wildlife recreation activities in the United States. The increase was primarily among those who fished and hunted.

Sportspersons rose from 33.9 million in 2006 to 37.4 million in 2011, and expenditures rose from $85.5 billion (in 2011 dollars) in 2006 to $89.8 billion in 2011.

In 2011, 33.1 million fished and 13.7 million hunted compared with 30.0 million who fished and 12.5 million who hunted in 2006. Although overall expenditures on fishing declined, expenditures for fishing equipment and trips were stable in 2011 compared to 2006. Expenditures for hunting equipment (firearms, ammunition, archery equipment, etc.) increased by 17 percent and for trips by 40 percent. The increase in sportspersons' expenditures was largely due to trip-related expenses, which went up 18 percent.

Equipment expenditures went down 5 percent. From 2006 to 2011 the number of wildlife watchers and their expenditures did not change significantly.

2006–2011 Wildlife-Associated Recreation Comparison of Participants
(Numbers in thousands)

	2006		2011	
	Number	Percent	Number	Percent
Total wildlife-related recreationists	**87,465**	**100**	**90,108**	**100**
Total sportspersons	**33,916**	**39**	**37,397**	**42**
Anglers	29,952	34	33,112	37
Hunters	12,510	14	13,674	15
Total wildlife-watching participants	**71,132**	**81**	**71,776**	**80**
Around the home	67,756	77	68,598	76
Away from home	22,977	26	22,496	25

2006–2011 Wildlife-Associated Recreation Comparison of Expenditures
(Numbers in billions of 2011 dollars)

	2006		2011	
	Number	Percent	Number	Percent
Total, wildlife-related recreation expenditures . . .	**136.4**	**100**	**144.7**	**100**
Total, fishing and hunting expenditures	**85.5**	**100**	**89.8**	**100**
Fishing expenditures, total	**47.0**	**100**	**41.8**	**100**
Trip-related	19.9	42	21.8	52
Equipment, total	20.9	45	15.5	37
Fishing equipment	5.9	13	6.1	15
Auxiliary equipment	0.9	2	1.1	3
Special equipment	14.1	30	8.3	20
Other	6.2	13	4.5	11
Hunting expenditures, total	**25.5**	**100**	**33.7**	**100**
Trip-related	7.5	29	10.4	31
Equipment, total	12.0	47	14.0	41
Hunting equipment	6.0	24	7.7	23
Auxiliary equipment	1.5	6	1.8	5
Special equipment	4.5	17	4.4	13
Other	6.1	24	9.3	28
Wildlife-watching expenditures, total	**50.9**	**100**	**54.9**	**100**
Trip-related	14.4	28	17.3	31
Equipment, total	25.9	51	27.2	49
Wildlife-watching equipment	11.0	22	11.3	21
Auxiliary equipment	1.2	2	1.6	3
Special equipment	13.7	27	14.3	26
Other	10.7	21	10.5	19

Fishing

Fishing Highlights

In 2011, 33.1 million U.S. residents 16 years old and older enjoyed a variety of fishing opportunities throughout the United States. Anglers fished 554 million days and took 455 million fishing trips. They spent $41.8 billion in fishing-related expenses during the year. Freshwater anglers numbered 27.5 million. They fished 456 million days and took 369 million trips to freshwater in 2011. Freshwater anglers spent $25.7 billion on freshwater fishing trips and equipment. Saltwater fishing attracted 8.9 million anglers who enjoyed 86 million trips on 99 million days. They spent $10.3 billion on their trips and equipment.

Fishing

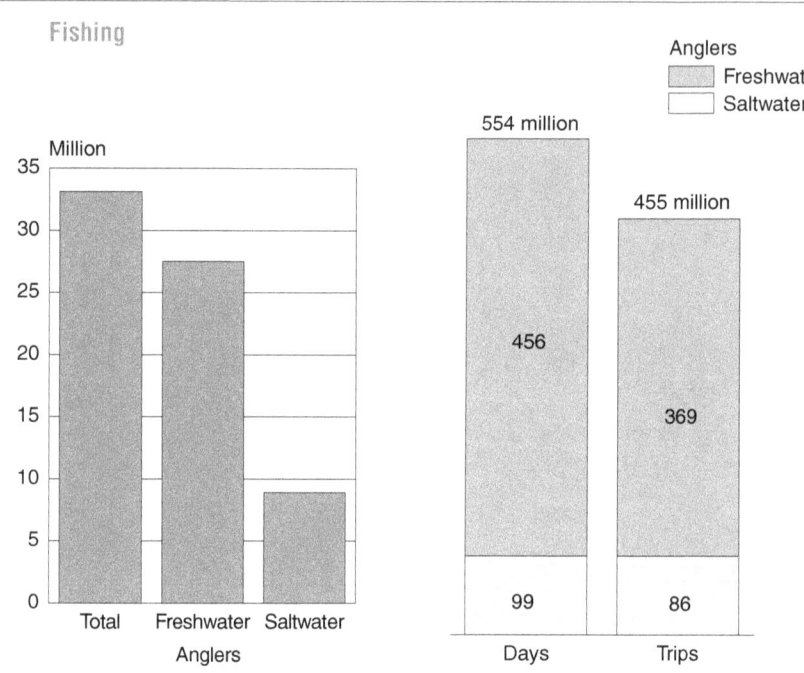

Note: Detail does not add to total because of multiple responses and nonresponse.

Total Fishing

Anglers	**33.1 million**
Freshwater.	27.5 million
Saltwater	8.9 million
Days	**553.8 million**
Freshwater.	455.9 million
Saltwater	99.5 million
Trips	**455.0 million**
Freshwater.	368.8 million
Saltwater	86.2 million
Expenditures	**$41.8 billion**
Freshwater*	25.7 billion
Saltwater*	10.3 billion
Nonspecific	5.8 billion

* Only includes trip-related and equipment expenditures

Note: Detail does not add to total because of multiple responses and nonresponse

Source: Tables 1, 12, 13, and 16

Fishing Expenditures

Anglers spent $41.8 billion in 2011 including $21.8 billion on travel-related items—52 percent of all fishing expenditures. Food and lodging accounted for $7.7 billion, 35 percent of all trip-related costs. Spending on transportation totaled $6.3 billion, 29 percent of trip-related expenditures. Other trip expenditures such as land use fees, guide fees, equipment rental, boating expenses, and bait cost anglers $7.8 billion—36 percent of all trip expenses.

Fishing equipment expenditures totaled $15.5 billion, 37 percent of all fishing expenditures. Anglers spent $6.1 billion on fishing equipment such as rods, reels, tackle boxes, depth finders, and artificial lures and flies. This amounted to 40 percent of all equipment expenditures. Auxiliary equipment expenditures, which include camping equipment, binoculars, and special fishing clothing, totaled $1.1 billion—7 percent of equipment costs. Expenditures for special equipment such as boats, vans, and cabins were $8.3 billion—53 percent of all equipment costs.

Anglers also spent a considerable amount on other fishing-related items, such as land leasing and ownership, membership dues, contributions, licenses, stamps, and permits. Land leasing and ownership spending totaled $3.4 billion, which is 8 percent of all expenditures. Expenditures on magazines, books, DVDs, membership dues and contributions, licenses, stamps, tags, and permits were $1.1 billion.

Total Fishing Expenditures

Total fishing expenditures	**$41.8 billion**
Total trip-related expenditures	**$21.8 billion**
Food and lodging	7.7 billion
Transportation	6.3 billion
Other trip costs	7.8 billion
Total equipment expenditures	**$15.5 billion**
Fishing equipment	6.1 billion
Auxiliary equipment	1.1 billion
Special equipment	8.3 billion
Total other fishing expenditures	**$4.5 billion**
Magazines, books, DVDs	0.1 billion
Membership dues and contributions	0.3 billion
Land leasing and ownership	3.4 billion
Licenses, stamps, tags, and permits	0.6 billion

Source: Table 12.

Fishing Expenditures by Type of Fishing
(Total expenditures: $41.8 billion)

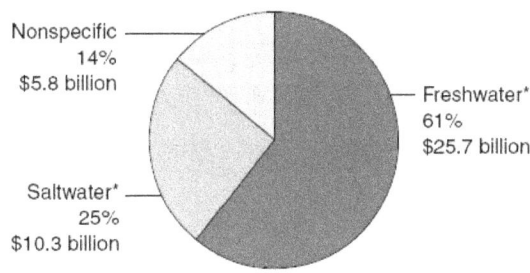

Nonspecific 14% $5.8 billion

Freshwater* 61% $25.7 billion

Saltwater* 25% $10.3 billion

* Only includes trip-related and equipment expenditures.

Percent of Total Fishing Expenditures
(Total expenditures: $41.8 billion)

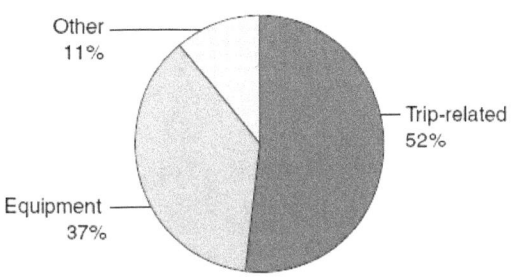

Other 11%

Trip-related 52%

Equipment 37%

Freshwater Fishing

Anglers	**27.5 million**
Freshwater except Great Lakes	27.1 million
Great Lakes	1.7 million
Days	**455.9 million**
Freshwater except Great Lakes	443.2 million
Great Lakes	19.7 million
Trips	**368.8 million**
Freshwater except Great Lakes	353.6 million
Great Lakes	15.2 million
Trip and equipment expenditures	**$25.7 billion**
Freshwater except Great Lakes	23.8 billion
Great Lakes	1.9 billion

Note: Detail does not add to total because of multiple response and nonresponse.
Source: Tables 1, 13, 14, and 15.

Freshwater Fishing Highlights

Freshwater fishing was the most popular type of fishing. In 2011, 27.5 million Americans fished 456 million days and took 369 million trips. Their expenditures for trips and equipment totaled $25.7 billion for the year. Freshwater fishing can be separated into Great Lakes and freshwater other than the Great Lakes.

There were 27.1 million anglers who fished for 443 million days on 354 million trips to freshwater other than the Great Lakes. Trip and equipment expenditures for non-Great Lakes freshwater fishing totaled $23.8 billion for an average of $879 per angler for the year. Food and lodging comprised $5.0 billion, 37 percent of total expenditures. Transportation costs were $4.5 billion or 33 percent of trip costs. Other trip expenses, which include guide fees, equipment rental, and bait were $4.0 billion for 30 percent.

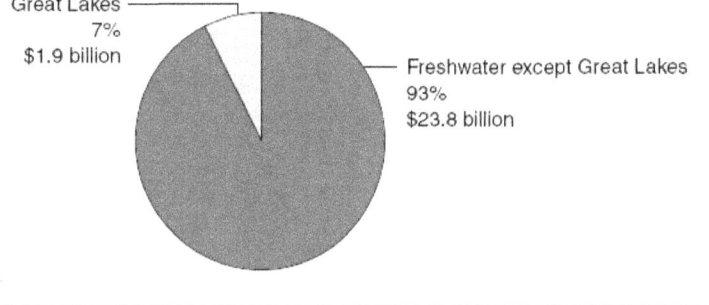

Freshwater Fishing Trip and Equipment Expenditures
(Total expenditures: $25.7 billion)

Great Lakes — 7% $1.9 billion

Freshwater except Great Lakes 93% $23.8 billion

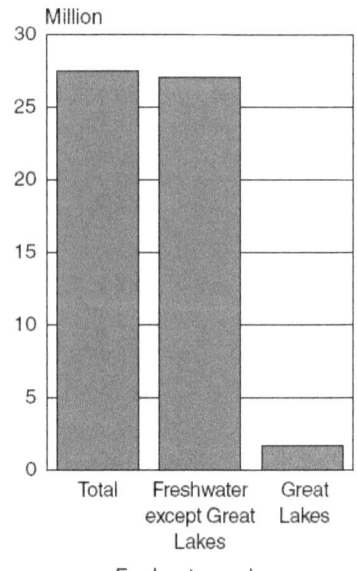

Freshwater Fishing

Million

Freshwater anglers

Note: Detail does not add to total because of multiple responses and nonresponse.

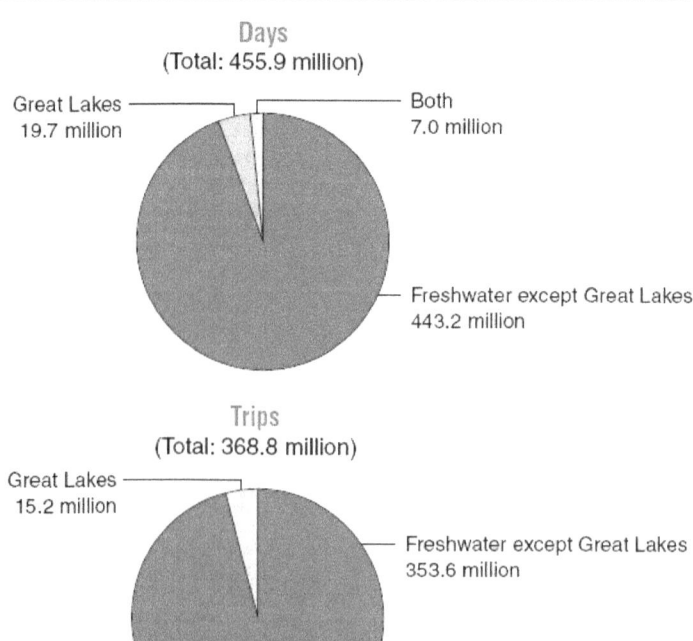

Days
(Total: 455.9 million)

Great Lakes 19.7 million

Both 7.0 million

Freshwater except Great Lakes 443.2 million

Trips
(Total: 368.8 million)

Great Lakes 15.2 million

Freshwater except Great Lakes 353.6 million

Freshwater Fishing Expenditures

Anglers spent over $10.4 billion on equipment for non-Great Lakes fresh-water fishing. Expenditures for fishing equipment, such as rods and reels, tackle boxes, depth finders, and artificial lures and flies, totaled $4.0 billion. Expenditures for auxiliary equipment such as binoculars and camping equipment were $560 million. Expenditures for special equipment such as boats, vans, and cabins accounted for $5.9 billion.

There were 1.7 million people who fished almost 20 million days on 15 million trips to the Great Lakes in 2011. Their Great Lakes-related expenditures totaled $1.9 billion for an average of $1,121 per angler for the year. Trip-related expenditures totaled $1.1 billion. Of these expenditures, $374 million was spent on food and lodging, 34 percent of trip costs; $252 million was spent on transportation, 23 percent of trip costs; and $465 million, or 43 percent, was spent on other items such as guide fees, equipment rental, and bait. Equipment expenditures totaled $777 million. Of this $777 million, $223 million was for fishing equipment (rods, reels, etc.), $83 million was for auxiliary equipment (camping equipment, binoculars, etc.) and $471 million was for special equipment (boats, vans, etc.).

Saltwater Fishing Highlights

In 2011, 8.9 million anglers enjoyed saltwater fishing on 86 million trips totaling 99 million days. Overall, they spent $10.3 billion during the year on trips and equipment. Of their expenditures, trip-related costs garnered the largest portion, $7.3 billion. Food and lodging cost $2.4 billion, 32 percent of trip expenditures; transportation costs totaled $1.5 billion, 21 percent of trip costs; and other trip costs such as equipment rental, bait, and guide fees were $3.4 billion.

Anglers spent a total of $2.9 billion on equipment for saltwater fishing. Of the $2.9 million, $1.4 billion was for fishing equipment (rods, reels, etc.), $217 million for auxiliary equipment (camping equipment, binoculars, etc.), and $1.3 billion for special equipment (boats, vans, etc.).

Saltwater Fishing

Anglers..........	8.9 million
Days............	99.5 million
Trips............	86.2 million
Trips and equipment expenditures.....	$10.3 billion

Source: Tables 1 and 16

Comparative Trip and Equipment Expenditures

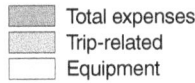
Total expenses
Trip-related
Equipment

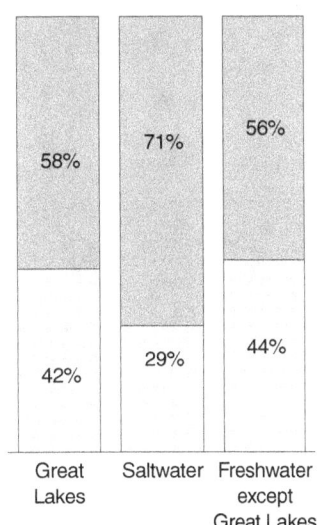

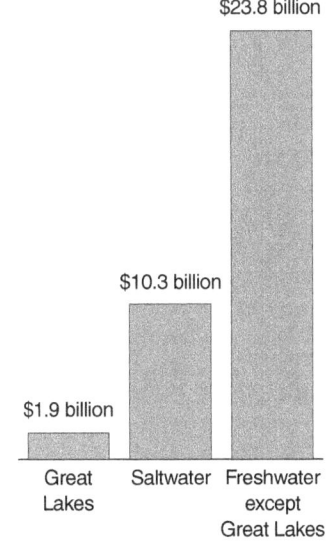

Comparative Fishing by Type of Fishing

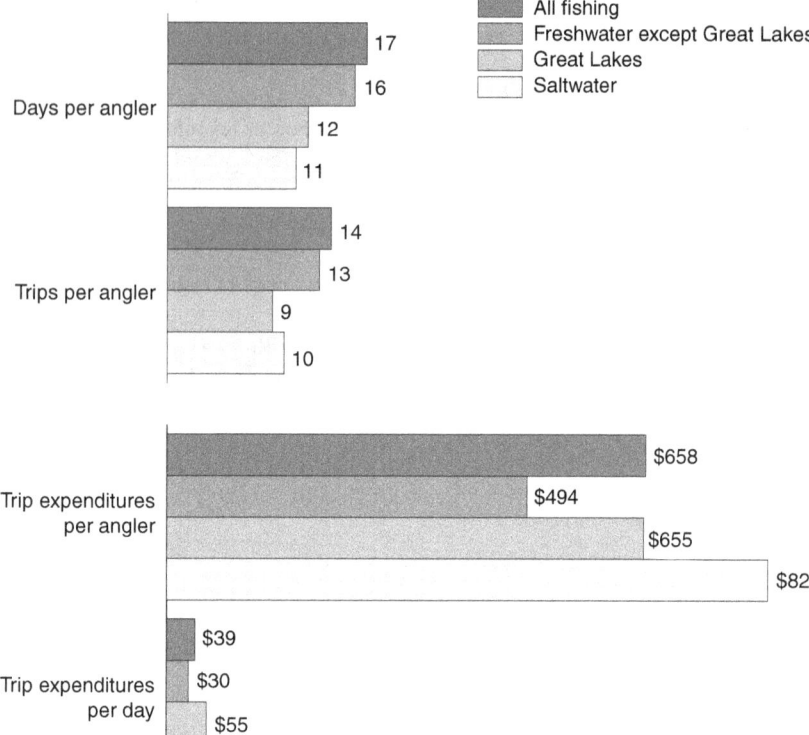

Legend:
- All fishing
- Freshwater except Great Lakes
- Great Lakes
- Saltwater

Days per angler: 17, 16, 12, 11

Trips per angler: 14, 13, 9, 10

Trip expenditures per angler: $658, $494, $655, $824

Trip expenditures per day: $39, $30, $55, $74

Selected Fish by Type of Fishing
(In millions)

Type of fishing	Anglers	Days
Freshwater except Great Lakes, total	**27.1**	**443**
Black bass	10.6	171
Panfish	7.3	97
Trout	7.2	76
Catfish/bullhead	7.0	96
Crappie	6.1	102
White bass, striped bass, and striped bass hybrids	4.4	61
Great Lakes, total	**1.7**	**20**
Walleye, sauger	0.6	6
Black bass	0.6	5
Perch	0.5	6
Salmon	0.4	5
Northern pike, pickerel, muskie, muskie hybrids	*0.2	*2
Lake trout	*0.2	*4
Saltwater, total	**8.9**	**99**
Striped bass	2.1	18
Flatfish (flounder, halibut)	2.0	22
Red drum (redfish)	1.5	21
Sea trout (weakfish)	1.1	15
Bluefish	1.0	10
Salmon	0.7	4

* Estimate based on a sample size of 10–29

Source: Tables 3, 4, and 5

Comparative Fishing Highlights

In 2011, anglers spent an average of 17 days fishing and took an average of 14 fishing trips. Freshwater, non-Great Lakes anglers averaged 16 days fishing and 13 trips while Great Lakes anglers averaged 12 days fishing and 9 trips. Saltwater anglers fished fewer days on average, 11, and averaged 10 trips.

Overall, anglers spent an average of $1,262 on fishing-related expenses in 2011. They averaged $658 per angler for their trip-related costs, a daily average of $39. Freshwater anglers, excluding the Great Lakes, averaged $494 per participant for their trips in 2011, equaling $30 per day. Great Lakes anglers spent an average of $655 on trip-related expenses, $55 per day. Saltwater anglers experienced the highest average expenditure amount at $824, an average of $74 per day.

Fishing for Selected Fish

The most popular fish species among the 27.1 million anglers who fished freshwater, other than the Great Lakes, was black bass. More than 10.6 million participants spent 171 million days fishing for black bass. Panfish were sought by 7.3 million anglers on 97 million days. Trout fishing attracted 7.2 million anglers on 76 million days. Catfish and bullheads drew 7.0 million anglers on 96 million days. Over 6.1 million anglers fished for crappie on 102 million days. Nearly 4.4 million anglers fished for white bass and striped bass on 61 million days. Freshwater anglers also commonly fished for walleye, northern pike, sauger, salmon, and steelhead.

In 2011, 1.7 million anglers fished the Great Lakes. Walleye and sauger, the most commonly sought fish for these waters, attracted 584 thousand anglers, fishing nearly 6 million days. Black bass attracted 559 thousand anglers who fished for them 5 million days. Perch, another popular fish, was fished for by 497 thousand anglers for 6 million days. Salmon drew 379 thousand anglers for almost 3 million days of fishing. Great Lakes anglers also commonly fished for northern pike, pickerel, and muskie, as well as steelhead and lake trout.

Among the nearly 8.9 million salt-water anglers, 2.1 million fished for striped bass for 18 million days. Two million anglers fished for flatfish, which includes flounder and halibut, on 22 million days. Also popular were red drum (redfish) and sea trout (weakfish) with 1.5 million and 1.1 million anglers who fished for 21 million and 15 million days, respectively. Other prominent saltwater species sought were mackerel with 650 thousand anglers, tuna with 564 thousand anglers, and mahi mahi (dolphinfish) with 538 thousand anglers.

Participation by Geographic Region

In 2011, 239 million people 16 years old and older lived in the United States and 1 in 7 of these U.S. residents went fishing. While the national participation rate was 14 percent, the regional rates ranged from 9 percent in the Pacific to 23 percent in the West North Central Region. The West North Central, East North Central, East South Central, West South Central, and Mountain Regions all reported participation rates above the national rate. The Middle Atlantic, South Atlantic, New England, and Pacific Regions fell below the national rate.

Fishing in State of Residence and in Other States

A large majority of the 33.1 million anglers who fished in 2011 did so within their home state. Approximately 30.0 million participants, 91 percent of all anglers, fished in their resident state. Nearly 7.0 million, 21 percent, fished out-of-state. Percentages do not add to 100 because those anglers who fished both in-state and out-of-state were included in both categories.

Of the 27.1 million non-Great Lakes anglers, 92 percent, 24.9 million, fished within their resident state. Over 4.5 million, 17 percent, of these freshwater anglers fished out-of-state. Ninety-two percent, 1.5 million, of all Great Lakes anglers enjoyed fishing

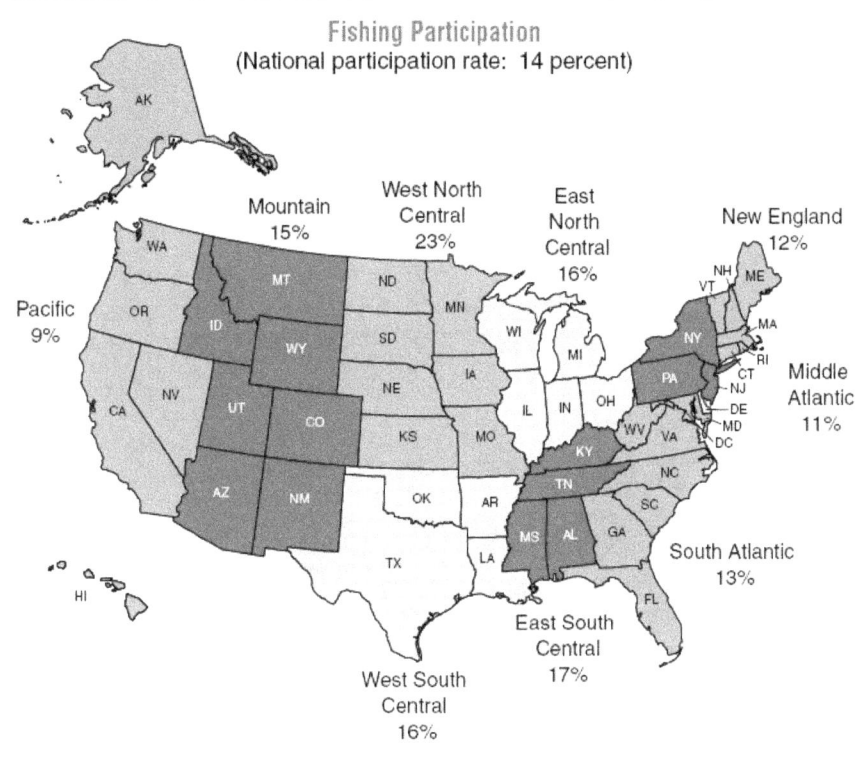

Fishing Participation
(National participation rate: 14 percent)

Pacific 9%
Mountain 15%
West North Central 23%
East North Central 16%
New England 12%
Middle Atlantic 11%
South Atlantic 13%
East South Central 17%
West South Central 16%

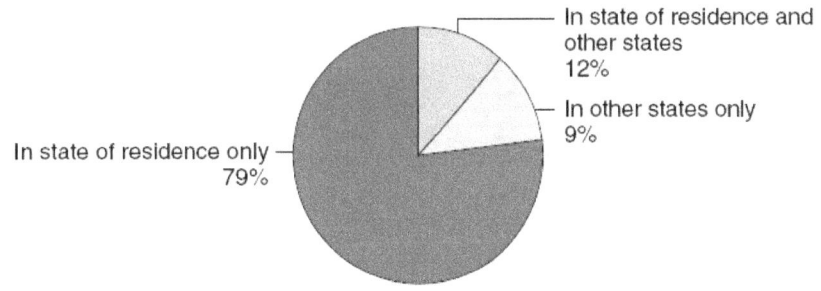

Percent of All Fishing in State of Residence and in Other States
(Total: 33.1 million participants)

In state of residence and other states 12%
In other states only 9%
In state of residence only 79%

within their home state in 2011. Thirteen percent, 224 thousand, of all Great Lakes anglers fished out-of-state.

Of the three different types of fishing, saltwater fishing had both the highest percentage of anglers fishing outside their resident state, 31 percent, and the lowest percentage fishing within their resident state, 74 percent. Nonresident saltwater anglers numbered 2.8 million and resident anglers 6.6 million.

Fishing in State of Residence and in Other States
(In millions)

	In state	Out of state
Total anglers	30.0	7.0
Freshwater except		
Great Lakes . . .	24.9	4.5
Great Lakes	1.5	0.2
Saltwater	6.6	2.8

Source: Table 2

Types of Freshwater Fished, Excluding Great Lakes
(In millions)

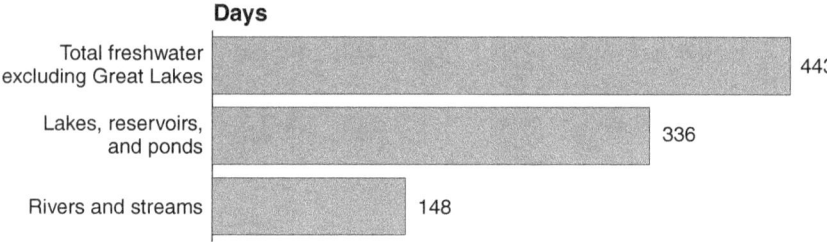

Anglers

Total freshwater excluding Great Lakes	27.1
Lakes, reservoirs, and ponds	22.8
Rivers and streams	11.9

Days

Total freshwater excluding Great Lakes	443
Lakes, reservoirs, and ponds	336
Rivers and streams	148

Great Lakes Fishing

	Anglers (thousands)	Percentage of all Great Lakes Anglers
Total, all Great Lakes	**1,665**	**100**
Lake Erie	639	38
Lake Michigan	413	25
Lake Huron	*262	*16
Tributaries to the Great Lakes	*159	*10
Lake Superior	*147	*9
Lake Ontario	*143	*9
St. Lawrence	...	...
Lake St. Clair	...	...

* Estimate based on a sample of 10–29
... Sample size too small to report data reliably

Source: Table 26

Types of Freshwater Fished, Excluding Great Lakes

Excluding the Great Lakes, 84 percent or 22.8 million of all freshwater anglers fished in reservoirs, lakes, and ponds. 44 percent or 11.9 million fished in rivers and streams. They spent 336 million days fishing in lakes, reservoirs, and ponds and 148 million days fishing in rivers and streams.

Great Lakes Anglers

Great Lakes fishing includes not only the Great Lakes, but also their tributaries—bodies of water that connect the Great Lakes, and the St. Lawrence River south of the bridge at Cornwall. The most popular of the Lakes among anglers was Lake Erie, attracting 38 percent of all Great Lakes anglers. They averaged 13 days of fishing in Lake Erie during 2011. Lake Michigan ranked second in popularity, hosting 25 percent of Great Lakes anglers with an average of 6 days per angler. Lake Huron attracted 16 percent of Great Lakes anglers for an average of 17 days per angler. Lake Superior drew 9 percent, as did Lake Ontario, of all Great Lakes fishing in 2011. Anglers fished an average of 15 days in Lake Ontario and 10 days in Lake Superior. The tributaries to the lakes drew 10 percent, 159 thousand anglers, who averaged 8 days of fishing there.

Sex and Age of Anglers

Although more men than women fished in 2011, a substantial number of women, 8.9 million, fished. Approximately 21 percent of all males 16 years old and older went fishing, while 7 percent of all females fished. Of the 33.1 million anglers who fished in the United States, 73 percent, 24.2 million, were male and 27 percent were female.

Of the age categories, 7.4 million anglers were 45 to 54 years old. They composed 22 percent of all anglers and had a participation rate of 16 percent. The 25- to 34-year-old age group accounted for 6.1 million anglers, 19 percent of all anglers. They had 15 percent participation. Six million anglers, 18 percent of all anglers, were 35 to 44 years old. Their participation rate was 15 percent of the U.S. population in that age group. The 5.9 million 55- to 64-year-olds who fished comprised 18 percent of all anglers and had a participation rate of 15 percent. The 2.7 million anglers 18 to 24 years old made up 8 percent of the angler population, and had a participation rate of 10 percent. Anglers 75 and older numbered 1.0 million, 3 percent of all anglers, and had a participation rate of 7 percent. The 16- and 17-year-olds added 942 thousand individuals to the angler population. They made up 3 percent of all anglers, and had a 12 percent participation rate.

Anglers by Sex and Age

Total, both sexes . . .	**33.1 million**
Male	24.2 million
Female	8.9 million
Total, all ages	**33.1 million**
16 and 17	0.9 million
18 to 24	2.7 million
25 to 34	6.1 million
35 to 44	6.0 million
45 to 54	7.4 million
55 to 64	5.9 million
65 and older	4.1 million

Source: Table 9

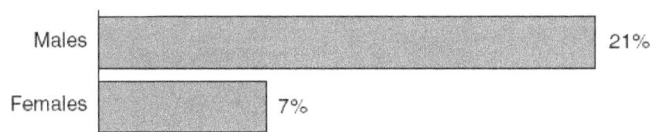

Percent of Males and Females Who Fished in the United States

- Males 21%
- Females 7%

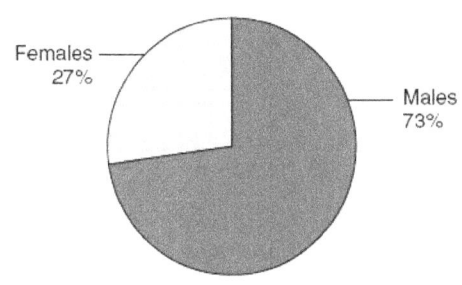

Percent of Anglers by Sex

- Females 27%
- Males 73%

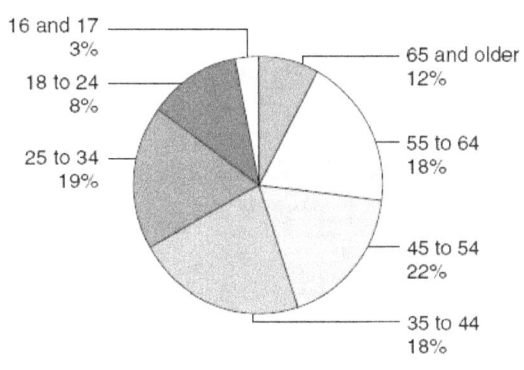

Percent of Anglers by Age

- 16 and 17 — 3%
- 18 to 24 — 8%
- 25 to 34 — 19%
- 35 to 44 — 18%
- 45 to 54 — 22%
- 55 to 64 — 18%
- 65 and older — 12%

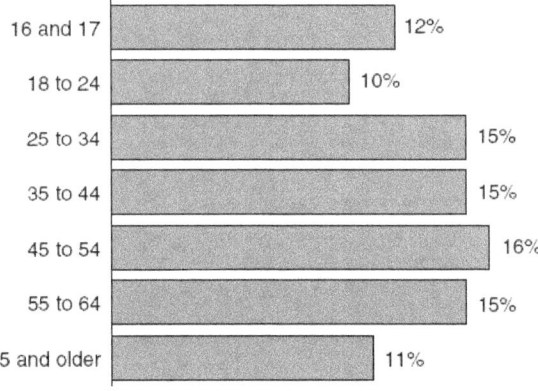

Percent of U.S. Population Who Fished by Age

- 16 and 17 — 12%
- 18 to 24 — 10%
- 25 to 34 — 15%
- 35 to 44 — 15%
- 45 to 54 — 16%
- 55 to 64 — 15%
- 65 and older — 11%

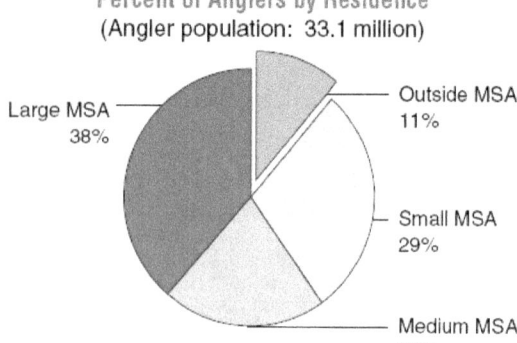

Percent of Anglers by Residence
(Angler population: 33.1 million)

Large MSA 38%
Outside MSA 11%
Small MSA 29%
Medium MSA 21%

Percent of U.S. Population Who Fished by Residence
(Total U.S. population that fished: 14 percent)

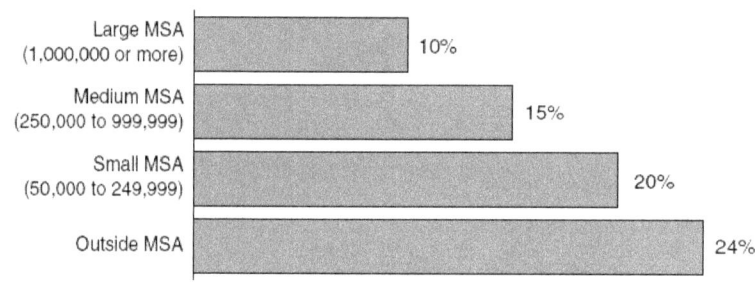

Large MSA (1,000,000 or more)	10%
Medium MSA (250,000 to 999,999)	15%
Small MSA (50,000 to 249,999)	20%
Outside MSA	24%

Percent of U.S. Population Who Fished by Household Income

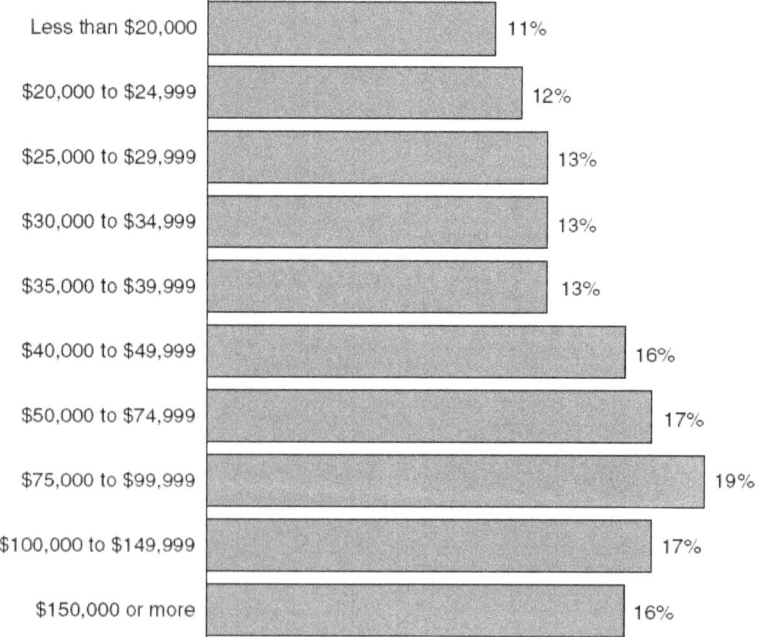

Less than $20,000	11%
$20,000 to $24,999	12%
$25,000 to $29,999	13%
$30,000 to $34,999	13%
$35,000 to $39,999	13%
$40,000 to $49,999	16%
$50,000 to $74,999	17%
$75,000 to $99,999	19%
$100,000 to $149,999	17%
$150,000 or more	16%

Metropolitan and Nonmetropolitan Anglers

While residents of metropolitan statistical areas (MSA)[1] had lower participation rates in fishing than non-MSA residents, they still accounted for the majority of anglers. Thirteen percent of all MSA residents fished in 2011, but they composed 89 percent of all anglers. By comparison, non-MSA residents composed 11 percent of all anglers, but their participation rate was almost twice as high at 24 percent.

Larger MSAs had lower participation rates in fishing than smaller MSAs but composed more of the angler population. Large MSAs with populations of 1,000,000 or more had the lowest participation rate at 10 percent, but they made up 38 percent of all anglers. Medium MSAs with a population of 250,000 to 999,999 had a 15 percent participation rate and made up 21 percent of all anglers. Those MSAs with a population from 50,000 to 249,999 had a participation rate of 20 percent and composed 29 percent of all anglers.

Household Income of Anglers

The participation rate in fishing tended to increase as household income increased. The participation rate is the percent of each income group that fished. The rate of those who reported incomes of $75,000 to $99,999 was the highest at 19 percent. Those with incomes of $50,000 to $74,999 and $100,000 to $149,999 had a slightly lower rate of 17 percent. Generally, the participation rate declined as income decreased with exception of those with incomes of $150,000 or more which had the same participation rate, 16 percent, as those with incomes of $40,000 to $49,999. Those with incomes of $25,000 to $39,999 had a 13 percent participation rate. Those with incomes under $20,000 had the lowest participation rate at 11 percent.

[1] See Appendix A for definition of metropolitan statistical area

The majority of anglers had household incomes of $50,000 or more. Among anglers who reported income, 60 percent were from households with incomes of $50,000 or more and 40 percent were from households with incomes less than $50,000.

Education, Race and Ethnicity

People of all educational backgrounds had similar participation rates. Those with 11 years of education or less had a participation rate of 12 percent. Those with 12 years of education had a participation rate of 13 percent. Those with 1 to 4 years of college had the highest participation rate at 15 percent. The second highest participation rate, 14 percent, was held by those with 5 years or more of college.

While the highest participation rate is among those with 1 to 4 years of college, participants with 12 years of education made up the largest share of anglers. Thirty-two percent, 10.5 million anglers, had 12 years of education.

Anglers by Education, Race, and Ethnicity

(In millions)

Total anglers **33.1**

Education
    11 years or less 3.7
    12 years 10.5
    1 to 3 years of college 8.5
    4 years of college 6.3
    5 years or more of college .   4.1

Race
    White 28.6
    African American 2.3
    Asian American 0.7
    Other 1.5

Ethnicity
    Hispanic 1.7
    Non-Hispanic 31.4

Source: Table 9

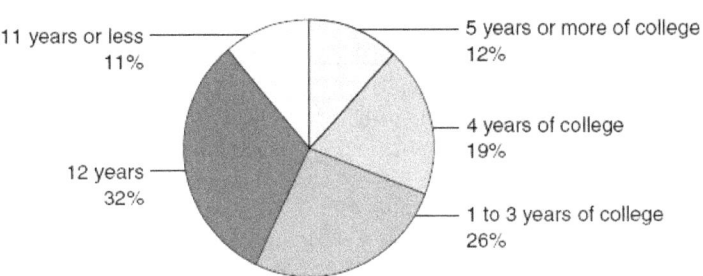

Percent of Anglers by Education

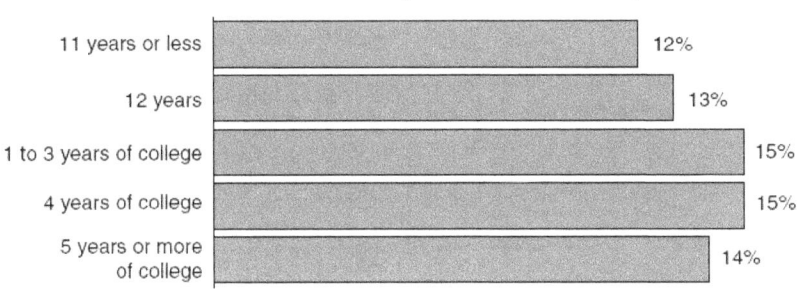

Percent of U.S. Population Who Fished by Education

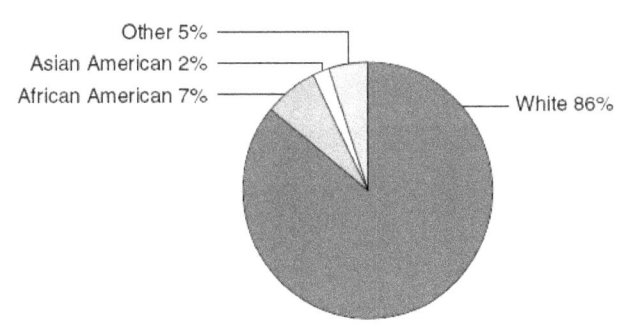

Percent of Anglers by Race

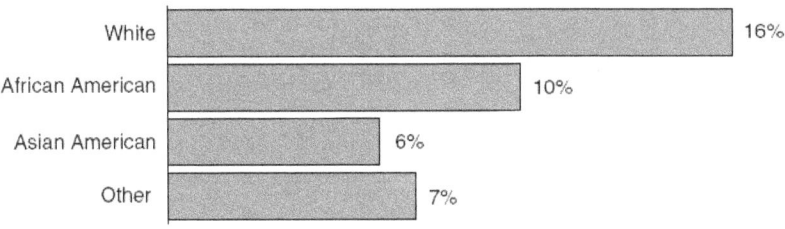

Percent of U.S. Population Who Fished by Race

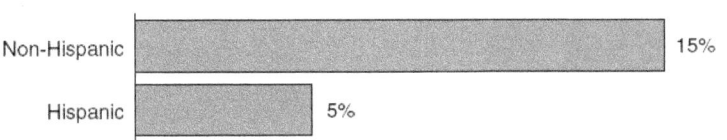

Percent of U.S. Population Who Fished by Ethnicity

Fishing was most popular among Whites and African Americans. Whites participated at a 16 percent rate and African Americans participated at a 10 percent rate. Other races, which include Native Americans, Pacific Islanders, and those of mixed race, participated at a 7 percent rate. Asian Americans participated at a 6 percent rate. Of all anglers, 86 percent were White, 7 percent were African American, 5 percent were other races, and 2 percent were Asian Americans.

2001–2011 Comparison of Fishing Activity

In 2011 the number of people fishing was 11 percent higher than in 2006.

Specifically, participation in freshwater, except Great Lakes, and saltwater fishing were up significantly, 8 and 15 percent, respectively. The number of Great Lakes anglers did not undergo a significant change. Days fishing, however, did not have statistically significant changes for any type of fishing, which means average days per freshwater, except Great Lakes, and Great Lakes anglers were slightly down. Expenditures for trip-related items and equipment decreased 11 percent overall, primarily due to a 41 percent drop in big-ticket special equipment such as cabins and boats.

Comparing fishing in 2011 to that in 2001, there was no significant differ-

ence in either the number of participants or days for any type of fishing. The drop in fishing from 2001 to 2006 was reversed across the board by the increase from 2006 to 2011. Total expenditures also did not change significantly, although when expenditures are broken down into its two components, trip-related and equipment items, there were differences. Anglers spent significantly more in 2011 for trip-related expenses and less for equipment purchases, particularly the big-ticket items.

Number of Anglers
(Millions)

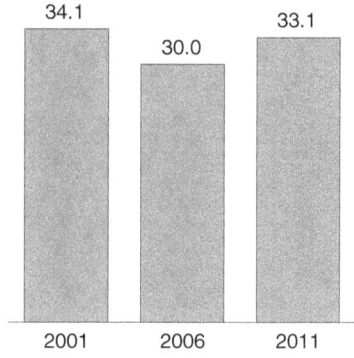

Days of Fishing
(Millions)

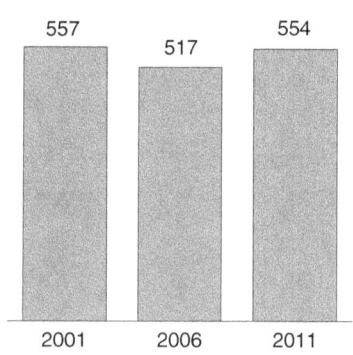

Fishing Expenditures
(Billions of 2011 dollars)

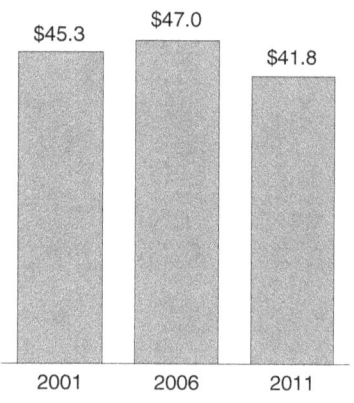

2001–2011 Fishing Participants, Days, and Expenditures
(U.S. population 16 years old and older. Numbers in thousands)

	2001		2011		2001–2011
	Number	Percent	Number	Percent	percent change
Anglers, total	**34,071**	**100**	**33,112**	**100**	NS–3
All freshwater	28,439	83	27,547	83	NS–3
Freshwater, except Great Lakes	27,913	82	27,060	82	NS–3
Great Lakes	1,847	5	1,665	5	NS–10
Saltwater	9,051	27	8,889	27	NS–2
Days, total	**557,394**	**100**	**553,841**	**100**	NS–1
All freshwater	466,984	84	455,862	82	NS–2
Freshwater, except Great Lakes	443,247	80	443,223	80	0
Great Lakes	23,138	4	19,661	4	NS–15
Saltwater	90,838	16	99,474	18	NS10
Fishing, total (2011 dollars)	**$45,257,393**	**100**	**$41,788,936**	**100**	NS–8
Trip-related	18,614,941	41	21,789,465	52	17
Equipment, total	21,545,781	48	15,506,433	37	–28
Fishing equipment	5,864,914	13	6,141,895	15	NS5
Auxiliary equipment	915,822	2	1,106,865	3	NS21
Special equipment	14,765,019	33	8,257,673	20	–44
Other	5,096,669	11	4,493,037	11	NS–12

NS Not different from zero at the 5 percent level of significance

2006–2011 Fishing Participants, Days, and Expenditures
(U.S. population 16 years old and older. Numbers in thousands)

	2006		2011		2006–2011
	Number	Percent	Number	Percent	percent change
Anglers, total	**29,952**	**100**	**33,112**	**100**	**11**
All freshwater	25,431	85	27,547	83	8
Freshwater, except Great Lakes	25,035	84	27,060	82	8
Great Lakes	1,420	5	1,665	5	NS17
Saltwater	7,717	26	8,889	27	15
Days, total	**516,781**	**100**	**553,841**	**100**	NS7
All freshwater	433,337	84	455,862	82	NS5
Freshwater, except Great Lakes	419,942	81	443,223	80	NS6
Great Lakes	18,016	3	19,661	4	NS9
Saltwater	85,663	17	99,474	18	NS16
Fishing, total (2011 dollars)	**$47,036,454**	**100**	**$41,788,936**	**100**	NS–11
Trip-related	19,948,340	29	21,789,465	52	NS9
Equipment, total	20,928,889	47	15,506,433	37	–26
Fishing equipment	5,949,727	23	6,141,895	15	NS3
Auxiliary equipment	868,894	6	1,106,865	3	NS27
Special equipment	14,110,268	18	8,257,673	20	–41
Other	6,159,225	24	4,493,037	11	–27

NS Not different from zero at the 5 percent level of significance

Hunting

Hunting Highlights

In 2011, 13.7 million people 16 years old and older enjoyed hunting a variety of animals within the United States. They hunted 282 million days and took 257 million trips. Hunting expenditures totaled $33.7 billion.

Big game hunting was the most popular type of hunting. Almost 11.6 million hunters pursued big game such as deer and elk on 212 million days. Big game-related expenditures for trips and equipment totaled $16.9 billion. There were 4.5 million hunters of small game including squirrels and rabbits. They hunted small game on 51 million days and spent $2.6 billion on small game hunting trips and equipment. Migratory bird hunters numbered 2.6 million. They spent 23 million days hunting birds such as waterfowl and doves. Migratory bird-related trip and equipment expenditures totaled $1.8 billion. Nearly 2.2 million hunters sought other animals such as raccoons and feral pigs on 34 million days, and their expenditures for trips and equipment were $858 million.

Hunting

Legend:
- Big game
- Small game
- Migratory bird
- Other animals

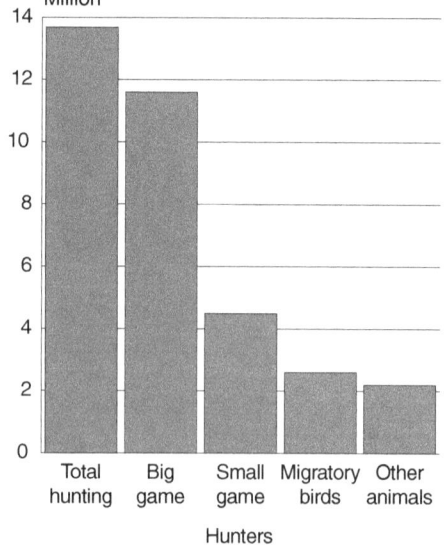

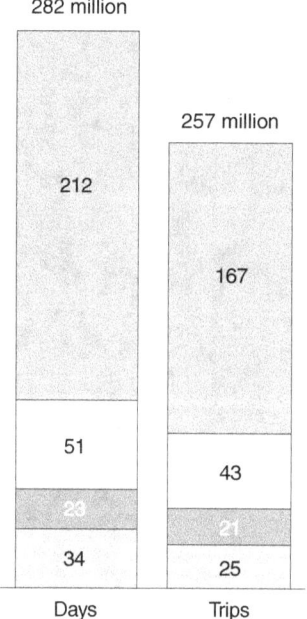

Note: Detail does not add to total because of multiple responses and nonresponse.

Total Hunting

Hunters	**13.7 million**
Big game	11.6 million
Small game	4.5 million
Migratory birds .	2.6 million
Other animals . .	2.2 million
Days	**282 million**
Big game	212 million
Small game	51 million
Migratory birds .	23 million
Other animals . .	34 million
Trips	**257 million**
Big game	167 million
Small game	43 million
Migratory birds .	21 million
Other animals . .	25 million
Expenditures	**$33.7 billion**
Big game	16.9 billion
Small game	2.6 billion
Migratory birds .	1.8 billion
Other animals . .	0.9 billion
Nonspecific	11.9 billion

Source: Tables 1 and 17–21

Hunting Expenditures

Of the $33.7 billion spent by hunters in 2011, 31 percent, $10.4 billion, was spent on trip-related expenses. Food and lodging totaled $3.9 billion, 37 percent of all trip-related expenses. Transportation spending was $4.8 billion, 46 percent of trip expenditures. Other trip expenses such as guide fees, land use fees, and equipment rental were $1.8 billion or 17 percent of all trip-related expenses.

Total equipment expenditures for hunting were $14.0 billion in 2011, 41 percent of all hunting expenses. Hunting equipment, such as guns and rifles, telescopic sights, and ammunition, composed $7.7 billion, or 55 percent of all equipment costs. Expenditures for auxiliary equipment, including camping equipment, binoculars, and special hunting clothing, accounted for $1.8 billion or 13 percent of all equipment expenses. Special equipment, such as campers or all-terrain vehicles, amounted to $4.4 billion or 31 percent of all equipment expenditures.

Land leasing and ownership for hunting was a large expenditure category. Hunters spent $7.1 billion on land leasing and ownership, which was 21 percent of all hunting-related expenditures. Expenditures for magazines, books, DVDs, membership dues, contributions, licenses, tags, and permits totaled $1.5 billion or 4 percent. Expenditures for plantings, $703 million, was 2 percent of all hunting expenditures.

Total Hunting Expenditures

Total hunting expenditures.	**$33.7 billion**
Total trip-related expenditures	**$10.4 billion**
Food and lodging	3.9 billion
Transportation	4.8 billion
Other trip costs	1.8 billion
Total equipment expenditures	**$14.0 billion**
Hunting equipment	7.7 billion
Auxiliary equipment	1.8 billion
Special equipment	4.4 billion
Total other hunting expenditures	**$9.3 billion**
Magazines, books, DVDs	0.1 billion
Membership dues and contributions	0.4 billion
Land leasing and ownership	7.1 billion
Licenses, stamps, tags, and permits	1.0 billion
Plantings	0.7 billion

Source: Table 17.

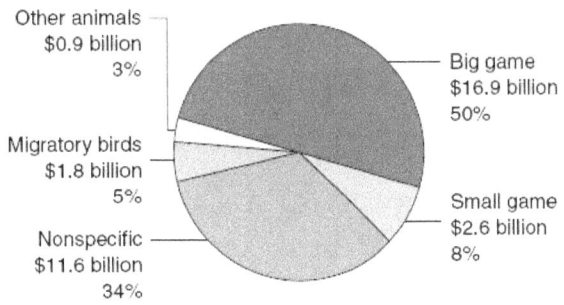

Hunting Expenditures by Type of Hunting
(Total expenditures: $33.7 billion)

Other animals $0.9 billion 3%
Big game $16.9 billion 50%
Migratory birds $1.8 billion 5%
Small game $2.6 billion 8%
Nonspecific $11.6 billion 34%

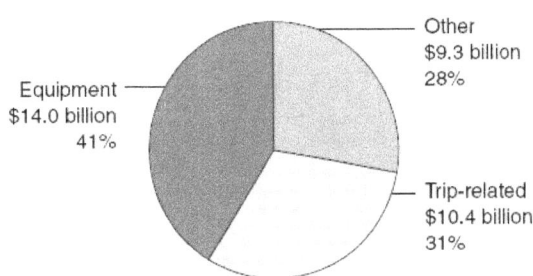

Percent of Total Hunting Expenditures
(Total expenditures: $33.7 billion)

Equipment $14.0 billion 41%
Other $9.3 billion 28%
Trip-related $10.4 billion 31%

Big Game Hunting

In 2011, a majority of hunters, 11.6 million, devoted 212 million days to hunting big game including deer, elk, bear, and wild turkey. They took 167 million trips and spent an average of 18 days hunting big game.

Trip and equipment expenditures for big game hunting totaled $16.9 billion. Trip-related expenses were $7.3 billion. Of that amount, food and lodging accounted for $2.6 billion or 37 percent of all trip-related costs. Transportation costs were $3.4 billion, 46 percent of trip costs. Other trip-related expenses amounted to $1.2 billion or 17 percent of trip costs.

Fifty-seven percent of big game-related expenditures were on equipment, which totaled $9.6 billion. Hunting equipment, which includes firearms, ammunition, bows, and arrows, accounted for $3.9 billion or 41 percent of all equipment. Purchases of auxiliary equipment such as tents and binoculars totaled $1.5 billion (16 percent). Special equipment such as campers and all-terrain vehicles accounted for $4.1 billion (43 percent).

Small Game Hunting

Small game such as rabbits, squirrels, pheasants, quail, and grouse was also popular with hunters. Just over 4.5 million hunters pursued small game for a total of 51 million days. They took 43 million trips and averaged 11 days in the field hunting small game.

These hunters spent $2.6 billion on trips and equipment for small game hunting. Trip expenditures totaled $1.6 billion. Spending on food and lodging was $658 million or 42 percent of trip expenditures. Transportation costs totaled $686 million or 43 percent of small game trip expenses. Other trip-related expenditures were $233 million or 15 percent of all trip costs.

Equipment expenditures for small game hunting were $984 million. For the pursuit of small game, hunters spent $854 million on hunting equipment (firearms, ammunition, etc.) and $85 million on auxiliary equipment, 87 and 9 percent of equipment expenditures, respectively.

Big Game

Hunters..........	11.6 million
Days............	212 million
Trips............	167 million
Trips and equipment expenditures	$16.9 billion

Source: Tables 1 and 18

Big Game Trip and Equipment Expenditures
(Total expenditures: $16.9 billion)

Equipment — $9.6 billion
Trip-related — $7.3 billion

Small Game

Hunters..........	4.5 million
Days............	51 million
Trips............	43 million
Trips and equipment expenditures	$2.6 billion

Source: Tables 1 and 19

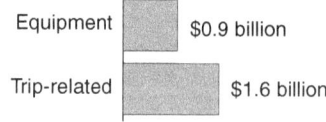

Small Game Trip and Equipment Expenditures
(Total expenditures: $2.6 billion)

Equipment — $0.9 billion
Trip-related — $1.6 billion

Migratory Bird Hunting

In 2011, 2.6 million migratory bird hunters devoted 23 million days on 21 million trips for hunting birds such as doves, ducks, and geese. Hunters averaged 9 days pursuing migratory birds for the year.

Migratory bird-related spending for trips and equipment was $1.8 billion in 2011. Of this amount, $942 million was spent on hunting trips. An estimated $316 million or 34 percent of all trip expenditures were on food and lodging, and $390 million (41 percent) were on transportation. Other trip expenses were $235 million (25 percent) of the total trip-related expenditures for migratory bird hunters.

Equipment purchases for migratory bird hunting totaled $866 million in 2011. Of this amount, $767 million was spent on hunting equipment (firearms, ammunition, etc.) and $59 million on auxiliary equipment, 89 and 7 percent of total equipment purchases, respectively.

Hunting Other Animals

Nearly 2.2 million hunters reported spending 34 million days on 25 million trips pursuing other animals such as groundhogs, feral pigs, raccoons, foxes, and coyotes. They averaged 16 days of hunting.

These hunters spent $858 million in 2011 on trips and equipment for the pursuit of other animals. Trip-related costs totaled $653 million. Of that, food and lodging were $259 million or 40 percent of all trip costs; transportation was $324 million, 50 percent of trip expenses; and other trip expenses were $70 million, 11 percent of all trip costs.

Equipment expenditures for hunting other animals totaled $205 million. For the pursuit of other animals, hunters spent $189 million on hunting equipment (firearms, ammunition, etc.) and $6 million on auxiliary equipment, 92 and 3 percent of total equipment expenditures, respectively.

Comparative Hunting Highlights

In 2011 big game hunters pursued big game an average of 18 days on 14 trips. Small game hunters pursued small game an average of 11 days on 10 trips. Migratory bird hunters hunted migratory birds an average of 9 days on 8 trips. Individuals hunting other animals did so an average of 16 days on 11 trips.

Average spending on trips and equipment was about twice as high for big game hunting than for any other type of hunting. For hunting big game, participants spent an average of $1,457 for the year. By comparison, spending on small game hunting by participants averaged $568, spending on migratory bird hunting by participants averaged $700, and spending on other animal hunting averaged $396.

During 2011 trip expenditures for all hunting averaged $762 per hunter, a daily average of $37. In pursuit of big game, hunters averaged trip expenditures of $627, which was $34 per day. Hunters spent an average of $350 while

---

Migratory Birds

Hunters	2.6 million
Days	23 million
Trips	21 million
Trips and equipment expenditures	$1.8 billion

Source: Tables 1 and 20

Migratory Bird Trip and Equipment Expenditures
(Total expenditures: $1.8 billion)

| Equipment | $0.9 billion |
| Trip-related | $0.9 billion |

Other Animals

Hunters	2.2 million
Days	34 million
Trips	25 million
Trips and equipment expenditures	$0.9 billion

Source: Tables 1 and 21

Trip and Equipment Expenditures for Hunting Other Animals
(Total expenditures: $0.9 billion)

| Equipment | $0.2 billion |
| Trip-related | $0.7 billion |

Comparative Hunting by Type of Hunting

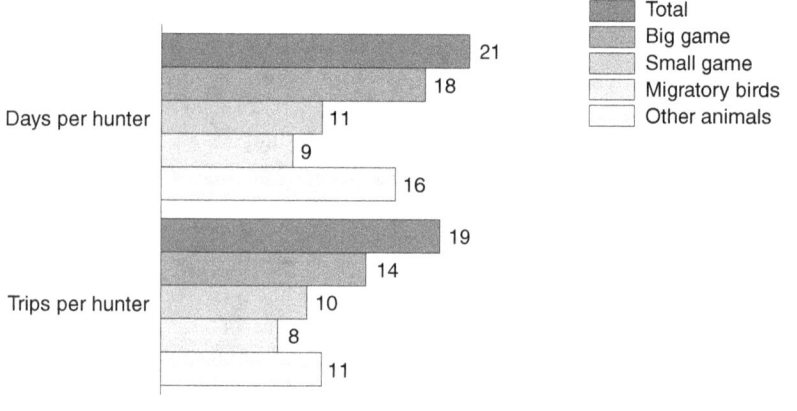

Legend:
- Total
- Big game
- Small game
- Migratory birds
- Other animals

Days per hunter: 21, 18, 11, 9, 16

Trips per hunter: 19, 14, 10, 8, 11

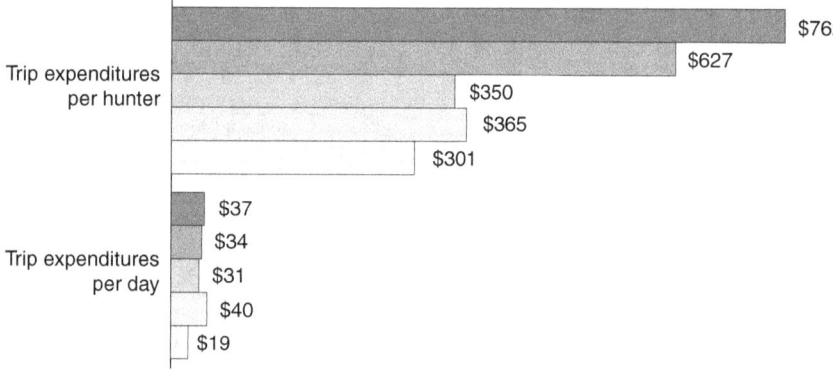

Trip expenditures per hunter: $762, $627, $350, $365, $301

Trip expenditures per day: $37, $34, $31, $40, $19

Selected Game by Type of Hunting

(In millions)

Type of hunting	Hunters	Days
Big game, total	**11.6**	**212**
Deer	10.9	168
Wild turkey	3.1	33
Elk	0.9	8
Bear	0.5	5
Small game, total	**4.5**	**51**
Squirrel	1.7	21
Rabbit and hare	1.5	17
Pheasant	1.5	10
Quail	0.8	9
Grouse/prairie chicken	0.8	8
Migratory birds, total	**2.6**	**23**
Ducks	1.4	15
Doves	1.3	7
Geese	0.8	9

Source: Table 7

seeking small game ($31 per day) and spent an average of $365 ($40 per day) while pursuing migratory birds. Hunters averaged $301 ($19 per day) while pursuing other animals.

Hunting for Selected Game

Among big game species, deer was the most popular animal pursued, attracting 10.9 million hunters for 168 million days. Wild turkey attracted 3.1 million hunters for 33 million days, while elk drew 867 thousand for 8 million days, and bear was hunted by 526 thousand for 5 million days. Moose was pursued by 106 thousand hunters for 1 million days. In addition, 305 thousand hunters spent 5 million days hunting other big game animals.

Among small game species, squirrels were the most popular quarry with 1.7 million small game hunters who hunted them 21 million days in 2011. Rabbits were hunted by 1.5 million participants for 17 million days, and pheasants attracted 1.5 million hunters for 10 million days. Quail was flushed by 841 thousand hunters on 9 million days, while grouse and prairie chicken were pursued by 812 thousand hunters on 8 million days. In addition, 299 thousand hunters spent 3 million days hunting other small game animals.

Among those hunting migratory birds, 1.4 million pursued ducks for 15 million days. There were 1.3 million hunters who pursued doves on 7 million days. On 9 million days, 781 thousand hunters hunted geese in 2011. Other migratory bird species attracted 227 thousand people who hunted for 2 million days.

Participation by Geographic Region

Regionally, participation rates in hunting ranged from 3 percent in the Pacific Region to 11 percent in the East South Central Region. The East North Central, West North Central, and West South Central Regions also had participation rates above the national average of 6 percent. Regions with participation rates below the national rate were New England, Middle Atlantic, South Atlantic, and Pacific. The rate in the Mountain Region was equal to the average at 6 percent.

Hunting in State of Residence and in Other States

A large majority of participants, 94 percent or 12.9 million, hunted within their resident state in 2011. Only 1.9 million, 14 percent, hunted in another state. Percentages do not add to 100 because those who hunted both in state and out of state were included in both categories.

The overall resident/nonresident pattern is relatively constant across all types of hunting. Eleven million big game hunters, 95 percent of all big game hunters, hunted within their state of residence, while 11 percent, 1.3 million people, traveled to another state to hunt big game. Four million small game hunters, 90 percent of all small game hunters, pursued game in their resident state. An estimated 708 thousand small game hunters, 16 percent ventured across state lines to hunt small game. Over 2.4 million migratory bird hunters, 94 percent of all migratory bird hunters, hunted within their resident state. Eleven percent or 284 thousand hunted out of state. Among sportspersons who hunted other animals, 92 percent, 2 million, hunted in state and 10 percent, 224 thousand participants, hunted out of state.

Hunting in State of Residence and in Other States

(In millions)

	In state	Out of state
All hunters	**12.9**	**1.9**
Big game	11.0	1.3
Small game	4.0	0.7
Migratory birds ..	2.4	0.3
Other animals ...	2.0	0.2

Source: Table 6

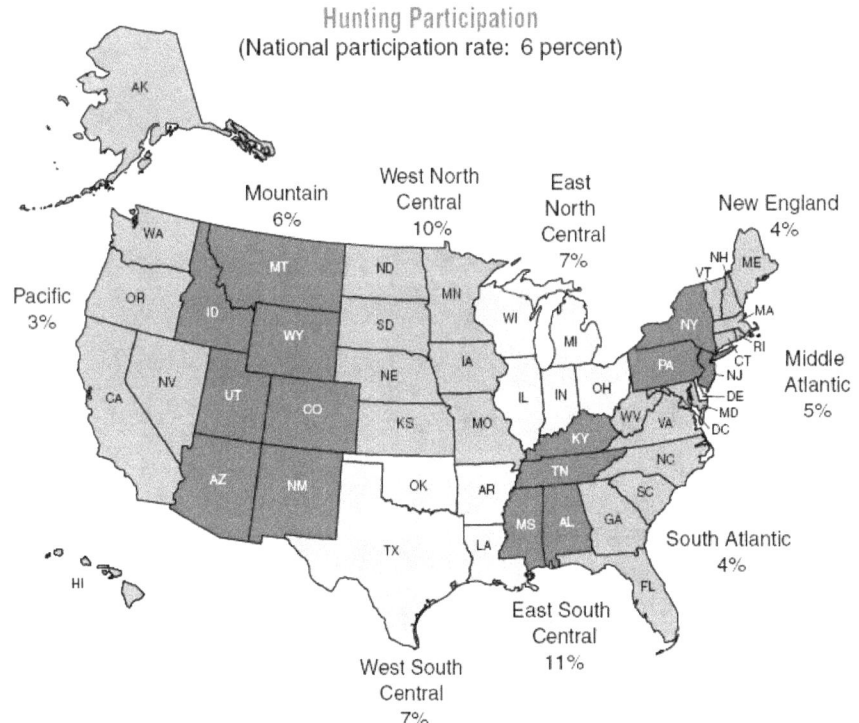

Hunting Participation
(National participation rate: 6 percent)

Hunting on Public and Private Lands

In 2011, 13.7 million hunters 16 years old and older hunted on public land, private land, or both. Of this number, 4.9 million or 36 percent hunted on publicly owned lands compared to 11.5 million or 84 percent who hunted on privately owned land. Some hunters hunted exclusively on public land and others hunted exclusively on private land—1.7 million, 13 percent of all hunters, used public lands only, and 8.4 million hunted only on private land, 61 percent of all hunters. Nearly 3.2 million hunters, 23 percent, hunted on both public and private lands.

During 2011, 4.9 million hunters used public lands on 61 million days, which represents 22 percent of all hunting days. Thirty-three percent of big game hunters pursued big game on public land for 39 million days. Thirty-one percent of all small game hunters, 1.4 million, pursued small game on public land for 14 million days. An estimated 923 thousand migratory bird hunters, 36 percent, hunted migratory birds on public lands for 8 million days. Twenty-four percent, 523 thousand, of all hunters pursued other animals on public land for over 5 million days.

The percent of hunters on private land is similar among different types of hunting. Eighty-four percent of big game hunters hunted on private land, which compares to 83 percent seeking small game, 77 percent seeking migratory birds, and 87 percent seeking other animals.

Of all days hunting, 78 percent or 219 million were on private land. The percent of hunting days on private land varied slightly more among types of hunting than the percent of hunters. Seventy-nine percent of big game hunting days, 73 percent of small game hunting days, 57 percent of migratory bird hunting days, and 79 percent of other animal days were on private land. Total hunting days pursuing these species on private land were as follows: big game 167 million, small game 37 million, migratory bird 13 million, and other animals 27 million.

Participation in Target Shooting

In preparation for hunting, 7.2 million hunters, 52 percent of all hunters, went target shooting. Twenty-two percent of all hunters, 2.9 million, used shooting ranges. The most commonly used firearms at a shooting range were shotguns and rifles (2.3 million hunters) and handguns (1.1 million).

Percent of All Hunting in State of Residence and in Other States
(Total: 13.7 million participants)

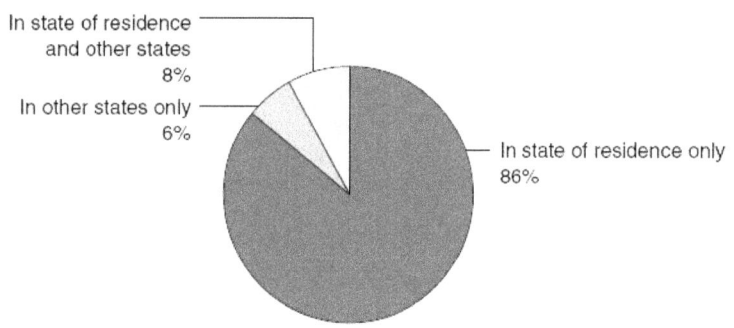

People Hunting on Public and Private Lands

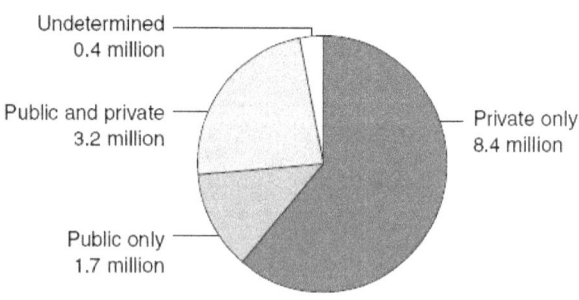

Number of Hunters Who Target Shoot and Use Shooting Ranges
(Total hunters: 13.7 million)

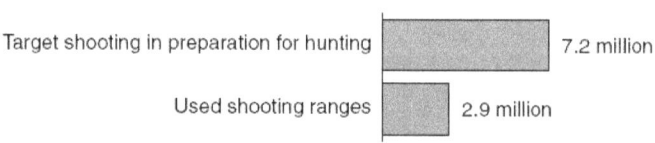

Sex and Age

Of the U.S. population 16 years old and older, 11 percent of the males and 1 percent of the females enjoyed hunting in 2011. Of the 13.7 million participants who hunted, 89 percent (12.2 million) were male and 11 percent (1.5 million) were female.

The participation rate in hunting tended to increase with age until individuals reached 65 years of age, and thereafter it declined. During 2011, 5 percent or 419 thousand 16- and 17-year-olds hunted. The participation rate was also 5 percent for 18- to 24-year olds and 25- to 34-year olds. The participation rate climbed to 6 percent for 35- to 44-year olds, and then to 7 percent for 45- to 54-year olds and 55- to 64-year olds. People 65 and older had a participation rate of 4 percent. However, of the 65 and older age group, those who were 65 to 74 years of age had a 5 percent hunting participation rate, while those who were 75 and older had a 2 percent rate.

The age group that contributed the most hunters was 45 to 54 years old. About 3.1 million hunters, which was 23 percent of all hunters, were 45 to 54. Individuals 55 to 64 years old were close in total number of hunters at 2.8 million.

Hunters by Sex and Age

Total, both sexes . . .	**13.7 million**
Male	12.2 million
Female	1.5 million
Total, all ages	**13.7 million**
16 and 17	0.4 million
18 to 24	1.3 million
25 to 34	2.1 million
35 to 44	2.4 million
45 to 54	3.1 million
55 to 64	2.8 million
65 and older	1.5 million

Source: Table 10

Percent of Males and Females Who Hunted in the United States

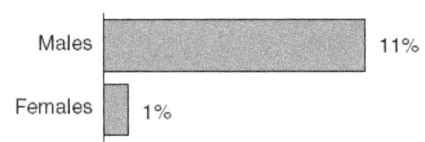

Percent of Hunters by Sex

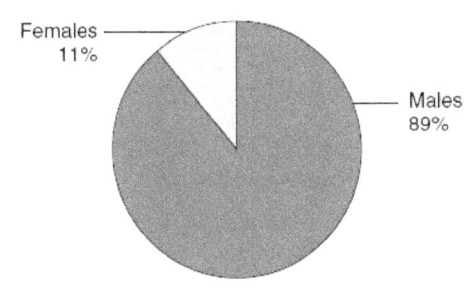

Percent of Hunters by Age

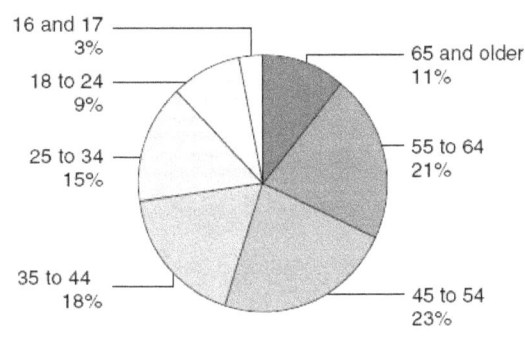

Percent of U.S. Population Who Hunted by Age

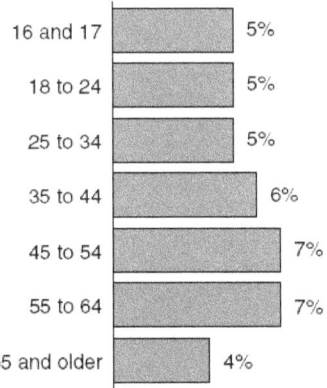

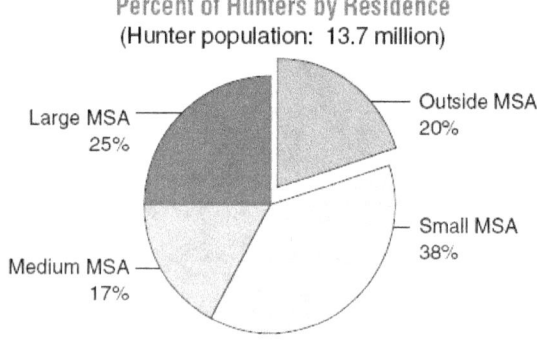

Percent of Hunters by Residence
(Hunter population: 13.7 million)

Outside MSA 20%
Small MSA 38%
Medium MSA 17%
Large MSA 25%

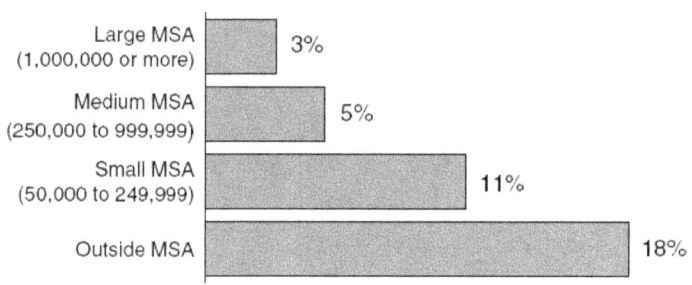

Percent of U.S. Population Who Hunted by Residence
(Total U.S. population that hunted: 6 percent)

Large MSA (1,000,000 or more) 3%
Medium MSA (250,000 to 999,999) 5%
Small MSA (50,000 to 249,999) 11%
Outside MSA 18%

Percent of U.S. Population Who Hunted by Household Income

Less than $20,000 — 3%
$20,000 to $24,999 — 4%
$25,000 to $29,999 — 5%
$30,000 to $34,999 — 5%
$35,000 to $39,999 — 5%
$40,000 to $49,999 — 7%
$50,000 to $74,999 — 8%
$75,000 to $99,999 — 9%
$100,000 to $149,999 — 8%
$150,000 or more — 5%

Metropolitan and Nonmetropolitan Hunters

As was the case for fishing, participation rates for hunting were the lowest among residents of the largest metropolitan statistical areas (MSAs)[1] and were the highest among non-MSA residents. Residents of the MSAs with a population of 1 million or more hunted at a 3 percent rate, which compares to 18 percent of those who resided outside MSAs. Furthermore the smaller the MSA the higher the participation rate. The rate among residents of MSAs of 50,000 to 249,999 was 11 percent and among residents of MSAs with 250,000 to 999,999 inhabitants the rate was 5 percent.

Despite the lower participation rates among MSA residents, they still made up the majority of hunters. Over 10.9 million hunters were MSA residents, compared to 2.8 million who were non-metropolitan residents.

Household Income of Hunters

The participation rate in hunting increased as household income increased until it reached incomes of $100,000 or more. The participation was highest among those with incomes of $75,000 to $99,999 at 9 percent. Participation rates for those who reported incomes of $50,000 to $74,999 and $100,000 to $149,999 was slightly lower at 8 percent. The participation rate in hunting for household incomes of $40,000 to $49,999 was 7 percent. A participation rate of 5 percent was reported for the following four income groups: $25,000 to $29,999; $30,000 to $34,999; $35,000 to $39,999; and $150,000 or more. The lowest participation rate was 3 percent reported for household incomes of less than $20,000.

The majority of hunters had household incomes of $50,000 or more. Among hunters who reported income, 64 percent had household incomes of $50,000 or more, and 36 percent had household incomes of less than

[1] See Appendix A for definition of metropolitan statistical area

$50,000. For the general population, 52 percent had incomes of $50,000 or more and 48 percent had incomes less than $50,000.

Education, Race, and Ethnicity of Hunters

Participation rates in hunting in 2011 varied little among people with different levels of educational attainment. The highest participation rate was 6 percent for the following three levels of attainment: 12 years, 1 to 3 years of college, and 4 years of college. The next highest rate, 5 percent, was reached by people with 11 years of education. The lowest rate, 4 percent, was for those people with an educational attainment of 5 years of college or more.

The two largest categories of education were 12 years and 1 to 3 years of college, composing 36 percent and 26 percent of all hunters, respectively. Those with 4 years of college composed 18 percent of all hunters, and those with 11 years or less composed 11 percent of all hunters. Individuals with 5 years or more of college made up 9 percent of all hunters.

Hunters by Education, Race, and Ethnicity
(In millions)

Total hunters **13.7**

Education
11 years or less	1.5
12 years.	5.0
1 to 3 years of college.	3.5
4 years of college	2.4
5 years or more of college. .	1.3

Race
White.	12.9
African American	0.4
Asian American.	*<0.1
Other	0.4

Ethnicity
Hispanic	0.3
Non-Hispanic	13.4

Source: Table 10
* Estimate based on a sample size of 10–29

While people of all races participate in hunting, the majority are White. Seven percent of the nation's White population, 2 percent of the African American population, 2 percent of those identified as other races, and less than 0.5 percent of the Asian American population went hunting in 2011.

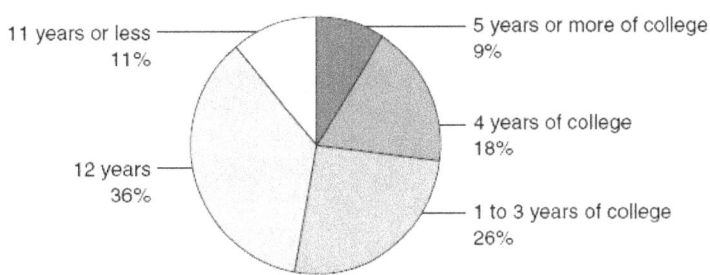

Percent of Hunters by Education

11 years or less 11%
5 years or more of college 9%
4 years of college 18%
1 to 3 years of college 26%
12 years 36%

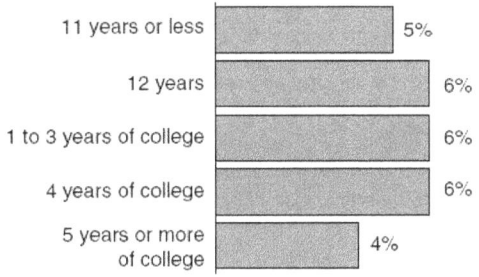

Percent of U.S. Population Who Hunted by Education

11 years or less	5%
12 years	6%
1 to 3 years of college	6%
4 years of college	6%
5 years or more of college	4%

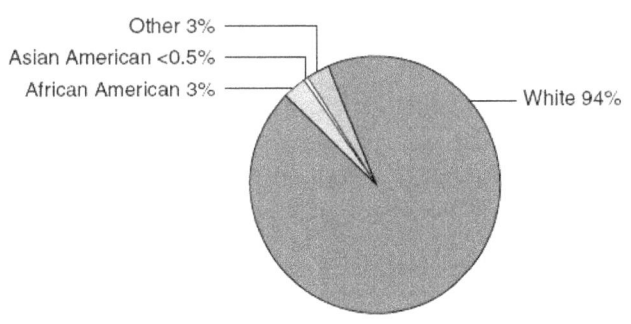

Percent of Hunters by Race

Other 3%
Asian American <0.5%
African American 3%
White 94%

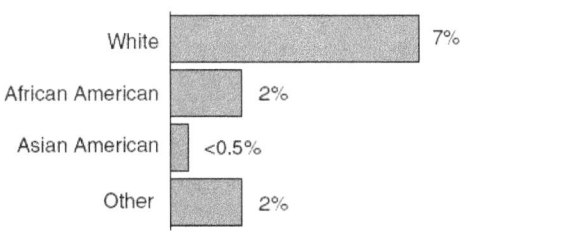

Percent of U.S. Population Who Hunted by Race

White	7%
African American	2%
Asian American	<0.5%
Other	2%

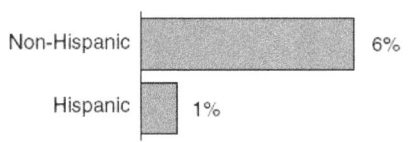

Percent of U.S. Population Who Hunted by Ethnicity

Non-Hispanic	6%
Hispanic	1%

Hispanics, who represent a growing percentage of the U.S population, hunted at a much lower rate than non-Hispanics. One percent of all Hispanics hunted in 2011 compared to 6 percent of non-Hispanics. The 271 thousand Hispanics who hunted in 2011 made up 2 percent of all hunters.

2001–2011 Comparison of Hunting Activity

The number of hunters increased 9 percent from 2006 to 2011. Other animal hunters increased 92 percent in number and the other types of hunting stayed level at the 95 percent level of significance. Total days of hunting went up 28 percent, primarily due to a 29 percent increase in big game hunting days. Other animal

hunting days also went up significantly. Trip-related, equipment, and other expenditures went up 29 percent. Trip-related expenditures increased 39 percent, equipment expenditures did not increase significantly, and other expenditures such as land leasing and owning went up 40 percent.

Comparing 2001 and 2011 estimates reveals no statistically significant change in the number of overall hunters, but does show increases in the number of days and expenditures. Small game hunting participant numbers went down, while other animal participant numbers went up. Days of big game and other animal hunting went up significantly, while small game and migratory bird hunting

days did not have a significant change. Turning to expenditures, the comparison is similar to 2006–2011. Overall expenditures went up, with trip-related and other items undergoing an increase and equipment staying level.

The across-the-board increases in 2011 hunting participation, day, and expenditure estimates run counter to the downward trends documented in the preceding three FHWAR National Surveys. From 1991 to 2006, hunting participation had dropped 11 percent and the number of hunting days had not significantly changed. The 9 percent participant and 28 percent day increases puts the 2011 hunting status on par with that of 1991 hunting, the high point of hunting in the last twenty years.

Number of Hunters
(Millions)

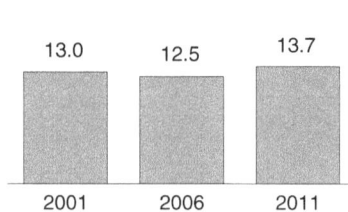

Days of Hunting
(Millions)

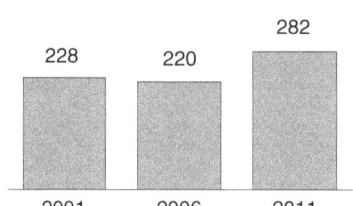

Hunting Expenditures
(Billions of 2011 dollars)

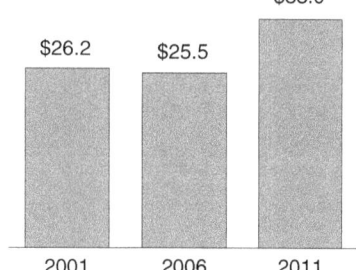

2001–2011 Hunting Participants, Days, and Expenditures

(U.S. population 16 years old and older. Numbers in thousands)

	2001		2011		2001-2011
	Number	Percent	Number	Percent	percent change
Hunters, total	**13,034**	**100**	**13,674**	**100**	NS5
Big game.........................	10,911	84	11,570	85	NS6
Small game......................	5,434	42	4,506	33	–17
Migratory birds....................	2,956	23	2,583	19	NS–13
Other animals	1,047	8	**2,168	16	107
Days, total......................	**228,368**	**100**	**281,884**	**100**	**23**
Big game.........................	153,191	67	212,116	75	38
Small game......................	60,142	26	50,884	18	NS–15
Migratory birds....................	29,310	13	23,263	8	NS–21
Other animals	19,207	8	**34,434	12	79
Hunting, total (2011 dollars)...........	**$26,178,562**	**100**	***$32,999,416	**100**	**26**
Trip-related	6,671,189	25	10,421,189	32	56
Equipment, total	13,160,387	50	13,972,490	42	NS 6
Hunting equipment	5,793,937	22	7,738,324	23	34
Auxiliary equipment	1,527,736	6	1,844,880	6	NS21
Special equipment..............	5,838,687	22	4,389,286	13	NS–25
Other.........................	6,346,987	24	***8,605,739	26	36

NS Not different from zero at the 5 percent level of significance
** Other animals redefined to include feral pigs
*** Plantings not included in 2011 expenditures for comparison purposes 2011 was first year plantings were included

2006–2011 Hunting Participants, Days, and Expenditures

(U.S. population 16 years old and older. Numbers in thousands)

	2006		2011		2006-2011
	Number	Percent	Number	Percent	percent change
Hunters, total	**12,510**	**100**	**13,674**	**100**	9
Big game.........................	10,682	85	11,570	85	NS8
Small game......................	4,797	38	4,506	33	NS–6
Migratory birds....................	2,293	18	2,583	19	NS13
Other animals	1,128	9	**2,168	16	92
Days, total......................	**219,925**	**100**	**281,884**	**100**	**28**
Big game.........................	164,061	75	212,116	75	29
Small game......................	52,395	24	50,884	18	NS–3
Migratory birds....................	19,770	9	23,263	8	NS18
Other animals	15,205	7	**34,434	12	126
Hunting, total (2011 dollars)...........	**$25,543,470**	**100**	***$32,999,416	**100**	**29**
Trip-related......................	7,451,789	29	10,421,189	32	40
Equipment, total...................	11,973,875	47	13,972,490	42	NS17
Hunting equipment..............	5,987,611	23	7,738,324	23	29
Auxiliary equipment.............	1,484,214	6	1,844,880	6	NS24
Special equipment	4,502,047	18	4,389,286	13	NS–3
Other	6,117,806	24	***8,605,739	26	41

NS Not different from zero at the 5 percent level of significance
** Other animals redefined to include feral pigs
*** Plantings not included in 2011 expenditures for comparison purposes 2011 was first year plantings were included

Wildlife Watching

Wildlife Watching Highlights

Nearly a third of the U.S. population enjoyed wildlife watching in 2011. Wildlife watching is defined here as closely observing, feeding, and photographing wildlife, visiting public parks around the home because of wildlife, and maintaining plantings and natural areas around the home for the benefit of wildlife. These activities are categorized as around the home (within a mile of home) or away from home (at least one mile from home).

The 2011 Survey counts wildlife watching as recreational activities, as defined above, in which the primary objective was to watch wildlife. Secondary or incidental participation, such as observing wildlife while doing something else, was not included in the Survey.

During 2011, 71.8 million U.S. residents, 30 percent of the U.S. population 16 years old or older, participated in wildlife-watching activities. People who took an interest in wildlife around their homes numbered 68.6 million, while those who took trips away from their homes to wildlife watch numbered 22.5 million people.

Wild Bird Observers

Of all the wildlife in the United States, birds attracted the biggest following. Approximately 46.7 million people observed birds around the home and on trips in 2011. A large majority, 88 percent (41.3 million), observed wild birds around the home, while 38 percent, 17.8 million, took trips away from home to observe wild birds. Participants averaged a startling 110 days of birding in 2011, due to the 119 days by around-the-home birders. Away-from-home birders averaged 13 days.

Wildlife-Watching Participants by Activity
(In millions)

Total wildlife-watching participants	**71.8**
Away from home	**22.5**
Observers	19.8
Photographers	12.4
Feeders	5.4
Around the home	**68.6**
Feeders	52.8
Observers	45.0
Photographers	25.4
Maintainers of plantings or natural areas.	13.4
Visitors of parks or natural areas.	12.3

Source: Table 35

Wildlife-Watching Participants
(In millions)

Total	71.8
Around the home	68.6
Away from home	22.5

Bird Watchers
(In millions)

Total	46.7
Around the home	41.3
Away from home	17.8

Wildlife-Watching Expenditures

Thirty-eight percent of all the dollars spent in 2011 for wildlife-related recreation was due to wildlife watching. Wildlife-watching participants 16 years old or older spent $54.9 billion, an average of $981 per spender. Seventy-eight percent of all wildlife watchers spent money on their avocation.

Wildlife watchers spent $17.3 billion on trips pursuing their activities. Food and lodging accounted for $9.3 billion (54 percent of all trip-related expenditures), transportation expenses totaled $6.0 billion (35 percent), and other trip costs, such as land use fees and equipment rental, amounted to $1.9 billion (11 percent) for the year.

These recreationists purchased $27.2 billion worth of equipment for wildlife watching. They spent $11.3 billion (42 percent of all equipment expenditures) on wildlife-watching equipment including binoculars, cameras, bird food, and special clothing. Expenditures for auxiliary equipment, such as tents and backpacking equipment, totaled $1.6 billion (6 percent) for the year. Participants spent $14.3 billion (53 percent) on special equipment, including off-road vehicles, campers, and boats.

Also for the year, wildlife watchers spent $5.7 billion on land leasing and owning; $2.2 billion on plantings for the benefit of wildlife; $2.2 billion on membership dues and contributions; and $0.4 billion on magazines, books, and DVDs.

Total Wildlife-Watching Expenditures

Total wildlife-watching expenditures	**$54.9 billion**
Total trip-related...............................	**$17.3 billion**
Food and lodging	9.3 billion
Transportation..............................	6.0 billion
Other trip costs	1.9 billion
Total equipment expenditures	**$27.2 billion**
Wildlife-watching equipment.....................	11.3 billion
Auxiliary equipment.........................	1.6 billion
Special equipment...........................	14.3 billion
Total other equipment........................	**$10.5 billion**
Land leasing and owning	5.7 billion
Plantings.................................	2.2 billion
Membership dues and contributions...............	2.2 billion
Magazines, books, DVDs......................	0.4 billion

Source: Table 40.

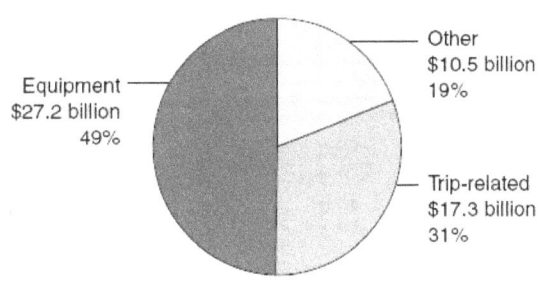

Wildlife-Watching Expenditures
(Total expenditures: $54.9 billion)

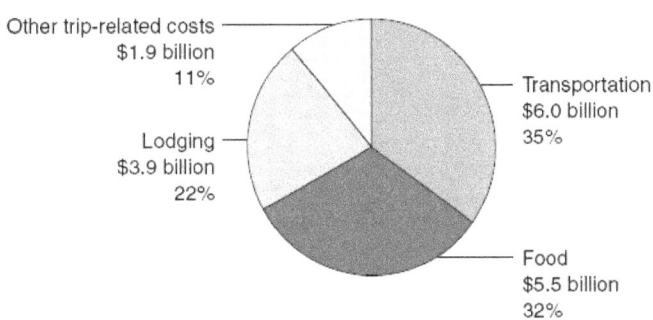

Trip-Related Expenditures
(Total expenditures: $17.3 billion)

Around-The-Home Wildlife-Watching Highlights

In 2011, around-the-home participants 16 years old and older numbered 68.6 million—96 percent of all wildlife-watching recreationists. The most popular activity, feeding birds and other wildlife, accounted for 52.8 million wildlife watchers—77 percent of all around-the-home participants. About 45 million people observed wildlife, representing 66 percent of all around-the-home participants.

Approximately 25.4 million recreationists (37 percent of all around-the-home wildlife watchers) photographed wildlife. About 13.4 million maintained plantings or natural areas for the benefit of wildlife. They made up 19 percent of all around-the-home participants. Finally, 12.3 million people visited parks or natural areas within one mile of their homes for wildlife watching. They comprised 18 percent of all around-the-home participants.

Around-The-Home Participants
(In millions)

Total participants	**68.6**
Feed wildlife	52.8
Observe wildlife	45.0
Photograph wildlife	25.4
Visits parks or natural areas	12.3
Maintain plantings	9.2
Maintain natural areas	8.0

Source: Table 37

Percent of Total Around-The-Home Participants by Activity
(Total: 68.6 million participants)

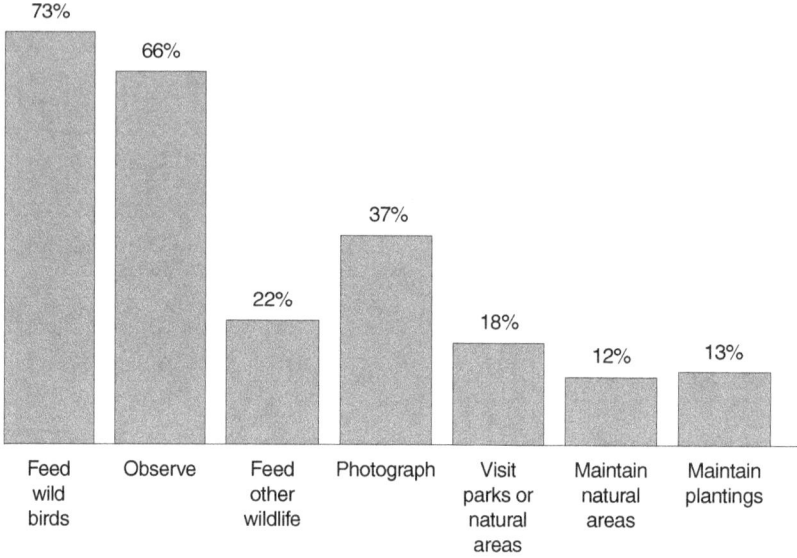

Wildlife Fed, Observed, or Photographed by Around-The-Home Participants

Of the 52.8 million people feeding wildlife around their homes in 2011, 95 percent (50.2 million) fed wild birds, while 28 percent (14.8 million) fed other wildlife.

Approximately 45.0 million participants closely observed wildlife around their homes, of which 41.3 million observed birds. Observing mammals was undertaken by 35.9 million participants. Insects and spiders attracted the attention of 16.6 million people; 14.1 million observed amphibians or reptiles; and 8.4 million people observed fish and other wildlife. The median number of days for around-the-home observations for all animals was a little over 87 days in 2011.

About 25.4 million people photographed wildlife around their homes. The median number of days people took pictures of wildlife around their homes in 2011 was 4 days, although 3.7 million people (15 percent) photographed wildlife 21 days or more.

Around-The-Home Wildlife Watchers by Geographic Region

In 2011, over 239 million people 16 years old or older lived in the United States. Of those, 29 percent wildlife watched around their homes. The participation rates of these around-the-home participants varied by region.

The percentages of regional populations that wildlife watched around their homes ranged from 24 percent in the Pacific Region to 35 percent in the East North Central Region. The New England, East North Central, West North Central, and East South Central had participation rates above the national average of 29 percent.

The regions making up the largest number of around-the-home wildlife watchers in the United States were the South Atlantic (12.8 million participants) and the East North Central Region (12.5 million participants).

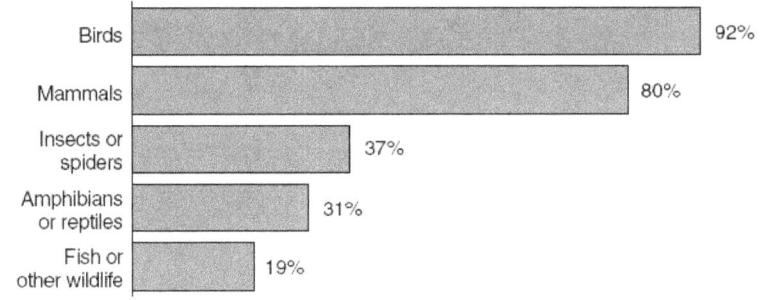

Percent of Around-The-Home Observers
by Type of Wildlife Observed
(Total wildlife observers: 45.0 million)

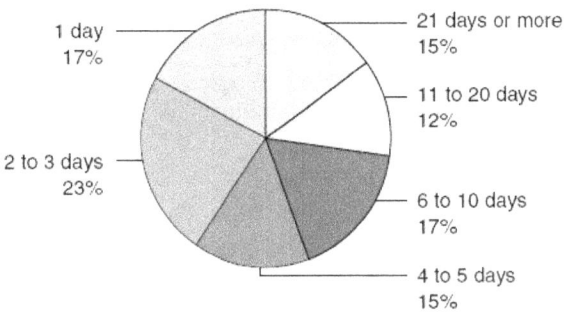

Percent of Around-The-Home Photographers
by Days Spent Photographing Wildlife
(Total wildlife photographers: 25.4 million)

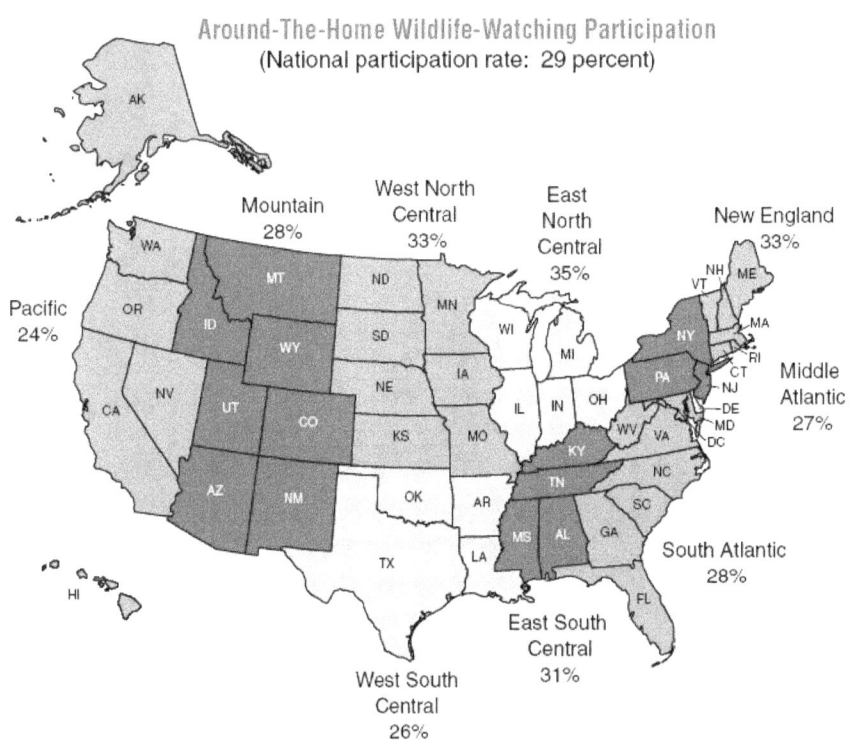

Around-The-Home Wildlife-Watching Participation
(National participation rate: 29 percent)

Percent of Males and Females Who Participated Around-The-Home

Males	27%
Females	30%

Percent of Around-The-Home Wildlife Watchers by Sex
(Total participants: 68.6 million)

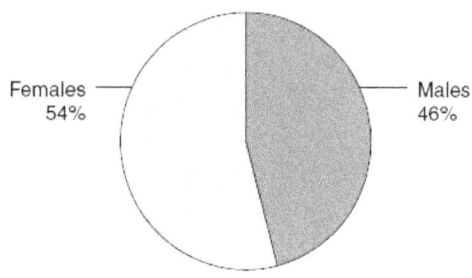

Females 54%   Males 46%

Percent of Around-The-Home Wildlife Watchers by Age
(Total participants: 68.6 million)

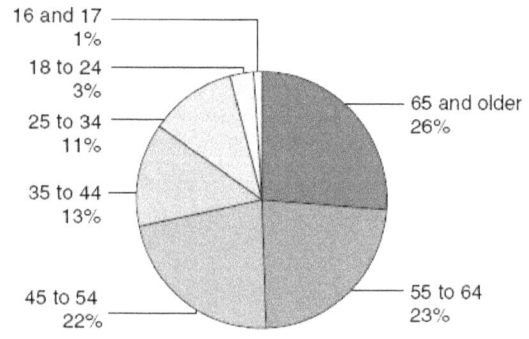

16 and 17 — 1%
18 to 24 — 3%
25 to 34 — 11%
35 to 44 — 13%
45 to 54 — 22%
55 to 64 — 23%
65 and older — 26%

Percent of U.S. Population Who Participated Around-The-Home by Age

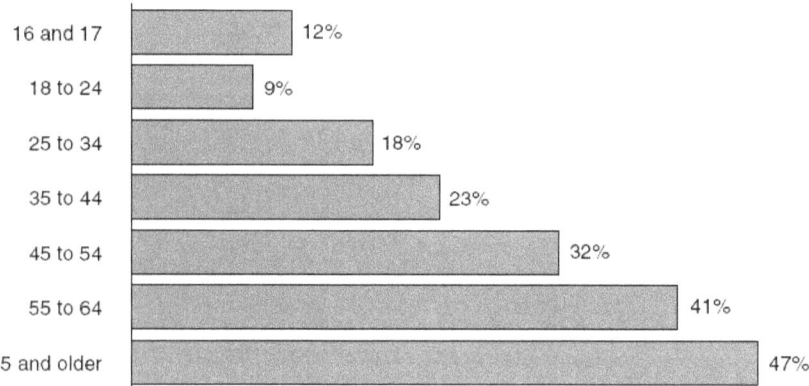

16 and 17	12%
18 to 24	9%
25 to 34	18%
35 to 44	23%
45 to 54	32%
55 to 64	41%
65 and older	47%

Sex and Age of Around-The-Home Wildlife Watchers

Females and males had similar participation rates for around-the-home wildlife watching. In 2011, 30 percent of females and 27 percent of males enjoyed around-the-home activities. Of the 68.6 million around-the-home wildlife watchers, 54 percent (37.3 million) were females and 46 percent (31.3 million) were males.

People in the 65- to 74-year-old age group were most likely to participate at 53 percent (11.9 million). People in the 18- to 24-year-old age group were the least likely to participate, with 9 percent (2.4 million). The disparity in participation rates between people 16 to 34 years old (14 percent) and those 35 years old and older (35 percent) is striking.

Around-The-Home Participants by Sex and Age
(In millions)

Total, both sexes. . . .	**68.6 million**
Male	31.3 million
Female.	37.3 million
Total, all ages	**68.6 million**
16 and 17.	0.9 million
18 to 24	2.4 million
25 to 34	7.3 million
35 to 44	9.3 million
45 to 54	14.9 million
55 to 64	15.8 million
65 and older.	18.1 million

Source: Table 42

Metropolitan and Nonmetropolitan Around-The-Home Participants

Approximately 91 percent of around-the-home wildlife watchers lived in metropolitan areas, as defined by the U.S. Census Bureau. Metropolitan statistical areas, or MSAs[1], with populations of 1 million or more had a participation rate of 25 percent, lower than any smaller MSA or non-MSA. Nonetheless, recreationists from the most populous MSAs comprised 46 percent of all around-the-home wildlife watchers. In MSAs of 250,000 to 999,999, the participation rate was 33 percent and they made up 23 percent of all around-the-home recreationists. About 22 percent of around-the-home wildlife watchers lived in MSAs with a population from 50,000 to 249,999. The population of these areas had a participation rate of 32 percent.

The participation rate for nonmetropolitan populations was 38 percent, higher than for any MSA. Six percent of the total U.S. population lived outside MSAs in 2011 and represented 9 percent of all around-the-home wildlife watchers.

[1] See Appendix A for definition of Metropolitan Statistical Area

Percent of U.S. Population Who Participated Around-The-Home by Residence

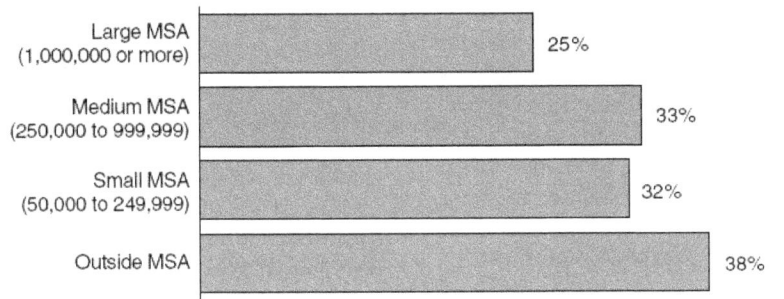

Percent of Around-The-Home Wildlife Watchers by Residence
(Total participants: 68.6 million)

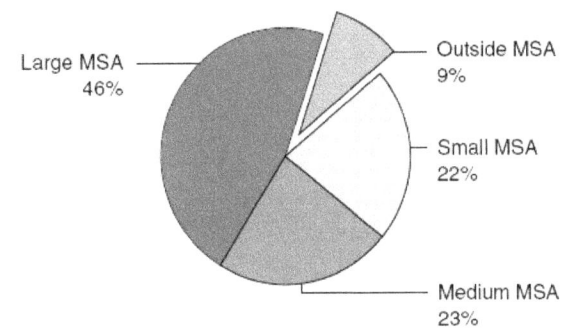

Household Income of Around-The-Home Participants

Participation rates ranged from 22 percent among U.S. residents living in households earning less than $20,000 per year and $25,000 to $29,999 per year to 36 percent of those living in households earning $150,000 or more annually. These participants made up 10 percent, 3 percent, and 9 percent, respectively, of the 68.6 million around-the-home wildlife watchers in 2011.

Participants in households earning $50,000 to $74,999 a year constituted the largest number, 11.7 million, and had a 35 percent participation rate. The next two income groups with the largest numbers of participants had household incomes of $75,000 to $99,999 and $100,000 to $149,999. The former contributed 8.6 million participants and had a 34 percent participation rate, while the latter contributed 8.3 million and had a 35 percent participation rate. The number of around-the-home recreationists contributed by other income groups ranged from 2.2 million participants with $25,000 to $29,999 household incomes and 22 percent participation rates to 6.1 million participants with $150,000 or more incomes and 36 percent participation rates.

Percent of U.S. Population Who Participated Around-The-Home
by Household Income

Income	Percent
Less than $20,000	22%
$20,000 to $24,999	27%
$25,000 to $29,999	22%
$30,000 to $34,999	35%
$35,000 to $39,999	28%
$40,000 to $49,999	29%
$50,000 to $74,999	35%
$75,000 to $99,999	34%
$100,000 to $149,999	35%
$150,000 or more	36%

Education, Race, and Ethnicity of Around-The-Home Participants

Looking at the educational background of participants, it was found that the rate of participation in around-the-home wildlife watching increased with the increase in educational attainment. The highest participation rate was among recreationists with 5 years or more of college, 43 percent. They made up 18 percent of all around-the-home wildlife watchers. The lowest participation rate, 17 percent, was among people with 11 years or less of education— 8 percent of all participants. Recreationists with 12 years of education, 30 percent of all around-the-home participants, had a participation rate of 25 percent. Participants with 1 to 3 years of college, 22 percent of all participants, had a participation rate of 28 percent. Recreationists with 4 years of college, 23 percent of all participants, had a participation rate of 36 percent.

A wide range of participation rates were found among the different races and ethnic groups. About 34 percent of the White population engaged in

Around-The-Home Participants by Education, Race, and Ethnicity
(In millions)

Total participants **68.6**

Education
11 years of less 5.4
12 years 20.3
1 to 3 years of college 15.3
4 years of college 15.5
5 years or more of college . 12.1

Race
White 62.5
African American 2.6
Asian American 1.0
Other 2.6

Ethnicity
Hispanic 3.4
Non-Hispanic 65.2

Source: Table 42

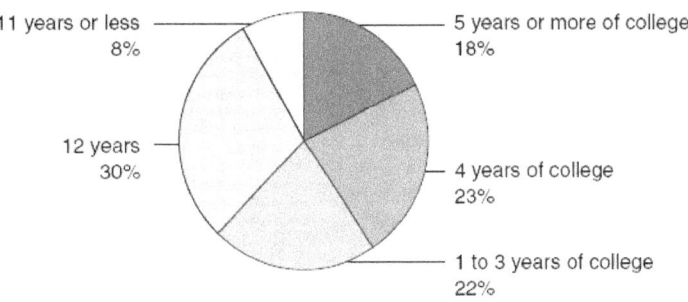

Percent of Around-The-Home Wildlife Watchers by Education
(Total: 68.6 million participants)

11 years or less 8%
5 years or more of college 18%
12 years 30%
4 years of college 23%
1 to 3 years of college 22%

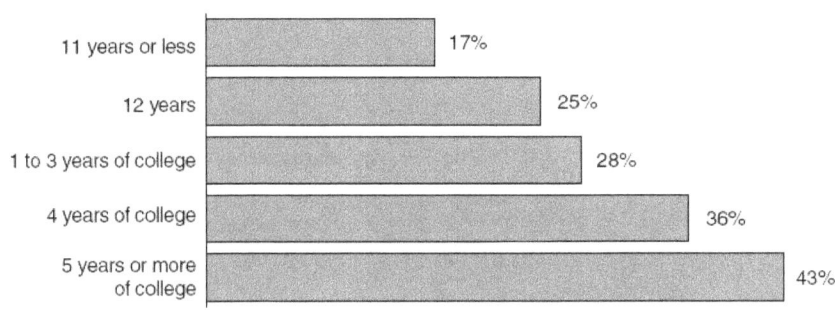

Percent of U.S. Population Who Participated Around-The-Home by Education

11 years or less 17%
12 years 25%
1 to 3 years of college 28%
4 years of college 36%
5 years or more of college 43%

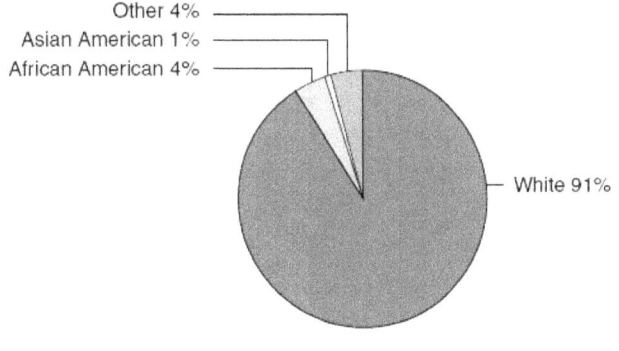

Percent of Around-The-Home Wildlife Watchers by Race
(Total: 68.6 million participants)

Other 4%
Asian American 1%
African American 4%
White 91%

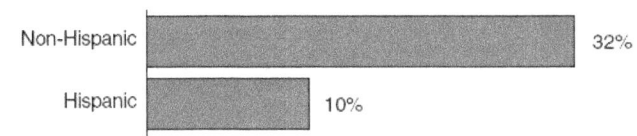

Percent of U.S. Population Who Participated Around-The-Home by Ethnicity

Non-Hispanic 32%
Hispanic 10%

around-the-home wildlife watching, contrasted with 11 percent of the African American population, 8 percent of the Asian American population, and 12 percent of individuals comprising other races. Of the total number of around-the-home participants, 91 percent were White, 4 percent were African Americans, 1 percent was Asian American, and 4 percent were all other races.

Ten percent of the U.S. Hispanic population engaged in wildlife watching around their homes in comparison with 32 percent of the non-Hispanic population. The 65.2 million non-Hispanic participants comprised 95 percent of all around-the-home wildlife watchers and the 3.4 million Hispanic participants made up 5 percent.

Away-From-Home Wildlife-Watching Highlights

In 2011, 22.5 million people 16 years old and older took trips away from home to feed, observe, or photograph wildlife. They comprised 31 percent of all wildlife watchers. Most popular with away-from-home participants was closely observing wildlife. About 19.8 million participants, 8 percent of the U.S. population 16 years old and older, observed wildlife an average of 14 days in 2011. Photographing wildlife was enjoyed by 12.4 million people, 5 percent of the U.S. population. They averaged 9 days per photographer.

Approximately 5.4 million people fed wildlife an average of 11 days and comprised 2 percent of the U.S. population.

About 82 percent of all away-from-home participants took trips within their resident state to participate in wildlife watching. Approximately 70 percent took trips only in their resident state, 12 percent took trips both inside and outside their resident state, and 18 percent took trips only to other states. Altogether, 30 percent of all away-from-home participants took at least some of their trips to other states.

Percent of U.S. Population Who Participated Away-From-Home by Type of Activity
(Total: 22.5 million participants)

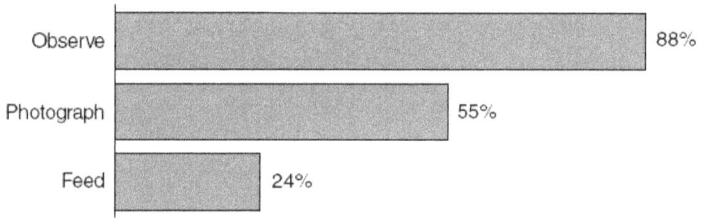

Percent of Away-From-Home Wildlife Watchers in State of Residence and Other States
(Total participants: 22.5 million)

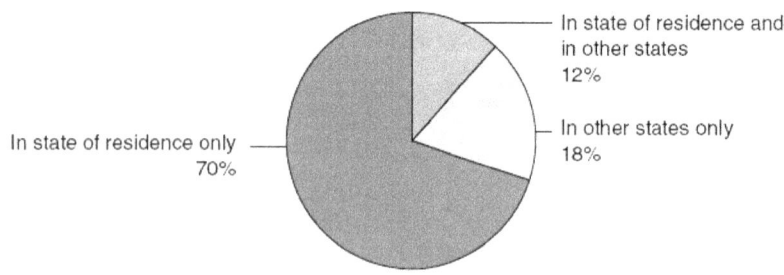

Away-From-Home Participants
(In millions)

Total participants	**22.5**
Observers	19.8
Photographers	12.4
Feeders	5.4
Total days	**336**
Observers	269
Photographers	110
Feeders	59

Source: Table 36

Away-From-Home Participants by Type of Wildlife Observed, Fed, or Photographed

(In millions)

Total participants	**22.5**
Birds, total	**18.9**
Waterfowl	13.3
Birds of prey	12.9
Songbirds	12.1
Other water birds	10.6
Other birds	6.9
Land mammals, total	**13.7**
Large land mammals	10.4
Small land mammals	10.3
Fish	**6.4**
Marine mammals	**4.0**
Other (turtles, butterflies, etc.)	**10.1**

Source: Table 38

Wildlife Observed, Fed, or Photographed by Away-From-Home Participants

Wild birds attracted the most interest from wildlife watchers on their trips—18.9 million people or 84 percent of all away-from-home participants. The most-watched birds, waterfowl (ducks and geese, primarily), were watched by 13.3 million people. Next on the list of most-watched were birds of prey which drew 12.9 million trip-takers, followed by songbirds with 12.1 million watchers. Herons, shore birds, and other water birds attracted 10.6 million recreationists. Lastly, other birds, such as road runners and turkeys, attracted 6.9 million wildlife watchers.

Land mammals, such as deer, bears, and coyotes, were observed, fed, or photographed by 13.7 million people—61 percent of all away-from-home participants. Fish attracted the attention of 6.4 million people or 28 percent of all away-from-home recreationists.

About 4.0 million people or 18 percent of all away-from-home participants observed, fed, or photographed marine mammals, such as whales, seals, and dolphins. Other wildlife, such as butterflies, snakes, and turtles, appealed to 10.1 million people or 45 percent of all away-from-home wildlife watchers.

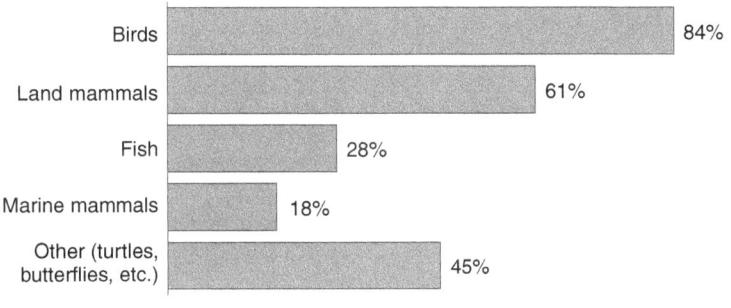

Percent of Away-From-Home Wildlife Watchers Who Observed, Fed, or Photographed Wildlife
(Total: 22.5 million participants)

Area Visited by Away-From-Home Participants

In 2011, the most visited areas for Americans to observe, feed, or photograph wildlife were publicly owned. Approximately 82 percent of all trip-taking wildlife watchers used public areas while just 34 percent used private areas. About 25 percent of all away-from-home participants, 5.5 million, visited both public and private areas. Approximately 12.8 million, 57 percent, visited only public areas to engage in their activities while 2.0 million, 9 percent, visited only private areas.

Away-From-Home Participants by Public and Private Land
(In millions)

Total participants	**22.5**
Public land only	12.8
Private land only	2.1
Public and private land . . .	5.5
Not reported	2.0

Source: Table 36

Percent of Away-From-Home Wildlife Watchers by Public and Private Land
(Total participants: 22.5 million)

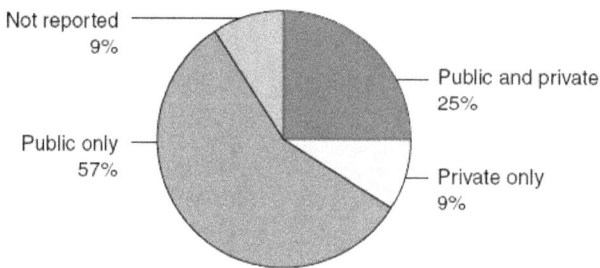

Away-From-Home Wildlife Watchers by Geographic Region

In 2011, 239 million people 16 years old and older lived in the United States—9 percent of whom took trips to wildlife watch.

Away-from-home participation rates ranged from 6 percent in the West South Central Region to 13 percent in the Mountain Region. The regions that had participation rates higher than the national average were New England, West North Central, East South Central, Mountain, and Pacific.

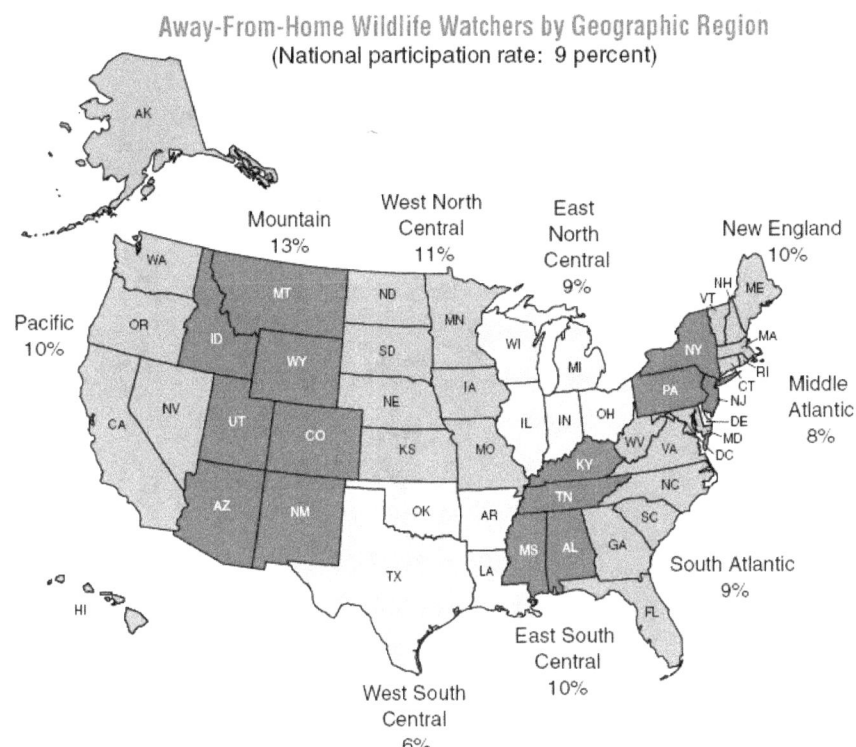

Away-From-Home Wildlife Watchers by Geographic Region
(National participation rate: 9 percent)

Percent of Males and Females Who Participated Away-From-Home

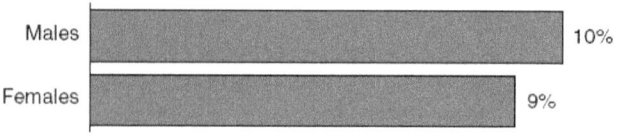

Males — 10%
Females — 9%

Percent of Away-From-Home Wildlife Watchers by Sex

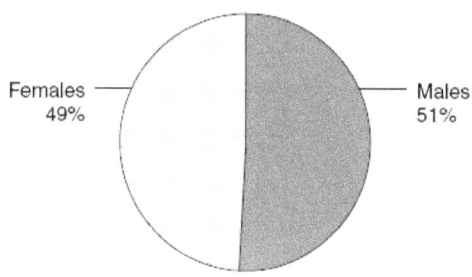

Females 49%   Males 51%

Percent of Away-From-Home Wildlife Watchers by Age

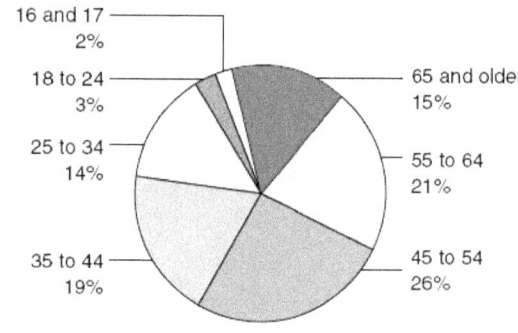

16 and 17 2%
18 to 24 3%
25 to 34 14%
35 to 44 19%
45 to 54 26%
55 to 64 21%
65 and older 15%

Percent of U.S. Population Who Participated by Age

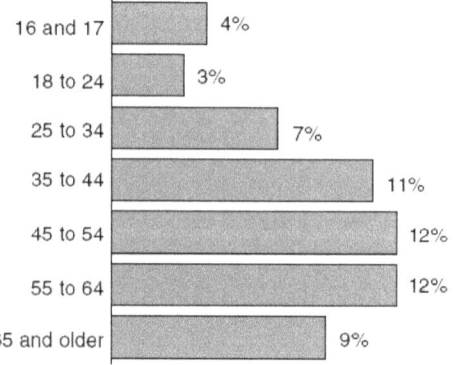

16 and 17 — 4%
18 to 24 — 3%
25 to 34 — 7%
35 to 44 — 11%
45 to 54 — 12%
55 to 64 — 12%
65 and older — 9%

Sex and Age of Away-From-Home Wildlife Watchers

A similar number of males and females participated in away-from-home wildlife watching in 2011. Fifty-one percent (11.5 million) of all participants were males and 49 percent (11.0 million) were females. Ten percent of males and 9 percent of females in the United States enjoyed observing, feeding, or photographing wildlife away from home.

The 45- to 54-year-old age group had the most away-from-home recreationists, 5.8 million. This age group, the 55- to 64-year-olds, and the 65- to 74-year olds had the highest participation rate, 12 percent. Another age group that had a high participation rate was the 35- to 44-year-old age group, 11 percent. The 18- to 24-year-olds had the lowest participation rate, at 3 percent.

Away-From-Home Participants by Sex and Age

(In millions)

Total, both sexes	**22.5**
Male	11.5
Female	11.0
Total, all ages	**22.5**
16 and 17	0.3
18 to 24	0.8
25 to 34	3.1
35 to 44	4.3
45 to 54	5.8
55 to 64	4.7
65 and older	3.4

Source: Table 41

Metropolitan and Nonmetropolitan Away-From-Home Participants

In 2011, 9 percent of all people living in MSAs[2] took trips primarily to enjoy wildlife. MSA residents comprised 92 percent of all away-from-home participants. In contrast, 12 percent of all people outside an MSA watched wildlife away from home.

As was the case with around-the-home wildlife watching, the biggest MSA had both the lowest participation rate and the highest number of participants. Residents of non-MSAs made up 8 percent of away-from-home participants and 9 percent of around-the-home participants.

Household Income of Away-From-Home Participants

Participation rates ranged from 5 percent for those in households earning less than $20,000 per year to 15 percent for those in households earning $75,000 to $99,999. There was a strong correlation between income and the likelihood to wildlife watch away from home, with an increase in one matched by an increase in the other. The income group that had the most participants was $50,000 to $74,999, with 4.8 million recreationists.

Median income was higher for away-from-home participants than for Americans as a whole, slightly under $68,000 for recreationists compared to about $52,000 for the U.S. population.

[2] See Appendix A for definition of Metropolitan Statistical Area

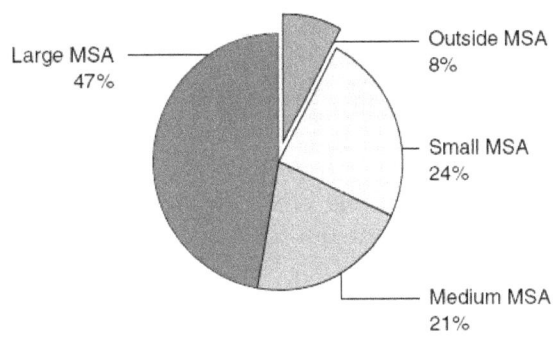

Percent of Away-From-Home Wildlife Watchers by Residence
(Total participants: 22.5 million)

- Large MSA 47%
- Outside MSA 8%
- Small MSA 24%
- Medium MSA 21%

Percent of U.S. Population Who Participated by Residence

- Large MSA (1,000,000 or more) — 8%
- Medium MSA (250,000 to 999,999) — 10%
- Small MSA (50,000 to 249,999) — 11%
- Outside MSA — 12%

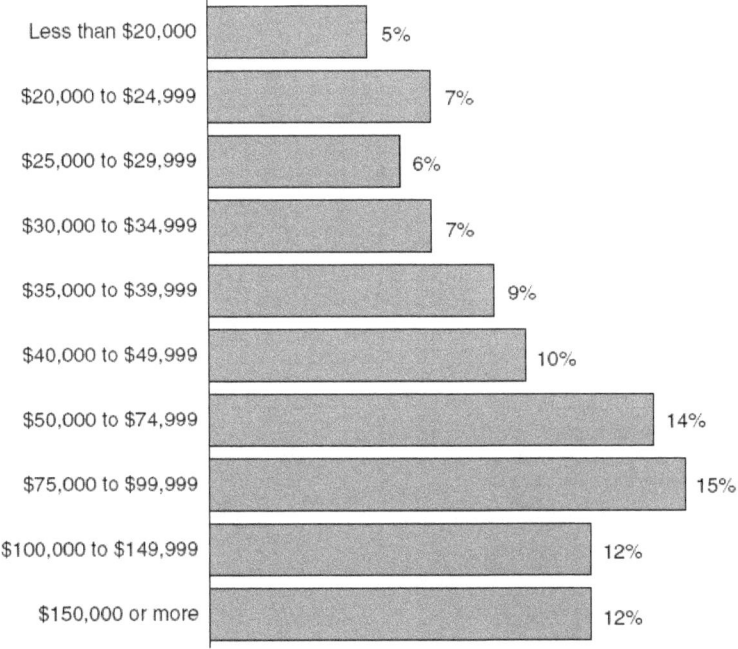

Percent of U.S. Population Who Participated Away-From-Home by Household Income

- Less than $20,000 — 5%
- $20,000 to $24,999 — 7%
- $25,000 to $29,999 — 6%
- $30,000 to $34,999 — 7%
- $35,000 to $39,999 — 9%
- $40,000 to $49,999 — 10%
- $50,000 to $74,999 — 14%
- $75,000 to $99,999 — 15%
- $100,000 to $149,999 — 12%
- $150,000 or more — 12%

Education, Race, and Ethnicity of Away-From-Home Participants

As in the case of household income, educational achievement and participation in away-from-home wildlife watching have a direct correlation. About 4 percent of the U.S. population with 11 years of education or less participated, compared to 19 percent of the population with 5 years or more of college. The educational cohort with the most participants was 4 years of college, with 5.4 million recreationists. The educational cohort with the fewest recreationists was 11 years or less, with 1.2 million.

The participation rates by race varied greatly. Approximately 11 percent of Whites and 5 percent of other races except African Americans and Asian Americans took trips to wildlife watch. In contrast, 3 percent of African Americans and 2 percent of Asian Americans participated. Of the total 22.5 million away-from-home participants, 92 percent were White, 3 percent were African Americans, 1 percent were Asian Americans, and 4 percent were other races.

Away-From-Home Participants by Education, Race and Ethnicity

(In millions)

Total participants **22.5**

Education
11 years or less	1.2
12 years	5.2
1 to 3 years of college	5.3
4 years of college	5.4
5 years or more of college .	5.3

Race
White	20.6
African American	0.6
Asian American	0.3
Other	1.0

Ethnicity
Hispanic	1.4
Non-Hispanic	21.1

Source: Table 41

About 1.4 million recreationists were Hispanic, 6 percent of all participants. Approximately 4 percent of the U.S. Hispanic population took trips to engage in wildlife watching. Of the non-Hispanic population, 10 percent (21.1 million participants) took trips to wildlife watch. They were 94 percent of all away-from-home wildlife watchers.

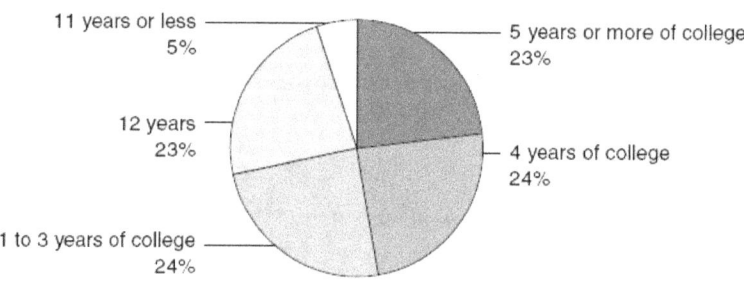

Percent of Away-From-Home Wildlife Watchers by Education
(Total participants: 22.5 million)

- 11 years or less 5%
- 5 years or more of college 23%
- 12 years 23%
- 4 years of college 24%
- 1 to 3 years of college 24%

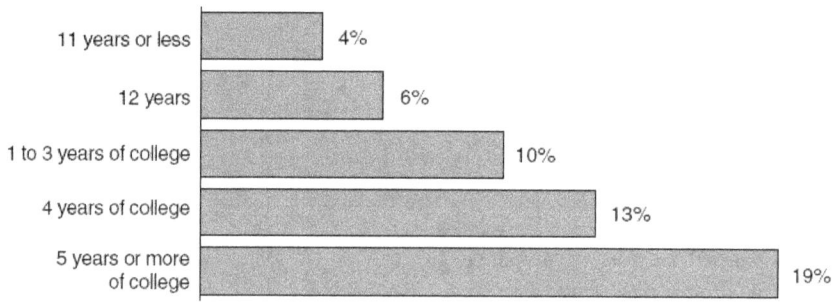

Percent of U.S. Population Who Participated Away-From-Home by Education

- 11 years or less 4%
- 12 years 6%
- 1 to 3 years of college 10%
- 4 years of college 13%
- 5 years or more of college 19%

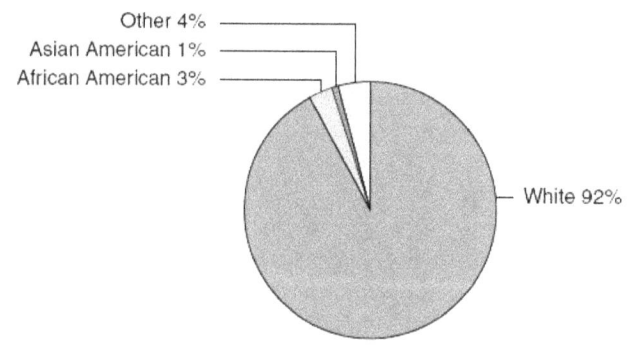

Percent of Away-From-Home Wildlife Watchers by Race
(Total participants: 22.5 million)

- Other 4%
- Asian American 1%
- African American 3%
- White 92%

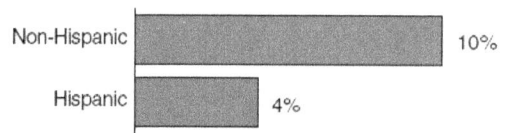

Percent of U.S. Population Who Participated Away-From-Home by Ethnicity

- Non-Hispanic 10%
- Hispanic 4%

2001–2011 Comparison of Wildlife-Watching Participation

Comparing 2006 and 2011 wildlife-watching measures finds no statistically significant change in the number of total participants, days, or expenditures. The increase in people photographing wildlife around the home was partially balanced by the decrease in people feeding wildlife. Away-from-home observers and feeders decreased in number, but not enough to affect overall away-from-home wildlife watching. The number of days of away-from-home wildlife watching did not change for any category. Similarly, the amount spent for wildlife watching was stable for all categories in 2006 and 2011.

From 2001 to 2011 the number of participants increased 9 percent. All categories of around-the-home wildlife watching increased or stayed level, led by the 82 percent increase in photographing wildlife. Overall away-from-home wildlife watching participant numbers stayed level, with the increase in photographers somewhat countered by the decrease in feeding wildlife. Similarly, the overall number of away-from-home days did not significantly change, with the increase in photographing days and decrease in feeding days roughly balancing each other. Trip-related expenditures increased significantly, but not enough to propel overall expenditures significantly higher. Equipment purchases, the largest component of wildlife-watching expenditures, did not increase or decrease significantly.

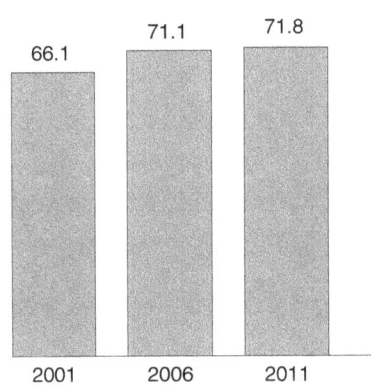

Number of Wildlife Watchers
(Millions)

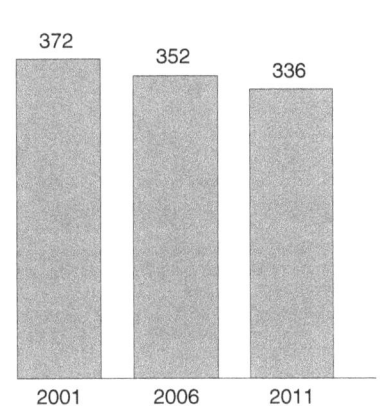

Days of Away-From-Home Wildlife Watching
(Millions)

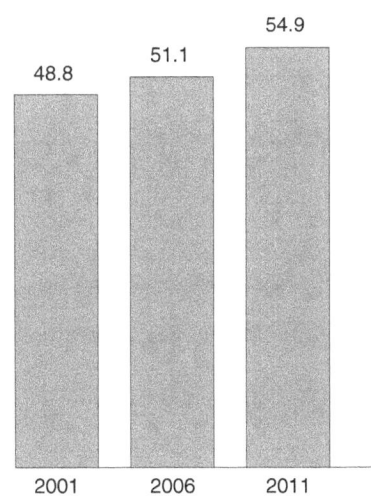

Wildlife-Watching Expenditures
(Billions of 2011 dollars)

2001–2011 Wildlife-Watching Participants, Days, and Expenditures

(U.S. population 16 years old and older. Numbers in thousands)

	2001		2011		2001-2011
	Number	Percent	Number	Percent	percent change
Wildlife-watching participants, total	**66,105**	**100**	**71,776**	**100**	9
Around the home	62,928	95	68,598	96	9
Observers	42,111	64	45,046	63	7
Photographers	13,937	21	25,370	35	82
Feeders	53,988	82	52,817	74	NS-2
Visitors of parks or natural areas	10,981	17	12,311	17	12
Maintainers of plantings or natural areas	13,072	20	13,399	19	NS3
Away from home	21,823	33	22,496	31	NS3
Observers	20,080	30	19,808	28	NS-1
Photographers	9,427	14	12,354	17	31
Feeders	7,077	11	5,399	8	-24
Days, away from home	372,006	100	335,625	100	NS-10
Observing	295,345	79	268,798	80	NS-9
Photographing	76,324	21	110,459	33	45
Feeding	103,307	28	59,255	18	-43
Wildlife-watching expenditures, total (2011 dollars)	**$48,791,172**	**100**	**$54,890,272**	**100**	NS13
Trip-related	10,367,312	21	17,274,675	31	67
Equipment, total	29,898,207	61	27,150,921	49	NS-9
Wildlife-watching equipment	9,340,464	19	11,323,179	21	21
Auxiliary equipment	910,552	2	1,555,374	3	71
Special equipment	19,647,191	40	14,272,368	26	NS-27
Other	8,525,654	17	10,464,677	19	NS23

NS Not different from zero at the 5 percent level of significance

2006–2011 Wildlife-Watching Participants, Days, and Expenditures

(U.S. population 16 years old and older. Numbers in thousands)

	2006		2011		2006-2011
	Number	Percent	Number	Percent	percent change
Wildlife-watching participants, total	**71,132**	**100**	**71,776**	**100**	NS1
Around the home.	67,756	95	68,598	96	NS1
Observers.	44,467	36	45,046	63	NS1
Photographers	18,763	26	25,370	35	35
Feeders.	55,512	78	52,817	74	–5
Visitors of parks or natural areas	13,271	19	12,311	17	NS–7
Maintainers of plantings or natural areas	14,508	20	13,399	19	NS–8
Away from home.	22,977	32	22,496	31	NS–2
Observers.	21,546	30	19,808	28	NS–8
Photographers	11,708	16	12,354	17	NS6
Feeders.	7,084	10	5,399	8	–24
Days, away from home.	352,070	100	335,625	100	NS–5
Observers.	291,027	82	268,798	80	NS–8
Photographers	103,872	30	110,459	33	NS6
Feeders.	77,329	22	59,255	18	NS–23
Wildlife-watching expenditures, total					
(2011 dollars).	**$51,133,555**	**100**	**$54,890,272**	**100**	NS7
Trip-related	14,420,170	28	17,274,675	31	NS20
Equipment, total	25,954,939	51	27,150,921	49	NS5
Wildlife-watching equipment.	11,054,094	22	11,323,179	21	NS2
Auxiliary equipment.	1,157,027	2	1,555,374	3	NS34
Special equipment	13,743,818	27	14,272,368	26	NS4
Other.	10,758,446	21	10,464,677	19	NS–3

NS Not different from zero at the 5 percent level of significance

Tables

Guide to Statistical Tables

Purpose and Coverage of Tables

The statistical tables of this report were designed to meet a wide range of needs for those interested in wildlife-related recreation. Special terms used in these tables are defined in Appendix A.

The tables are based on responses to the 2011 Survey, which was designed to collect data about participation in wildlife-related recreation. To have taken part in the Survey, a respondent must have been a U.S. resident (a resident of one of the 50 states or the District of Columbia). No one residing outside the United States (including U.S. citizens) was eligible for interviewing. Therefore, reported national totals do not include participation by those who were not U.S. residents or who were U.S. citizens residing outside the United States.

Comparability With Previous Surveys

The numbers reported can be compared with those in the 1991, 1996, 2001, and 2006 Survey Reports. The methodology used in 2011 was similar to that used in those Surveys. These results should not be directly compared to results from Surveys earlier than 1991 since there were major changes in methodology. These changes were made to improve accuracy in the information provided. Trends further back than 1991 are presented in Appendix C. These trends were developed using parts of the Surveys that were comparable.

Coverage of an Individual Table

Since the Survey covers many activities in various places by participants of different ages, all table titles, headnotes, stubs, and footnotes are designed to identify and articulate each item being reported in the table. For example, the title of Table 1 shows that data about anglers and hunters, their days of participation, and their number of trips are reported by type of activity. By contrast, the title of Table 3 indicates that it contains data on freshwater anglers and the days they fished for different species.

Percentages Reported in the Tables

Percentages are reported in the tables for the convenience of the user. When exclusive groups are being reported, the base of a percentage is apparent from its context because the percents add to 100 percent (plus or minus a rounding error). For example, Table 1 reports the number of trips taken by big game hunters (65 percent), those taken by small game hunters (17 percent), those taken by migratory bird hunters (8 percent), and those taken by hunters pursuing other animals (10 percent). These comprise 100 percent because they are exclusive categories.

Percents should not add to 100 when nonexclusive groups are being reported. Using Table 1 as an example again, note that adding the percentages associated with the total number of big game hunters (85 percent), total small game hunters (33 percent), total migratory bird hunters (19 percent), and total hunters of other animals (16 percent) will not yield total hunters (100 percent) because respondents could hunt for more than one type of game.

When the base of the percentage is not apparent in context, it is identified in a footnote. For example, Table 6 reports three percentages with different bases: one for the number of hunters, one for the number of trips, and one for days of hunting. Footnotes are used to clarify the bases of the reported percentages.

Footnotes to the Tables

Footnotes are used to clarify the information or items that are being reported in a table. Symbols in the body of a table indicate important footnotes. The following symbols are used in the tables to refer to the same footnote each time they appear:

*   Estimate based on a sample size of 10–29.

...   Sample size too small to report data reliably.

Z   Less than 0.5 percent.

X   Not applicable.

NA Not available.

Estimates based upon fewer than ten responses are regarded as being based on a sample size that is too small for reliable reporting. An estimate based upon at least 10 but fewer than 30 responses is treated as an estimate based on a small sample size. Other footnotes appear, as necessary, to qualify or clarify the estimates reported in the tables. In addition, these two important footnotes appear frequently:

- Detail does not add to total because of multiple responses.

- Detail does not add to total because of multiple responses and nonresponse.

"Multiple responses" is a term used to reflect the fact that individuals or their characteristics fall into more than one category. Using Table 2 as an example, those who fished in saltwater and freshwater appear in both of these totals. Yet each angler is represented only once in the "Total, all fishing" column. Similarly, in Table 6, those who hunt for big game and small game are counted only once as a hunter in the "Total, all hunting" column. Therefore, totals will be smaller than the sum of subcategories when multiple responses exist.

"Nonresponse" exists because the Survey questions were answered voluntarily, and some respondents did not or could not answer all the questions. The effect of nonresponse is illustrated in Table 27, where the total days of hunting is greater than the sum of hunting days on private land and hunting days on public land. This occurs because some respondents did not answer the days hunted on private/public land questions. As a result, it is known how many days hunters hunted but not known if those days were on public or private land. In this case, totals are greater than the sum of subcategories when nonresponses have occurred.

Table 1. Anglers and Hunters 16 Years Old and Older, Days of Participation, and Trips by Type of Fishing and Hunting: 2011

(Population 16 years old and older. Numbers in thousands)

Type of fishing and hunting	Participants		Days of participation		Trips	
	Number	Percent	Number	Percent	Number	Percent
Total sportspersons.....................	37,397	100	835,725	100	711,645	100
FISHING						
Total, all fishing........................	33,112	100	553,841	100	455,005	100
Total, all freshwater	27,547	83	455,862	82	368,805	81
Freshwater, except Great Lakes	27,060	82	443,223	80	353,620	78
Great Lakes	1,665	5	19,661	4	15,185	3
Saltwater	8,889	27	99,474	18	86,200	19
HUNTING						
Total, all hunting......................	13,674	100	281,884	100	256,640	100
Big game	11,570	85	212,116	75	167,320	65
Small game	4,506	33	50,884	18	43,135	17
Migratory birds	2,583	19	23,263	8	21,315	8
Other animals	2,168	16	34,434	12	24,869	10

Note: Detail does not add to total because of multiple responses

Table 2. Anglers, Trips, and Days of Fishing by Type of Fishing: 2011

(Population 16 years old and older. Numbers in thousands)

Anglers, trips, and days of fishing	Total, all fishing		Freshwater						Saltwater	
			Total, all freshwater		Freshwater, except Great Lakes		Great Lakes			
	Number	Percent	Number	Percent	Number	Percent	Number	Percent	Number	Percent
ANGLERS										
Total in U S	33,112	100	27,547	100	27,060	100	1,665	100	8,889	100
In state of residence	30,037	91	25,403	92	24,914	92	1,525	92	6,600	74
In other states	6,964	21	4,641	17	4,540	17	224	13	2,764	31
TRIPS										
Total in U S	455,005	100	368,805	100	353,620	100	15,185	100	86,200	100
In state of residence	419,908	92	344,190	93	329,785	93	14,405	95	75,718	88
In other states	35,096	8	24,615	7	23,835	7	781	5	10,481	12
DAYS OF FISHING										
Total in U S	553,841	100	455,862	100	443,223	100	19,661	100	99,474	100
In state of residence	502,008	91	421,155	92	403,207	91	18,231	93	86,027	86
In other states	57,499	10	43,861	10	42,801	10	1,503	8	13,681	14
Average days per angler	17	(X)	17	(X)	16	(X)	12	(X)	11	(X)

(X) Not applicable

Note: Detail for participants does not add to total because of multiple responses Percents shown are based on the respective "Total in U S " rows

Table 3. Freshwater Anglers and Days of Fishing by Type of Fish: 2011

(Population 16 years old and older. Numbers in thousands. Excludes Great Lakes fishing)

Type of fish	Anglers		Days of fishing		Average days per angler
	Number	Percent	Number	Percent	
Total, all types of fish	**27,060**	**100**	**443,223**	**100**	**16**
Black bass (largemouth, smallmouth, etc)	10,626	39	171,279	39	16
White bass, striped bass and striped bass hybrids	4,374	16	60,998	14	14
Panfish	7,263	27	96,925	22	13
Crappie	6,123	23	101,958	23	17
Catfish and Bullheads	7,048	26	95,749	22	14
Walleye	2,493	9	38,361	9	15
Sauger	219	1	3,795	1	17
Northern pike, pickerel, muskie, muskie hybrids	1,642	6	23,420	5	14
Trout	7,157	26	75,748	17	11
Salmon	1,160	4	12,402	3	11
Steelhead	594	2	8,585	2	14
Anything[1]	3,360	12	37,224	8	11
Another type of freshwater fish	1,327	5	20,268	5	15

[1] Respondent fished for no specific species and identified "Anything" from a list of categories of fish

Note: Detail for participants does not add to total because of multiple responses

Table 4. Great Lakes Anglers and Days of Fishing by Type of Fish: 2011

(Population 16 years old and older. Numbers in thousands)

Type of fish	Anglers		Days of fishing		Average days per angler
	Number	Percent	Number	Percent	
Total, all types of fish	**1,665**	**100**	**19,661**	**100**	**12**
Black bass (largemouth, smallmouth, etc)	559	34	4,830	25	9
Walleye, Sauger	584	35	5,612	29	10
Northern pike, pickerel, muskie, muskie hybrids	*224	*13	*2,271	*12	*10
Perch	497	30	5,805	30	12
Salmon	379	23	5,297	27	14
Steelhead	*198	*12	*3,092	*16	*16
Lake trout	*215	*13	*3,573	*18	*17
Other trout	*97	*6	*700	*4	*7
Anything[1]	*148	*9	*1,464	*7	*10
Another type of Great Lakes fish	*179	*11	*1,722	*9	*10

* Estimate based on a sample size of 10–29

[1] Respondent fished for no specific species and identified "Anything" from a list of categories of fish

Note: Detail for participants does not add to total because of multiple responses

Table 5. Saltwater Anglers and Days of Fishing by Type of Fish: 2011

(Population 16 years old and older. Numbers in thousands)

Type of fish	Anglers		Days of fishing		Average days per angler
	Number	Percent	Number	Percent	
Total, all types of fish	**8,889**	**100**	**99,474**	**100**	**11**
Salmon	671	8	3,965	4	6
Striped bass	2,142	24	17,757	18	8
Flatfish (flounder, halibut)	2,005	23	22,473	23	11
Bluefish	1,028	12	10,044	10	10
Red drum (redfish)	1,548	17	21,130	21	14
Sea trout (weakfish)	1,089	12	15,261	15	14
Mackerel	650	7	7,732	8	12
Mahi Mahi (dolphinfish)	538	6	7,352	7	14
Tuna	564	6	3,339	3	6
Shellfish	561	6	3,950	4	7
Anything[1]	1,962	22	16,082	16	8
Another type of saltwater fish	3,388	38	38,065	38	11

[1] Respondent fished for no specific species and identified "Anything" from a list of categories of fish

Note: Detail for participants does not add to total because of multiple responses

Table 6. Hunters, Trips, and Days of Hunting by Type of Hunting: 2011

(Population 16 years old and older. Numbers in thousands)

Hunters, trips, and days of hunting	Total, all hunting		Big game		Small game		Migratory birds		Other animals	
	Number	Percent	Number	Percent	Number	Percent	Number	Percent	Number	Percent
HUNTERS										
Total in U S	**13,674**	**100**	**11,570**	**100**	**4,506**	**100**	**2,583**	**100**	**2,168**	**100**
In state of residence	12,890	94	10,976	95	4,040	90	2,418	94	1,994	92
In other states	1,942	14	1,282	11	708	16	284	11	224	10
TRIPS										
Total in U S	**256,640**	**100**	**167,320**	**100**	**43,135**	**100**	**21,315**	**100**	**24,869**	**100**
In state of residence	244,202	95	159,894	96	39,918	93	20,341	95	24,050	97
In other states	12,438	5	7,426	4	3,218	7	974	5	819	3
DAYS OF HUNTING										
Total in U S	**281,884**	**100**	**212,116**	**100**	**50,884**	**100**	**23,263**	**100**	**34,434**	**100**
In state of residence	263,038	93	198,537	94	46,115	91	21,927	94	32,839	95
In other states	20,291	7	14,581	7	4,975	10	1,409	6	1,687	5
Average days per hunter	21	(X)	18	(X)	11	(X)	9	(X)	16	(X)

(X) Not applicable

Note: Detail does not add to total because of multiple responses Percents shown are based on the respective "Total in U S " rows

Table 7.   Hunters and Days of Hunting by Type of Game: 2011

(Population 16 years old and older. Numbers in thousands)

Type of game	Hunters		Days of hunting		Average days per hunter
	Number	Percent	Number	Percent	
Total, all big game......................	**11,570**	**100**	**212,116**	**100**	**18**
Deer	10,851	94	167,658	79	15
Elk	867	7	7,715	4	9
Bear	526	5	4,824	2	9
Wild turkey	3,115	27	33,341	16	11
Moose	106	1	1,139	1	11
Other big game	305	3	4,911	2	16
Total, all small game....................	**4,506**	**100**	**50,884**	**100**	**11**
Rabbit, hare	1,545	34	16,893	33	11
Quail	841	19	9,419	19	11
Grouse/prairie chicken	812	18	7,541	15	9
Squirrel	1,691	38	20,542	40	12
Pheasant	1,474	33	9,670	19	7
Ptarmigan	*32	*1	*233	*(Z)	*7
Other small game	299	7	3,493	7	12
Total, all migratory birds................	**2,583**	**100**	**23,263**	**100**	**9**
Water fowl (geese and/or ducks)	1,517	59	16,757	72	11
Geese	781	30	8,684	37	11
Ducks	1,371	53	15,295	66	11
Doves	1,271	49	7,041	30	6
Other Migratory birds	227	9	1,576	7	7
Total, all other animals (fox, raccoon, groundhog, alligator, etc.)...............	**2,168**	**100**	**34,434**	**100**	**16**

* Estimate based on a sample size of 10–29   (Z) Less than 0 5 percent

Note: Detail does not add to total because of multiple responses

Table 8. Selected Characteristics of Anglers and Hunters: 2011

(Population 16 years old and older. Numbers in thousands)

Characteristic	U S population		Sportspersons (fished or hunted)			Fished only		
	Number	Percent	Number	Percent who participated	Percent	Number	Percent who participated	Percent
Total persons	**239,313**	**100**	**37,397**	**16**	**100**	**23,714**	**10**	**100**
Population Density of Residence								
Urban	180,723	76	21,989	12	59	16,184	9	68
Rural	58,589	24	15,407	26	41	7,530	13	32
Population Size of Residence								
Metropolitan Statistical Area (MSA)	224,025	94	32,747	15	88	21,824	10	92
1,000,000 or more	127,462	53	13,733	11	37	10,366	8	44
250,000 to 999,999	48,157	20	7,777	16	21	5,403	11	23
50,000 to 249,999	48,406	20	11,238	23	30	6,055	13	26
Outside MSA	15,288	6	4,649	30	12	1,890	12	8
Census Geographic Division								
New England	11,593	5	1,441	12	4	1,021	9	4
Middle Atlantic	32,392	14	3,966	12	11	2,408	7	10
East North Central	36,199	15	6,766	19	18	4,078	11	17
West North Central	15,860	7	3,980	25	11	2,320	15	10
South Atlantic	46,417	19	6,749	15	18	4,871	10	21
East South Central	14,206	6	3,010	21	8	1,479	10	6
West South Central	27,195	11	4,855	18	13	2,946	11	12
Mountain	17,013	7	2,976	17	8	1,933	11	8
Pacific	38,438	16	3,654	10	10	2,658	7	11
Age								
16 to 17 years	7,652	3	1,103	14	3	685	9	3
18 to 24 years	26,517	11	2,886	11	8	1,597	6	7
25 to 34 years	41,613	17	6,750	16	18	4,671	11	20
35 to 44 years	40,779	17	6,723	16	18	4,299	11	18
45 to 54 years	46,167	19	8,365	18	22	5,222	11	22
55 to 64 years	38,469	16	6,886	18	18	4,043	11	17
65 years and older	38,117	16	4,684	12	13	3,196	8	13
65 to 74 years	22,655	9	3,506	15	9	2,285	10	10
75 and older	15,461	6	1,177	8	3	911	6	4
Sex								
Male, total	114,705	48	28,093	24	75	15,867	14	67
16 to 17 years	3,922	2	839	21	2	510	13	2
18 to 24 years	12,909	5	2,160	17	6	1,145	9	5
25 to 34 years	20,350	9	4,720	23	13	2,934	14	12
35 to 44 years	19,738	8	5,081	26	14	2,837	14	12
45 to 54 years	22,426	9	6,163	27	16	3,411	15	14
55 to 64 years	18,252	8	5,418	30	14	2,704	15	11
65 years and older	17,108	7	3,711	22	10	2,326	14	10
65 to 74 years	10,832	5	2,808	26	8	1,675	15	7
75 and older	6,276	3	903	14	2	651	10	3
Female, total	124,608	52	9,304	7	25	7,846	6	33
16 to 17 years	3,730	2	264	7	1	175	5	1
18 to 24 years	13,608	6	726	5	2	453	3	2
25 to 34 years	21,263	9	2,030	10	5	1,736	8	7
35 to 44 years	21,041	9	1,642	8	4	1,463	7	6
45 to 54 years	23,741	10	2,202	9	6	1,811	8	8
55 to 64 years	20,216	8	1,467	7	4	1,339	7	6
65 years and older	21,008	9	973	5	3	870	4	4
65 to 74 years	11,824	5	699	6	2	611	5	3
75 and older	9,185	4	274	3	1	260	3	1
Ethnicity								
Hispanic	32,557	14	1,793	6	5	1,522	5	6
Non-Hispanic	206,756	86	35,603	17	95	22,192	11	94
Race								
White	182,872	76	32,706	18	87	19,846	11	84
African American	23,402	10	2,341	10	6	1,928	8	8
Asian American	11,647	5	737	6	2	710	6	3
All others	21,392	9	1,612	8	4	1,230	6	5
Annual Household Income								
Less than $20,000	30,550	13	3,610	12	10	2,619	9	11
$20,000 to $24,999	12,713	5	1,748	14	5	1,215	10	5
$25,000 to $29,999	10,441	4	1,481	14	4	986	9	4
$30,000 to $34,999	11,504	5	1,648	14	4	1,092	9	5
$35,000 to $39,999	11,441	5	1,714	15	5	1,108	10	5
$40,000 to $49,999	17,091	7	3,085	18	8	1,956	11	8
$50,000 to $74,999	33,850	14	6,725	20	18	4,114	12	17
$75,000 to $99,999	25,236	11	5,517	22	15	3,138	12	13
$100,000 to $149,999	23,790	10	4,799	20	13	2,868	12	12
$150,000 or more	17,151	7	2,940	17	8	2,079	12	9
Not reported	45,545	19	4,131	9	11	2,540	6	11
Education								
11 years or less	31,574	13	4,225	13	11	2,743	9	12
12 years	81,984	34	12,329	15	33	7,346	9	31
1 to 3 years of college	55,014	23	9,486	17	25	5,976	11	25
4 years of college	42,552	18	6,995	16	19	4,548	11	19
5 years or more of college	28,188	12	4,361	15	12	3,101	11	13

See footnotes at end of table

(Population 16 years old and older. Numbers in thousands)

Characteristic	Hunted only			Fished and hunted		
	Number	Percent who participated	Percent	Number	Percent who participated	Percent
Total persons	**4,285**	**2**	**100**	**9,389**	**4**	**100**
Population Density of Residence						
Urban	1,774	1	41	4,023	2	43
Rural	2,511	4	59	5,366	9	57
Population Size of Residence						
Metropolitan Statistical Area (MSA)	3,306	1	77	7,610	3	81
1,000,000 or more	1,064	1	25	2,303	2	25
250,000 to 999,999	706	1	16	1,668	3	18
50,000 to 249,999	1,536	3	36	3,638	8	39
Outside MSA	979	6	23	1,780	12	19
Census Geographic Division						
New England	86	1	2	334	3	4
Middle Atlantic	471	1	11	1,087	3	12
East North Central	905	3	21	1,783	5	19
West North Central	390	2	9	1,271	8	14
South Atlantic	587	1	14	1,283	3	14
East South Central	566	4	13	965	7	10
West South Central	556	2	13	1,353	5	14
Mountain	390	2	9	653	4	7
Pacific	335	1	8	661	2	7
Age						
16 to 17 years	*161	*2	*4	258	3	3
18 to 24 years	218	1	5	1,070	4	11
25 to 34 years	616	1	14	1,463	4	16
35 to 44 years	761	2	18	1,654	4	18
45 to 54 years	937	2	22	2,206	5	23
55 to 64 years	1,000	3	23	1,842	5	20
65 years and older	590	2	14	897	2	10
65 to 74 years	455	2	11	766	3	8
75 and older	135	1	3	131	1	1
Sex						
Male, total	3,867	3	90	8,351	7	89
16 to 17 years	*106	*3	*2	224	6	2
18 to 24 years	188	1	4	827	6	9
25 to 34 years	561	3	13	1,225	6	13
35 to 44 years	676	3	16	1,560	8	17
45 to 54 years	831	4	19	1,921	9	20
55 to 64 years	980	5	23	1,734	9	18
65 years and older	525	3	12	860	5	9
65 to 74 years	395	4	9	738	7	8
75 and older	130	2	3	122	2	1
Female, total	418	(Z)	10	1,039	1	11
16 to 17 years						
18 to 24 years				*243	*2	*3
25 to 34 years				238	1	3
35 to 44 years	*85	*(Z)	*2	94	(Z)	1
45 to 54 years	*107	*(Z)	*2	285	1	3
55 to 64 years				*108	*1	*1
65 years and older	*65	*(Z)	*2	*37	*(Z)	*(Z)
65 to 74 years				*28	*(Z)	*(Z)
75 and older						
Ethnicity						
Hispanic	*118	*(Z)	*3	153	(Z)	2
Non-Hispanic	4,167	2	97	9,236	4	98
Race						
White	4,146	2	97	8,706	5	93
African American				358	2	4
Asian American				*23	*(Z)	*(Z)
All others	*79	*(Z)	*2	303	1	3
Annual Household Income						
Less than $20,000	343	1	8	648	2	7
$20,000 to $24,999	*174	*1	*4	358	3	4
$25,000 to $29,999	117	1	3	378	4	4
$30,000 to $34,999	204	2	5	352	3	4
$35,000 to $39,999	*193	*2	*4	413	4	4
$40,000 to $49,999	364	2	9	765	4	8
$50,000 to $74,999	874	3	20	1,737	5	18
$75,000 to $99,999	669	3	16	1,702	7	18
$100,000 to $149,999	669	3	16	1,263	5	13
$150,000 or more	218	1	5	643	4	7
Not reported	460	1	11	1,131	2	12
Education						
11 years or less	521	2	12	961	3	10
12 years	1,826	2	43	3,149	4	34
1 to 3 years of college	991	2	23	2,519	5	27
4 years of college	653	2	15	1,794	4	19
5 years or more of college	293	1	7	967	3	10

* Estimate based on a sample size of 10–29   ... Sample size too small (less than 10) to report data reliably   (Z) Less than 0 5 percent

Note: Percent who participated columns show the percent of each row's population who participated in the activity named by the column Percent columns show the percent of each column's participants who are described by the row heading Demographic variables we could include but haven't are (1) relationship to head of household, (2) marital status, (3) population size of area participant grew up, (4) years participant lived in resident state, (5) whether or not participant has a job, and (6) whether or not participant is going to school, keeping house, or retired

Table 9. Selected Characteristics of Anglers by Type of Fishing: 2011

(Population 16 years old and older. Numbers in thousands)

Characteristic	U S population		Total, all fishing			Total freshwater		
	Number	Percent	Number	Percent who participated	Percent	Number	Percent who participated	Percent
Total persons	**239,313**	**100**	**33,112**	**14**	**100**	**27,547**	**12**	**100**
Population Density of Residence								
Urban	180,723	76	20,216	11	61	15,918	9	58
Rural	58,589	24	12,896	22	39	11,629	20	42
Population Size of Residence								
Metropolitan Statistical Area (MSA)	224,025	94	29,442	13	89	24,133	11	88
1,000,000 or more	127,462	53	12,669	10	38	9,802	8	36
250,000 to 999,999	48,157	20	7,071	15	21	5,565	12	20
50,000 to 249,999	48,406	20	9,702	20	29	8,766	18	32
Outside MSA	15,288	6	3,670	24	11	3,414	22	12
Census Geographic Division								
New England	11,593	5	1,355	12	4	1,000	9	4
Middle Atlantic	32,392	14	3,496	11	11	2,409	7	9
East North Central	36,199	15	5,861	16	18	5,266	15	19
West North Central	15,860	7	3,591	23	11	3,421	22	12
South Atlantic	46,417	19	6,163	13	19	4,254	9	15
East South Central	14,206	6	2,444	17	7	2,274	16	8
West South Central	27,195	11	4,298	16	13	3,760	14	14
Mountain	17,013	7	2,586	15	8	2,499	15	9
Pacific	38,438	16	3,319	9	10	2,663	7	10
Age								
16 to 17 years	7,652	3	942	12	3	766	10	3
18 to 24 years	26,517	11	2,668	10	8	2,228	8	8
25 to 34 years	41,613	17	6,133	15	19	5,250	13	19
35 to 44 years	40,779	17	5,962	15	18	4,923	12	18
45 to 54 years	46,167	19	7,428	16	22	6,131	13	22
55 to 64 years	38,469	16	5,886	15	18	4,993	13	18
65 years and older	38,117	16	4,093	11	12	3,255	9	12
65 to 74 years	22,655	9	3,051	13	9	2,415	11	9
75 and older	15,461	6	1,042	7	3	840	5	3
Sex								
Male	114,705	48	24,226	21	73	20,359	18	74
Female	124,608	52	8,885	7	27	7,188	6	26
Ethnicity								
Hispanic	32,557	14	1,675	5	5	1,267	4	5
Non-Hispanic	206,756	86	31,436	15	95	26,280	13	95
Race								
White	182,872	76	28,560	16	86	23,995	13	87
African American	23,402	10	2,286	10	7	1,750	7	6
Asian American	11,647	5	733	6	2	472	4	2
All others	21,392	9	1,533	7	5	1,331	6	5
Annual Household Income								
Less than $20,000	30,550	13	3,266	11	10	2,677	9	10
$20,000 to $24,999	12,713	5	1,573	12	5	1,421	11	5
$25,000 to $29,999	10,441	4	1,364	13	4	1,132	11	4
$30,000 to $34,999	11,504	5	1,444	13	4	1,190	10	4
$35,000 to $39,999	11,441	5	1,521	13	5	1,276	11	5
$40,000 to $49,999	17,091	7	2,721	16	8	2,412	14	9
$50,000 to $74,999	33,850	14	5,851	17	18	5,000	15	18
$75,000 to $99,999	25,236	11	4,848	19	15	4,182	17	15
$100,000 to $149,999	23,790	10	4,131	17	12	3,366	14	12
$150,000 or more	17,151	7	2,722	16	8	2,047	12	7
Not reported	45,545	19	3,671	8	11	2,845	6	10
Education								
11 years or less	31,574	13	3,705	12	11	3,062	10	11
12 years	81,984	34	10,503	13	32	8,766	11	32
1 to 3 years of college	55,014	23	8,495	15	26	7,331	13	27
4 years of college	42,552	18	6,342	15	19	5,324	13	19
5 years or more of college	28,188	12	4,068	14	12	3,064	11	11

See footnotes at end of table

Table 9. Selected Characteristics of Anglers by Type of Fishing: 2011—Continued

(Population 16 years old and older. Numbers in thousands)

Characteristic	Freshwater, except Great Lakes Number	Percent who participated	Percent	Great Lakes Number	Percent who participated	Percent	Saltwater Number	Percent who participated	Percent
Total persons	27,060	11	100	1,665	1	100	8,889	4	100
Population Density of Residence									
Urban	15,656	9	58	907	1	54	6,654	4	75
Rural	11,404	19	42	758	1	46	2,235	4	25
Population Size of Residence									
Metropolitan Statistical Area (MSA)	23,759	11	88	1,416	1	85	8,519	4	96
1,000,000 or more	9,598	8	35	555	(Z)	33	4,658	4	52
250,000 to 999,999	5,498	11	20	485	1	29	2,191	5	25
50,000 to 249,999	8,663	18	32	376	1	23	1,669	3	19
Outside MSA	3,301	22	12	*249	*2	*15	370	2	4
Census Geographic Division									
New England	996	9	4				661	6	7
Middle Atlantic	2,343	7	9	395	1	24	1,425	4	16
East North Central	4,871	13	18	1,139	3	68	533	1	6
West North Central	3,418	22	13	*66	*(Z)	*4	*63	*(Z)	*1
South Atlantic	4,241	9	16	*35	*(Z)	*2	3,101	7	35
East South Central	2,274	16	8				360	3	4
West South Central	3,760	14	14				1,092	4	12
Mountain	2,494	15	9				170	1	2
Pacific	2,663	7	10				1,482	4	17
Age									
16 to 17 years	754	10	3				234	3	3
18 to 24 years	2,228	8	8				530	2	6
25 to 34 years	5,127	12	19	*320	*1	*19	1,505	4	17
35 to 44 years	4,847	12	18	232	1	14	1,571	4	18
45 to 54 years	5,954	13	22	483	1	29	2,161	5	24
55 to 64 years	4,911	13	18	359	1	22	1,730	4	19
65 years and older	3,239	8	12	*137	*(Z)	*8	1,157	3	13
65 to 74 years	2,403	11	9	*117	*1	*7	913	4	10
75 and older	836	5	3				244	2	3
Sex									
Male	20,033	17	74	1,257	1	75	6,610	6	74
Female	7,026	6	26	408	(Z)	25	2,279	2	26
Ethnicity									
Hispanic	1,267	4	5				603	2	7
Non-Hispanic	25,793	12	95	1,644	1	99	8,286	4	93
Race									
White	23,562	13	87	1,561	1	94	7,383	4	83
African American	1,701	7	6				764	3	9
Asian American	472	4	2				373	3	4
All others	1,326	6	5				369	2	4
Annual Household Income									
Less than $20,000	2,631	9	10				725	2	8
$20,000 to $24,999	1,416	11	5				*98	*1	*1
$25,000 to $29,999	1,132	11	4				428	4	5
$30,000 to $34,999	1,155	10	4				310	3	3
$35,000 to $39,999	1,276	11	5				256	2	3
$40,000 to $49,999	2,346	14	9	*153	*1	*9	611	4	7
$50,000 to $74,999	4,921	15	18	278	1	17	1,731	5	19
$75,000 to $99,999	4,032	16	15	*321	*1	*19	1,367	5	15
$100,000 to $149,999	3,308	14	12	334	1	20	1,167	5	13
$150,000 or more	2,022	12	7	*72	*(Z)	*4	1,050	6	12
Not reported	2,821	6	10	*123	*(Z)	*7	1,146	3	13
Education									
11 years or less	3,040	10	11				706	2	8
12 years	8,596	10	32	517	1	31	2,399	3	27
1 to 3 years of college	7,126	13	26	488	1	29	2,282	4	26
4 years of college	5,263	12	19	344	1	21	1,828	4	21
5 years or more of college	3,035	11	11	*177	*1	*11	1,673	6	19

* Estimate based on a sample size of 10–29   ... Sample size too small (less than 10) to report data reliably   (Z) Less than 0 5 percent

Note: Percent who participated columns show the percent of each row's population who participated in the activity named by the column Percent columns show the percent of each column's participants who are described by the row heading Demographic variables we could include but haven't are (1) relationship to head of household, (2) marital status, (3) population size of area participant grew up, (4) years participant lived in resident state, (5) whether or not participant has a job, and (6) whether or not participant is going to school, keeping house, or retired

Table 10. Selected Characteristics of Hunters by Type of Hunting: 2011

(Population 16 years old and older. Numbers in thousands)

Characteristic	U S population		Total, all hunting			Big game		
	Number	Percent	Number	Percent who participated	Percent	Number	Percent who participated	Percent
Total persons	**239,313**	**100**	**13,674**	**6**	**100**	**11,570**	**5**	**100**
Population Density of Residence								
Urban	180,723	76	5,797	3	42	4,470	2	39
Rural	58,589	24	7,877	13	58	7,099	12	61
Population Size of Residence								
Metropolitan Statistical Area (MSA)	224,025	94	10,915	5	80	9,059	4	78
1,000,000 or more	127,462	53	3,367	3	25	2,693	2	23
250,000 to 999,999	48,157	20	2,374	5	17	1,898	4	16
50,000 to 249,999	48,406	20	5,174	11	38	4,468	9	39
Outside MSA	15,288	6	2,759	18	20	2,510	16	22
Census Geographic Division								
New England	11,593	5	420	4	3	335	3	3
Middle Atlantic	32,392	14	1,558	5	11	1,530	5	13
East North Central	36,199	15	2,688	7	20	2,336	6	20
West North Central	15,860	7	1,661	10	12	1,368	9	12
South Atlantic	46,417	19	1,870	4	14	1,653	4	14
East South Central	14,206	6	1,531	11	11	1,416	10	12
West South Central	27,195	11	1,909	7	14	1,537	6	13
Mountain	17,013	7	1,043	6	8	730	4	6
Pacific	38,438	16	996	3	7	666	2	6
Age								
16 to 17 years	7,652	3	419	5	3	385	5	3
18 to 24 years	26,517	11	1,288	5	9	1,049	4	9
25 to 34 years	41,613	17	2,079	5	15	1,677	4	14
35 to 44 years	40,779	17	2,416	6	18	2,110	5	18
45 to 54 years	46,167	19	3,143	7	23	2,719	6	24
55 to 64 years	38,469	16	2,842	7	21	2,478	6	21
65 years and older	38,117	16	1,487	4	11	1,151	3	10
65 to 74 years	22,655	9	1,221	5	9	968	4	8
75 and older	15,461	6	266	2	2	182	1	2
Sex								
Male	114,705	48	12,217	11	89	10,220	9	88
Female	124,608	52	1,457	1	11	1,350	1	12
Ethnicity								
Hispanic	32,557	14	271	1	2	214	1	2
Non-Hispanic	206,756	86	13,403	6	98	11,356	5	98
Race								
White	182,872	76	12,852	7	94	10,855	6	94
African American	23,402	10	413	2	3	364	2	3
Asian American	11,647	5	*27	*(Z)	*(Z)	*18	*(Z)	*(Z)
All others	21,392	9	382	2	3	333	2	3
Annual Household Income								
Less than $20,000	30,550	13	991	3	7	876	3	8
$20,000 to $24,999	12,713	5	533	4	4	496	4	4
$25,000 to $29,999	10,441	4	495	5	4	447	4	4
$30,000 to $34,999	11,504	5	556	5	4	486	4	4
$35,000 to $39,999	11,441	5	606	5	4	523	5	5
$40,000 to $49,999	17,091	7	1,129	7	8	908	5	8
$50,000 to $74,999	33,850	14	2,610	8	19	2,332	7	20
$75,000 to $99,999	25,236	11	2,371	9	17	2,087	8	18
$100,000 to $149,999	23,790	10	1,932	8	14	1,433	6	12
$150,000 or more	17,151	7	861	5	6	662	4	6
Not reported	45,545	19	1,591	3	12	1,320	3	11
Education								
11 years or less	31,574	13	1,482	5	11	1,411	4	12
12 years	81,984	34	4,975	6	36	4,454	5	38
1 to 3 years of college	55,014	23	3,510	6	26	2,874	5	25
4 years of college	42,552	18	2,447	6	18	1,915	4	17
5 years or more of college	28,188	12	1,260	4	9	916	3	8

See footnotes at end of table

Table 10. Selected Characteristics of Hunters by Type of Hunting: 2011—Continued

(Population 16 years old and older. Numbers in thousands)

Characteristic	Small game			Migratory birds			Other animals		
	Number	Percent who participated	Percent	Number	Percent who participated	Percent	Number	Percent who participated	Percent
Total persons	**4,506**	**2**	**100**	**2,583**	**1**	**100**	**2,168**	**1**	**100**
Population Density of Residence									
Urban	2,118	1	47	1,172	1	45	1,065	1	49
Rural	2,389	4	53	1,411	2	55	1,103	2	51
Population Size of Residence									
Metropolitan Statistical Area (MSA)	3,612	2	80	2,134	1	83	1,699	1	78
1,000,000 or more	1,255	1	28	668	1	26	612	(Z)	28
250,000 to 999,999	819	2	18	465	1	18	325	1	15
50,000 to 249,999	1,539	3	34	1,001	2	39	762	2	35
Outside MSA	894	6	20	449	3	17	469	3	22
Census Geographic Division									
New England	174	2	4	60	1	2	59	1	3
Middle Atlantic	550	2	12	*71	*(Z)	*3	*261	*1	*12
East North Central	810	2	18	477	1	18	367	1	17
West North Central	735	5	16	326	2	13	192	1	9
South Atlantic	534	1	12	392	1	15	237	1	11
East South Central	455	3	10	167	1	6	183	1	8
West South Central	584	2	13	602	2	23	596	2	27
Mountain	333	2	7	200	1	8	163	1	8
Pacific	331	1	7	287	1	11	*112	*(Z)	*5
Age									
16 to 17 years	*102	*1	*2	*64	*1	*2	*68	*1	*3
18 to 24 years	364	1	8	291	1	11	175	1	8
25 to 34 years	801	2	18	619	1	24	436	1	20
35 to 44 years	837	2	19	449	1	17	473	1	22
45 to 54 years	963	2	21	475	1	18	402	1	19
55 to 64 years	935	2	21	405	1	16	452	1	21
65 years and older	503	1	11	281	1	11	162	(Z)	7
65 to 74 years	407	2	9	235	1	9	135	1	6
75 and older	97	1	2	*46	*(Z)	*2	*27	*(Z)	*1
Sex									
Male	4,251	4	94	2,353	2	91	2,020	2	93
Female	255	(Z)	6	*231	*(Z)	*9	*148	*(Z)	*7
Ethnicity									
Hispanic	*91	*(Z)	*2	*54	*(Z)	*2			
Non-Hispanic	4,415	2	98	2,529	1	98	2,058	1	95
Race									
White	4,183	2	93	2,486	1	96	2,055	1	95
African American	*106	*(Z)	*2						
Asian American									
All others	202	1	4	*90	*(Z)	*4	*77	*(Z)	*4
Annual Household Income									
Less than $20,000	269	1	6	*100	*(Z)	*4	*49	*(Z)	*2
$20,000 to $24,999	104	1	2	*30	*(Z)	*1			
$25,000 to $29,999	148	1	3	*120	*1	*5	*93	*1	*4
$30,000 to $34,999	201	2	4	*79	*1	*3	*119	*1	*5
$35,000 to $39,999	237	2	5	*84	*1	*3	*92	*1	*4
$40,000 to $49,999	496	3	11	274	2	11	*279	*2	*13
$50,000 to $74,999	762	2	17	453	1	18	367	1	17
$75,000 to $99,999	769	3	17	500	2	19	338	1	16
$100,000 to $149,999	719	3	16	428	2	17	326	1	15
$150,000 or more	319	2	7	161	1	6	210	1	10
Not reported	483	1	11	354	1	14	255	1	12
Education									
11 years or less	393	1	9	189	1	7	234	1	11
12 years	1,578	2	35	655	1	25	728	1	34
1 to 3 years of college	1,248	2	28	785	1	30	700	1	32
4 years of college	780	2	17	674	2	26	309	1	14
5 years or more of college	508	2	11	281	1	11	197	1	9

* Estimate based on a sample size of 10–29   … Sample size too small (less than 10) to report data reliably   (Z) Less than 0 5 percent

Note: Percent who participated columns show the percent of each row's population who participated in the activity named by the column Percent columns show the percent of each column's participants who are described by the row heading Demographic variables we could include but haven't are (1) relationship to head of household, (2) marital status, (3) population size of area participant grew up, (4) years participant lived in resident state, (5) whether or not participant has a job, and (6) whether or not participant is going to school, keeping house, or retired Detail does not add to total because of multiple responses and nonresponse

Table 11. Summary of Expenditures for Fishing and Hunting: 2011

(Population 16 years old and older)

Expenditure item	Expenditures		Spenders		
	Amount (thousands of dollars)	Average per sportsperson (dollars)[1]	Number (thousands)	Percent of sportspersons	Average per spender (dollars)[1]
Total, all items..	89,761,524	2,400	35,990	96	2,494
TRIP-RELATED EXPENDITURES					
Total trip-related..	32,210,653	861	33,507	90	961
Food and lodging, total................................	11,592,622	310	29,048	78	399
Food	8,653,068	231	28,773	77	301
Lodging	2,939,554	79	7,422	20	396
Transportation, total..................................	11,029,451	295	29,691	79	371
Public	1,107,975	30	2,760	7	401
Private	9,921,476	265	28,843	77	344
Other trip costs[2].......................................	9,588,580	256	26,804	72	358
EQUIPMENT EXPENDITURES					
Fishing equipment	6,179,132	165	21,920	59	282
Hunting equipment	8,182,297	219	11,585	31	706
Auxiliary equipment[3]	3,736,648	100	11,198	30	334
Special equipment[4]	25,129,326	672	3,990	11	6,298
OTHER EXPENDITURES					
Magazines, books, DVDs	319,781	9	6,053	16	53
Membership dues and contributions	1,122,787	30	5,394	14	208
Land leasing and ownership	10,563,362	282	2,935	8	3,600
Licenses, stamps, tags, and permits	1,614,937	43	24,099	64	67
Plantings (for hunting)	702,601	19	1,273	3	552

[1] Average expenditures are annual estimates

[2] Other trip costs include guide fees, pack trip or package fees, public and private land use fees, equipment rental, boating costs (which include launching, mooring, storage, maintenance, insurance, pumpout fees, and fuel), bait, ice, and heating and cooking fuel

[3] Auxiliary equipment includes camping equipment, binoculars, special fishing and hunting clothing, processing and taxidermy costs, foul weather gear, boots, waders, field glasses, telescopes, and electronic equipment such as a GPS device

[4] Special equipment includes boats, campers, cabins, trail bikes, dune buggies, 4 x 4 vehicles, ATVs, 4-wheelers, snowmobiles, pickups, vans, travel and tent trailers, motor homes, house trailers, recreational vehicles (RVs) and other special equipment

Note: Detail does not add to total because of multiple responses Detail in subsequent tables may not add to totals shown here because of nonresponse to individual questions

Table 12. Expenditures for Fishing: 2011

(Population 16 years old and older)

Expenditure item	Expenditures		Spenders		
	Amount (thousands of dollars)	Average per angler (dollars)[1]	Number (thousands)	Percent of anglers	Average per spender (dollars)[1]
Total, all items...	41,788,936	1,262	30,289	91	1,380
TRIP-RELATED EXPENDITURES					
Total trip-related..	21,789,465	658	29,309	89	743
Food and lodging, total..	7,711,318	233	25,158	76	307
Food	5,435,208	164	24,891	75	218
Lodging	2,276,110	69	5,983	18	380
Transportation, total..	6,261,536	189	25,293	76	248
Public	803,771	24	2,222	7	362
Private	5,457,766	165	24,504	74	223
Other trip costs, total..	7,816,610	236	25,143	76	311
Guide fees, pack trip or package fees	1,102,375	33	2,946	9	374
Public land use fees	237,887	7	4,190	13	57
Private land use fees	243,705	7	1,744	5	140
Equipment rental	245,547	7	1,872	6	131
Boating costs[2]	3,815,819	115	7,929	24	481
Bait	1,497,445	45	19,717	60	76
Ice	509,494	15	13,400	40	38
Heating and cooking fuel	164,337	5	3,810	12	43
EQUIPMENT EXPENDITURES					
Fishing equipment, total..	6,141,895	185	21,527	65	285
Rods, reels, poles, and rodmaking components	2,366,774	71	10,651	32	222
Lines and leaders	593,398	18	13,756	42	43
Artificial lures, flies, baits, and dressing for flies or lines	1,169,092	35	15,560	47	75
Hooks, sinkers, swivels, and other items attached to a line except lures and baits	628,600	19	16,496	50	38
Tackle boxes	141,789	4	4,271	13	33
Creels, stringers, fish bags, landing nets, and gaff hooks	131,515	4	3,655	11	36
Minnow traps, seines, and bait containers	81,008	2	3,172	10	26
Depth finders, fish finders, and other electronic fishing devices	469,849	14	938	3	501
Ice fishing equipment	241,328	7	637	2	379
Other fishing equipment	318,542	10	4,228	13	75
Auxiliary equipment, total.......................................	1,106,865	33	4,420	13	250
Camping equipment	385,633	12	1,976	6	195
Binoculars, field glasses, telescopes, etc	85,522	3	410	1	208
Special fishing clothing, rubber boots, waders, and foul weather gear	318,382	10	2,472	7	129
Processing and taxidermy costs	82,766	2	188	1	440
Other	234,562	7	720	2	326
Special equipment[3]	8,257,673	249	2,296	7	3,596
OTHER EXPENDITURES					
Magazines, books, DVDs	108,308	3	2,483	8	44
Membership dues and contributions	321,990	10	1,728	5	186
Land leasing and ownership	3,434,097	104	924	3	3,716
Licenses, stamps, tags, and permits, total	628,642	19	17,166	52	37
Licenses	551,824	17	16,233	49	34
Stamps, tags, and permits	76,819	2	3,726	11	21

[1] Average expenditures are annual estimates

[2] Boating costs include launching, mooring, storage, maintenance, insurance, pumpout fees, and fuel

[3] Special equipment includes boats, campers, cabins, trail bikes, dune buggies, 4 x 4 vehicles, ATVs, 4-wheelers, snowmobiles, pickups, vans, travel and tent trailers, motor homes, house trailers, recreational vehicles (RVs) and other special equipment

Note: Detail does not add to total because of multiple responses Detail in Tables 13 to 16 may not add to totals shown here because of multiple responses and nonresponse

Table 13.   Trip and Equipment Expenditures for Freshwater Fishing: 2011

(Population 16 years old and older)

Expenditure item	Expenditures		Spenders		
	Amount (thousands of dollars)	Average per angler (dollars)[1]	Number (thousands)	Percent of anglers	Average per spender (dollars)[1]
Total, all items	**25,732,493**	**934**	**25,498**	**93**	**1,009**
TRIP-RELATED EXPENDITURES					
Total trip-related	**14,463,533**	**525**	**25,020**	**91**	**578**
Food and lodging, total	**5,334,362**	**194**	**21,469**	**78**	**248**
Food	3,811,899	138	21,316	77	179
Lodging	1,522,464	55	4,559	17	334
Transportation, total	**4,714,131**	**171**	**21,565**	**78**	**219**
Public	479,435	17	1,393	5	344
Private	4,234,697	154	21,092	77	201
Other trip costs, total	**4,415,039**	**160**	**21,102**	**77**	**209**
Guide fees, pack trip or package fees	525,501	19	1,460	5	360
Public land use fees	188,463	7	3,568	13	53
Private land use fees	112,358	4	1,475	5	76
Equipment rental	183,811	7	1,468	5	125
Boating costs[2]	1,980,784	72	6,231	23	318
Bait	950,729	35	16,644	60	57
Ice	323,059	12	11,162	41	29
Heating and cooking fuel	150,335	5	3,490	13	43
EQUIPMENT EXPENDITURES					
Fishing equipment, total	**4,269,676**	**155**	**17,043**	**62**	**251**
Rods, reels, poles, and rodmaking components	1,597,184	58	8,174	30	195
Lines and leaders	387,736	14	10,282	37	38
Artificial lures, flies, baits, and dressing for flies or lines	914,388	33	12,375	45	74
Hooks, sinkers, swivels, and other items attached to a line except lures and baits	416,799	15	12,350	45	34
Tackle boxes	92,797	3	2,990	11	31
Creels, stringers, fish bags, landing nets, and gaff hooks	95,022	3	2,726	10	35
Minnow traps, seines, and bait containers	43,532	2	2,278	8	19
Depth finders, fish finders, and other electronic fishing devices	303,931	11	709	3	428
Ice fishing equipment	241,196	9	625	2	386
Other fishing equipment	177,091	6	2,787	10	64
Auxiliary equipment, total	**646,603**	**23**	**2,741**	**10**	**236**
Camping equipment	150,712	5	800	3	188
Binoculars, field glasses, telescopes, etc	65,985	2	242	1	273
Special fishing clothing, rubber boots, waders, and foul weather gear	209,291	8	1,645	6	127
Processing and taxidermy costs	*59,678	*2	*126	*(Z)	*473
Other	160,936	6	501	2	321
Special equipment[3]	**6,352,682**	**231**	**1,764**	**6**	**3,602**

* Estimate based on a sample size of 10–29   (Z) Less than 0 5 percent

[1] Average expenditures are annual estimates

[2] Boating costs include launching, mooring, storage, maintenance, insurance, pumpout fees, and fuel

[3] Special equipment includes boats, campers, cabins, trail bikes, dune buggies, 4 x 4 vehicles, ATVs, 4-wheelers, snowmobiles, pickups, vans, travel and tent trailers, motor homes, house trailers, recreational vehicles (RVs) and other special equipment

Note: Detail does not add to total because of multiple responses

Table 14. Trip and Equipment Expenditures for Freshwater Fishing, Except Great Lakes: 2011

(Population 16 years old and older)

Expenditure item	Expenditures		Spenders		
	Amount (thousands of dollars)	Average per angler (dollars)[1]	Number (thousands)	Percent of anglers	Average per spender (dollars)[1]
Total, all items	**23,782,678**	**879**	**24,989**	**92**	**952**
TRIP-RELATED EXPENDITURES					
Total trip-related	**13,373,390**	**494**	**24,539**	**91**	**545**
Food and lodging, total	**4,960,614**	**183**	**20,962**	**77**	**237**
Food	3,583,331	132	20,823	77	172
Lodging	1,377,283	51	4,324	16	319
Transportation, total	**4,462,519**	**165**	**21,091**	**78**	**212**
Public	466,090	17	1,344	5	347
Private	3,996,429	148	20,591	76	194
Other trip costs, total	**3,950,256**	**146**	**20,600**	**76**	**192**
Guide fees, pack trip or package fees	469,003	17	1,289	5	364
Public land use fees	173,406	6	3,477	13	50
Private land use fees	107,225	4	1,381	5	78
Equipment rental	158,371	6	1,336	5	119
Boating costs[2]	1,695,453	63	5,847	22	290
Bait	896,405	33	16,299	60	55
Ice	309,180	11	10,897	40	28
Heating and cooking fuel	141,213	5	3,292	12	43
EQUIPMENT EXPENDITURES					
Fishing equipment, total	**3,971,636**	**147**	**16,440**	**61**	**242**
Rods, reels, poles, and rodmaking components	1,534,749	57	7,883	29	195
Lines and leaders	360,198	13	9,836	36	37
Artificial lures, flies, baits, and dressing for flies or lines	871,255	32	11,871	44	73
Hooks, sinkers, swivels, and other items attached to a line except lures and baits	376,457	14	11,826	44	32
Tackle boxes	87,079	3	2,834	10	31
Creels, stringers, fish bags, landing nets, and gaff hooks	86,298	3	2,573	10	34
Minnow traps, seines, and bait containers	38,918	1	2,096	8	19
Depth finders, fish finders, and other electronic fishing devices	284,072	10	691	3	411
Ice fishing equipment	178,447	7	605	2	295
Other fishing equipment	154,162	6	2,520	9	61
Auxiliary equipment, total	**560,314**	**21**	**2,598**	**10**	**216**
Camping equipment	138,054	5	764	3	181
Binoculars, field glasses, telescopes, etc	65,985	2	242	1	273
Special fishing clothing, rubber boots, waders, and foul weather gear	182,239	7	1,573	6	116
Processing and taxidermy costs	*26,581	*1	*71	*(Z)	*372
Other	147,456	5	462	2	319
Special equipment[3]	**5,877,338**	**217**	**1,653**	**6**	**3,555**

* Estimate based on a sample size of 10–29   (Z) Less than 0 5 percent

[1] Average expenditures are annual estimates

[2] Boating costs include launching, mooring, storage, maintenance, insurance, pumpout fees, and fuel

[3] Special equipment includes boats, campers, cabins, trail bikes, dune buggies, 4 x 4 vehicles, ATVs, 4-wheelers, snowmobiles, pickups, vans, travel and tent trailers, motor homes, house trailers, recreational vehicles (RVs) and other special equipment

Note: Detail does not add to total because of multiple responses

Table 15. Trip and Equipment Expenditures for Great Lakes Fishing: 2011

(Population 16 years old and older)

Expenditure item	Expenditures		Spenders		
	Amount (thousands of dollars)	Average per angler (dollars)[1]	Number (thousands)	Percent of anglers	Average per spender (dollars)[1]
Total, all items..	1,867,098	1,121	1,583	95	1,180
TRIP-RELATED EXPENDITURES					
Total trip-related..	1,090,143	655	1,583	95	689
Food and lodging, total..	373,748	224	1,497	90	250
Food	228,567	137	1,484	89	154
Lodging	145,181	87	399	24	364
Transportation, total...	251,612	151	1,418	85	177
Public					
Private	238,268	143	1,403	84	170
Other trip costs, total..	464,783	279	1,486	89	313
Guide fees, pack trip or package fees	*56,498	*34	*216	*13	*262
Public land use fees	*15,057	*9	*116	*7	*130
Private land use fees					
Equipment rental	*25,440	*15	*142	*9	*180
Boating costs[2]	285,330	171	660	40	432
Bait	54,324	33	1,016	61	53
Ice	13,879	8	712	43	20
Heating and cooking fuel	*9,122	*5	*302	*18	*30
EQUIPMENT EXPENDITURES					
Fishing equipment, total......................................	222,925	134	630	38	354
Rods, reels, poles, and rodmaking components	*49,524	*30	*281	*17	*176
Lines and leaders	24,424	15	402	24	61
Artificial lures, flies, baits, and dressing for flies or lines	38,319	23	382	23	100
Hooks, sinkers, swivels, and other items attached to a line except lures and baits	26,938	16	420	25	64
Tackle boxes					
Creels, stringers, fish bags, landing nets, and gaff hooks					
Minnow traps, seines, and bait containers					
Depth finders, fish finders, and other electronic fishing devices					
Ice fishing equipment					
Other fishing equipment	*19,738	*12	*210	*13	*94
Auxiliary equipment, total.....................................	*83,388	*50	*126	*8	*660
Camping equipment					
Binoculars, field glasses, telescopes, etc					
Special fishing clothing, rubber boots, waders, and foul weather gear					
Processing and taxidermy costs					
Other					
Special equipment[3]...	*470,642	*283	*103	*6	*457

* Estimate based on a sample size of 10–29   ... Sample size too small (less than 10) to report data reliably

[1] Average expenditures are annual estimates

[2] Boating costs include launching, mooring, storage, maintenance, insurance, pumpout fees, and fuel

[3] Special equipment includes boats, campers, cabins, trail bikes, dune buggies, 4 x 4 vehicles, ATVs, 4-wheelers, snowmobiles, pickups, vans, travel and tent trailers, motor homes, house trailers, recreational vehicles (RVs) and other special equipment

Note: Detail does not add to total because of multiple responses

Table 16. Trip and Equipment Expenditures for Saltwater Fishing: 2011

(Population 16 years old and older)

Expenditure item	Expenditures		Spenders		
	Amount (thousands of dollars)	Average per angler (dollars)[1]	Number (thousands)	Percent of anglers	Average per spender (dollars)[1]
Total, all items..	10,266,904	1,155	8,115	91	1,265
TRIP-RELATED EXPENDITURES					
Total trip-related...	7,325,932	824	8,046	91	911
Food and lodging, total..	2,376,956	267	6,920	78	343
Food	1,623,310	183	6,767	76	240
Lodging	753,647	85	1,677	19	449
Transportation, total..	1,547,405	174	6,809	77	227
Public	324,336	36	979	11	331
Private	1,223,069	138	6,199	70	197
Other trip costs, total..	3,401,571	383	6,885	77	494
Guide fees, pack trip or package fees	576,874	65	1,596	18	361
Public land use fees	49,424	6	894	10	55
Private land use fees	131,347	15	289	3	454
Equipment rental	61,736	7	493	6	125
Boating costs[2]	1,835,036	206	2,230	25	823
Bait	546,716	62	4,725	53	116
Ice	186,435	21	3,534	40	53
Heating and cooking fuel	14,003	2	482	5	29
EQUIPMENT EXPENDITURES					
Fishing equipment, total..	1,424,590	160	3,936	44	362
Rods, reels, poles, and rodmaking components	608,539	68	1,880	21	324
Lines and leaders	154,622	17	2,622	30	59
Artificial lures, flies, baits, and dressing for flies or lines	180,156	20	2,288	26	79
Hooks, sinkers, swivels, and other items attached to a line except lures and baits	163,544	18	3,139	35	52
Tackle boxes	29,830	3	731	8	41
Creels, stringers, fish bags, landing nets, and gaff hooks	27,856	3	645	7	43
Minnow traps, seines, and bait containers	28,270	3	587	7	48
Depth finders, fish finders, and other electronic fishing devices	127,941	14	158	2	809
Other fishing equipment	103,831	12	997	11	104
Auxiliary equipment, total...	216,557	24	858	10	252
Camping equipment	*41,261	*5	*164	*2	*252
Binoculars, field glasses, telescopes, etc	*17,818	*2	*132	*1	*135
Special fishing clothing, rubber boots, waders, and foul weather gear	76,434	9	621	7	123
Processing and taxidermy costs	*14,690	*2	*48	*1	*309
Other	66,354	7	159	2	417
Special equipment[3]..	1,299,825	146	332	4	3,912

* Estimate based on a sample size of 10–29

[1] Average expenditures are annual estimates

[2] Boating costs include launching, mooring, storage, maintenance, insurance, pumpout fees, and fuel

[3] Special equipment includes boats, campers, cabins, trail bikes, dune buggies, 4 x 4 vehicles, ATVs, 4-wheelers, snowmobiles, pickups, vans, travel and tent trailers, motor homes, house trailers, recreational vehicles (RVs) and other special equipment

Note: Detail does not add to total because of multiple responses

Table 17. Expenditures for Hunting: 2011

(Population 16 years old and older)

Expenditure item	Expenditures		Spenders		
	Amount (thousands of dollars)	Average per hunter (dollars)[1]	Number (thousands)	Percent of hunters	Average per spender (dollars)[1]
Total, all items	**33,702,017**	**2,465**	**13,364**	**98**	**2,522**
TRIP-RELATED EXPENDITURES					
Total trip-related	**10,421,189**	**762**	**11,914**	**87**	**875**
Food and lodging, total	**3,881,304**	**284**	**10,289**	**75**	**377**
Food	3,217,859	235	10,253	75	314
Lodging	663,444	49	1,881	14	353
Transportation, total	**4,767,915**	**349**	**10,990**	**80**	**434**
Public	304,204	22	648	5	469
Private	4,463,711	326	10,885	80	410
Other trip costs, total	**1,771,970**	**130**	**4,581**	**34**	**387**
Guide fees, pack trip or package fees	493,913	36	1,024	7	482
Public land use fees	40,447	3	709	5	57
Private land use fees	755,087	55	1,193	9	633
Equipment rental	62,747	5	490	4	128
Boating costs[2]	213,817	16	519	4	412
Heating and cooking fuel	205,959	15	2,817	21	73
EQUIPMENT EXPENDITURES					
Hunting equipment, total	**7,738,324**	**566**	**10,400**	**76**	**744**
Firearms	3,050,322	223	3,007	22	1,015
Rifles	1,429,097	105	1,695	12	843
Shotguns	914,619	67	1,213	9	754
Muzzleloaders, primitive firearms	122,035	9	370	3	330
Pistols, handguns	584,570	43	901	7	649
Bows, arrows, archery equipment	934,847	68	2,829	21	331
Telescopic sights	530,655	39	1,748	13	304
Decoys and game calls	301,995	22	2,738	20	110
Ammunition	1,298,456	95	8,828	65	147
Hand loading equipment	199,019	15	1,262	9	158
Hunting dogs and associated costs	951,110	70	1,007	7	945
Other	471,920	35	3,125	23	151
Auxiliary equipment, total	**1,844,880**	**135**	**5,101**	**37**	**362**
Camping equipment	159,853	12	570	4	280
Binoculars, field glasses, telescopes, etc	287,186	21	1,210	9	237
Special hunting clothing, rubber boots, waders, and foul weather gear	570,308	42	3,082	23	185
Processing and taxidermy costs	672,759	49	2,055	15	327
Other	154,774	11	619	5	250
Special equipment[3]	**4,389,286**	**321**	**613**	**4**	**7,159**
OTHER EXPENDITURES					
Magazines, books, DVDs	107,272	8	1,934	14	55
Membership dues and contributions	382,817	28	1,885	14	203
Land leasing and ownership	7,129,265	521	2,279	17	3,128
Licenses, stamps, tags, and permits, total	986,385	72	10,214	75	97
Licenses	786,227	57	9,746	71	81
Federal duck stamps	33,094	2	2,206	16	15
Stamps, tags, and permits	167,064	12	3,554	26	47
Plantings	702,601	51	1,273	9	552

[1] Average expenditures are annual estimates

[2] Boating costs include launching, mooring, storage, maintenance, insurance, pumpout fees, and fuel

[3] Special equipment includes boats, campers, cabins, trail bikes, dune buggies, 4 x 4 vehicles, ATVs, 4-wheelers, snowmobiles, pickups, vans, travel and tent trailers, motor homes, house trailers, recreational vehicles (RVs) and other special equipment

Note: Detail does not add to total because of multiple responses Detail in Tables 18 to 21 may not add to totals shown here because of multiple responses and nonresponse

Table 18. Trip and Equipment Expenditures for Big Game Hunting: 2011

(Population 16 years old and older)

Expenditure item	Expenditures		Spenders		
	Amount (thousands of dollars)	Average per hunter (dollars)[1]	Number (thousands)	Percent of hunters	Average per spender (dollars)[1]
Total, all items...	16,853,654	1,457	10,832	94	1,556
TRIP-RELATED EXPENDITURES					
Total trip-related..	7,250,037	627	10,035	87	722
Food and lodging, total..	2,648,161	229	8,599	74	308
Food	2,249,911	194	8,564	74	263
Lodging	398,250	34	1,205	10	330
Transportation, total..	3,368,532	291	9,146	79	368
Public	187,802	16	459	4	409
Private	3,180,730	275	9,072	78	351
Other trip costs, total...	1,233,345	107	3,579	31	345
Guide fees, pack trip or package fees	321,270	28	635	5	506
Public land use fees	29,685	3	521	5	57
Private land use fees	550,410	48	878	8	627
Equipment rental	55,106	5	362	3	152
Boating costs[2]	122,485	11	187	2	655
Heating and cooking fuel	154,388	13	2,426	21	64
EQUIPMENT EXPENDITURES					
Hunting equipment, total......................................	3,943,190	341	7,451	64	529
Firearms	1,357,095	117	1,610	14	843
Rifles	960,161	83	1,155	10	831
Shotguns	155,790	13	349	3	447
Muzzleloaders, primitive firearms	115,257	10	336	3	343
Pistols, handguns	125,887	11	149	1	845
Bows, arrows, archery equipment	880,239	76	2,628	23	335
Telescopic sights	429,382	37	1,356	12	317
Decoys and game calls	90,590	8	1,474	13	61
Ammunition	628,379	54	5,193	45	121
Hand loading equipment	80,039	7	809	7	99
Hunting dogs and associated costs	*186,857	*16	*194	*2	*963
Other	290,609	25	2,033	18	143
Auxiliary equipment, total.....................................	1,549,539	134	4,176	36	371
Camping equipment	144,504	12	425	4	340
Binoculars, field glasses, telescopes, etc	248,233	21	913	8	272
Special hunting clothing, rubber boots, waders, and foul weather gear	434,845	38	2,245	19	194
Processing and taxidermy costs	614,547	53	1,862	16	330
Other	107,410	9	492	4	218
Special equipment[3]...	4,110,887	355	534	5	7,697

* Estimate based on a sample size of 10–29

[1] Average expenditures are annual estimates

[2] Boating costs include launching, mooring, storage, maintenance, insurance, pumpout fees, and fuel

[3] Special equipment includes boats, campers, cabins, trail bikes, dune buggies, 4 x 4 vehicles, ATVs, 4-wheelers, snowmobiles, pickups, vans, travel and tent trailers, motor homes, house trailers, recreational vehicles (RVs) and other special equipment

Note: Detail does not add to total because of multiple responses

Table 19. Trip and Equipment Expenditures for Small Game Hunting: 2011

(Population 16 years old and older)

Expenditure item	Expenditures		Spenders		
	Amount (thousands of dollars)	Average per hunter (dollars)[1]	Number (thousands)	Percent of hunters	Average per spender (dollars)[1]
Total, all items...	2,560,859	568	3,789	84	676
TRIP-RELATED EXPENDITURES					
Total trip-related...............................	1,576,453	350	3,544	79	445
Food and lodging, total.............................	657,647	146	2,950	65	223
Food	484,121	107	2,915	65	166
Lodging	173,526	39	571	13	304
Transportation, total.............................	685,655	152	3,209	71	214
Public	*96,961	*22	*296	*7	*327
Private	588,693	131	3,148	70	187
Other trip costs, total............................	233,152	52	1,108	25	210
Guide fees, pack trip or package fees	97,596	22	403	9	242
Public land use fees	4,954	1	144	3	34
Private land use fees	97,989	22	255	6	385
Equipment rental	*2,114	*(Z)	*84	*2	*25
Boating costs[2]	*10,573	*2	*53	*1	*199
Heating and cooking fuel	19,926	4	558	12	36
EQUIPMENT EXPENDITURES					
Hunting equipment, total............................	854,403	190	1,632	36	523
Firearms	363,391	81	495	11	735
Rifles	59,291	13	117	3	506
Shotguns	247,430	55	328	7	753
Muzzleloaders, primitive firearms					
Pistols, handguns	*55,453	*12	*89	*2	*625
Bows, arrows, archery equipment					
Telescopic sights	*17,965	*4	*102	*2	*177
Decoys and game calls	14,130	3	184	4	77
Ammunition	124,259	28	1,090	24	114
Hand loading equipment	*7,918	*2	*82	*2	*97
Hunting dogs and associated costs	290,947	65	376	8	775
Other	27,901	6	308	7	91
Auxiliary equipment, total............................	84,992	19	411	9	207
Camping equipment					
Binoculars, field glasses, telescopes, etc	*6,479	*1	*82	*2	*79
Special hunting clothing, rubber boots, waders, and foul weather gear	31,707	7	259	6	122
Processing and taxidermy costs					
Other					
Special equipment[3]............................	...	...	...	...	...

* Estimate based on a sample size of 10–29   ... Sample size too small (less than 10) to report data reliably   (Z) Less than 0 5 percent

[1] Average expenditures are annual estimates

[2] Boating costs include launching, mooring, storage, maintenance, insurance, pumpout fees, and fuel

[3] Special equipment includes boats, campers, cabins, trail bikes, dune buggies, 4 x 4 vehicles, ATVs, 4-wheelers, snowmobiles, pickups, vans, travel and tent trailers, motor homes, house trailers, recreational vehicles (RVs) and other special equipment

Note: Detail does not add to total because of multiple responses

Table 20. Trip and Equipment Expenditures for Migratory Bird Hunting: 2011

(Population 16 years old and older)

Expenditure item	Expenditures		Spenders		
	Amount (thousands of dollars)	Average per hunter (dollars)[1]	Number (thousands)	Percent of hunters	Average per spender (dollars)[1]
Total, all items	**1,808,030**	**700**	**2,321**	**90**	**779**
TRIP-RELATED EXPENDITURES					
Total trip-related	**942,005**	**365**	**2,254**	**87**	**418**
Food and lodging, total	**316,443**	**122**	**1,819**	**70**	**174**
Food	266,521	103	1,819	70	147
Lodging	49,922	19	170	7	293
Transportation, total	**390,169**	**151**	**2,027**	**78**	**193**
Public					
Private	381,398	148	2,020	78	189
Other trip costs, total	**235,393**	**91**	**757**	**29**	**311**
Guide fees, pack trip or package fees	*38,139	*15	*139	*5	*274
Public land use fees	*5,173	*2	*121	*5	*43
Private land use fees	86,532	33	212	8	408
Equipment rental	*3,818	*1	*73	*3	*53
Boating costs[2]	77,227	30	320	12	241
Heating and cooking fuel	24,503	9	210	8	117
EQUIPMENT EXPENDITURES					
Hunting equipment, total	**766,927**	**297**	**1,198**	**46**	**640**
Firearms	190,253	74	209	8	910
Rifles					
Shotguns	190,253	74	209	8	910
Muzzleloaders, primitive firearms					
Pistols, handguns					
Bows, arrows, archery equipment					
Telescopic sights					
Decoys and game calls	129,258	50	460	18	281
Ammunition	144,494	56	927	36	156
Hand loading equipment					
Hunting dogs and associated costs	253,925	98	231	9	1,098
Other	*38,806	*15	*155	*6	*250
Auxiliary equipment, total	**59,300**	**23**	**303**	**12**	**196**
Camping equipment					
Binoculars, field glasses, telescopes, etc					
Special hunting clothing, rubber boots, waders, and foul weather gear	34,231	13	197	8	174
Processing and taxidermy costs					
Other					
Special equipment[3]	...	...	...	...	...

* Estimate based on a sample size of 10–29   ... Sample size too small (less than 10) to report data reliably

[1] Average expenditures are annual estimates

[2] Boating costs include launching, mooring, storage, maintenance, insurance, pumpout fees, and fuel

[3] Special equipment includes boats, campers, cabins, trail bikes, dune buggies, 4 x 4 vehicles, ATVs, 4-wheelers, snowmobiles, pickups, vans, travel and tent trailers, motor homes, house trailers, recreational vehicles (RVs) and other special equipment

Note: Detail does not add to total because of multiple responses

Table 21. Trip and Equipment Expenditures for Hunting Other Animals: 2011

(Population 16 years old and older)

Expenditure item	Expenditures		Spenders		
	Amount (thousands of dollars)	Average per hunter (dollars)[1]	Number (thousands)	Percent of hunters	Average per spender (dollars)[1]
Total, all items	**857,607**	**396**	**1,589**	**73**	**540**
TRIP-RELATED EXPENDITURES					
Total trip-related	**652,693**	**301**	**1,536**	**71**	**425**
Food and lodging, total	**259,053**	**119**	**1,275**	**59**	**203**
Food	217,306	100	1,274	59	171
Lodging	*41,747	*19	*167	*8	*251
Transportation, total	**323,560**	**149**	**1,388**	**64**	**233**
Public	*10,670	*5	*39	*2	*273
Private	312,889	144	1,380	64	227
Other trip costs, total	**70,080**	**32**	**412**	**19**	**170**
Guide fees, pack trip or package fees	*36,908	*17	*68	*3	*543
Public land use fees					
Private land use fees					
Equipment rental					
Boating costs[2]					
Heating and cooking fuel	7,143	3	325	15	22
EQUIPMENT EXPENDITURES					
Hunting equipment, total	**189,043**	**87**	**348**	**16**	**543**
Firearms	*116,770	*54	*141	*7	*826
Rifles					
Shotguns					
Muzzleloaders, primitive firearms					
Pistols, handguns	*27,687	*13	*38	*2	*724
Bows, arrows, archery equipment					
Telescopic sights					
Decoys and game calls	*9,554	*4	*130	*6	*74
Ammunition	*31,230	*14	*230	*11	*136
Hand loading equipment					
Hunting dogs and associated costs					
Other					
Auxiliary equipment, total	***5,889**	***3**	***55**	***3**	***107**
Camping equipment					
Binoculars, field glasses, telescopes, etc					
Special hunting clothing, rubber boots, waders, and foul weather gear					
Processing and taxidermy costs					
Other					
Special equipment[3]	**...**	**...**	**...**	**...**	**...**

* Estimate based on a sample size of 10–29   ... Sample size too small (less than 10) to report data reliably

[1] Average expenditures are annual estimates

[2] Boating costs include launching, mooring, storage, maintenance, insurance, pumpout fees, and fuel

[3] Special equipment includes boats, campers, cabins, trail bikes, dune buggies, 4 x 4 vehicles, ATVs, 4-wheelers, snowmobiles, pickups, vans, travel and tent trailers, motor homes, house trailers, recreational vehicles (RVs) and other special equipment

Note: Detail does not add to total because of multiple responses

Table 22. Special Equipment Expenditures for Fishing and Hunting: 2011

(Population 16 years old and older)

Special equipment item	Expenditures		Spenders		
	Amount (thousands of dollars)	Average per sportsperson (dollars)[1]	Number (thousands)	Percent of sportsperson	Average per spender (dollars)[1]
Total, all items	**25,129,326**	**672**	**3,990**	**11**	**6,298**
Motor boat (other than bass boat)	2,767,043	74	425	1	6,509
Bass boat	1,176,261	31	354	1	3,319
Canoe, other nonmotor boat	223,387	6	471	1	474
Boat motor, trailer or hitch, or other boat accessories	1,311,836	35	1,292	3	1,016
Travel or tent trailer, pickup, camper, van, motor home, recreational vehicle (RV), house trailer	14,994,726	401	1,174	3	12,775
Cabin	*654,369	*17	*78	*(Z)	*8,337
Trail bike, dune buggy, 4x4 vehicle, 4-wheeler, snowmobile	3,606,009	96	573	2	6,289
Other	395,695	11	392	1	1,009

* Estimate based on a sample size of 10–29   (Z) Less than 0 5 percent

[1] Average expenditures are annual estimates

Note: Detail does not add to total because of multiple responses

Table 23. Anglers and Hunters Who Purchased Licenses or Were Exempt: 2011

(Population 16 years old and older. Numbers in thousands)

Sportspersons	Anglers		Hunters	
	Number	Percent	Number	Percent
Total sportspersons	**33,112**	**100**	**13,674**	**100**
Total license purchasers[1]	**21,473**	**65**	**10,626**	**78**
Sportspersons purchasing license				
In state of residence	19,367	58	10,004	73
In other states	3,798	11	1,398	10
Total exempt from purchasing licenses	**5,890**	**18**	**2,741**	**20**
Sportspersons exempt from license purchase				
In state of residence	5,298	16	2,701	20
In other states	743	2	234	2
Other[2]	**6,832**	**21**	**1,099**	**8**
Not reported	**839**	**3**	**282**	**2**

[1] Includes persons who had licenses bought for them Does not include persons who purchased licenses and did not fish or hunt in 2011

[2] Includes persons engages in activities requiring no licenses or exemptions and those who failed to buy a license for activities requiring a license

Note: Detail does not add to total because of multiple responses and nonresponse Respondents could have been licensed in one state and exempt in another

Table 24. Selected Characteristics of Anglers and Hunters Who Purchased Licenses: 2011

(Population 16 years old and older. Numbers in thousands)

Characteristic	Anglers Total		Anglers Purchased a license[1]		Anglers Did not purchase a license[2]		Hunters Total		Hunters Purchased a license[1]		Hunters Did not purchase a license[2]	
	Number	Percent	Number	Percent	Number	Percent	Number	Percent	Number	Percent	Number	Percent
Total persons	**33,112**	**100**	**21,473**	**65**	**11,639**	**35**	**13,674**	**100**	**10,626**	**78**	**3,049**	**22**
Population Density of Residence												
Urban	20,216	100	13,243	66	6,973	34	5,797	100	4,585	79	1,212	21
Rural	12,896	100	8,230	64	4,666	36	7,877	100	6,041	77	1,837	23
Population Size of Residence												
Metropolitan Statistical Area (MSA)	29,442	100	19,144	65	10,298	35	10,915	100	8,515	78	2,400	22
1,000,000 or more	12,669	100	7,792	62	4,877	38	3,367	100	2,577	77	791	23
250,000 to 999,999	7,071	100	4,720	67	2,351	33	2,374	100	1,957	82	418	18
50,000 to 249,999	9,702	100	6,632	68	3,070	32	5,174	100	3,982	77	1,192	23
Outside MSA	3,670	100	2,329	63	1,341	37	2,759	100	2,111	76	648	24
Census Geographic Division												
New England	1,355	100	896	66	459	34	420	100	316	75	104	25
Middle Atlantic	3,496	100	1,799	51	1,697	49	1,558	100	1,208	78	349	22
East North Central	5,861	100	4,339	74	1,521	26	2,688	100	2,249	84	439	16
West North Central	3,591	100	2,793	78	798	22	1,661	100	1,395	84	265	16
South Atlantic	6,163	100	3,191	52	2,972	48	1,870	100	1,340	72	530	28
East South Central	2,444	100	1,533	63	911	37	1,531	100	1,001	65	530	35
West South Central	4,298	100	2,138	50	2,160	50	1,909	100	1,451	76	458	24
Mountain	2,586	100	2,166	84	420	16	1,043	100	929	89	114	11
Pacific	3,319	100	2,617	79	702	21	996	100	736	74	260	26
Age												
16 to 17 years	942	100	499	53	444	47	419	100	356	85	*63	*15
18 to 24 years	2,668	100	1,874	70	794	30	1,288	100	967	75	322	25
25 to 34 years	6,133	100	3,819	62	2,314	38	2,079	100	1,537	74	542	26
35 to 44 years	5,962	100	4,221	71	1,740	29	2,416	100	2,021	84	395	16
45 to 54 years	7,428	100	5,148	69	2,280	31	3,143	100	2,670	85	473	15
55 to 64 years	5,886	100	4,074	69	1,812	31	2,842	100	2,220	78	622	22
65 years and older	4,093	100	1,838	45	2,256	55	1,487	100	856	58	632	42
65 to 74 years	3,051	100	1,513	50	1,538	50	1,221	100	707	58	514	42
75 and older	1,042	100	325	31	717	69	266	100	149	56	118	44
Sex												
Male	24,226	100	16,599	69	7,627	31	12,217	100	9,587	78	2,630	22
Female	8,885	100	4,873	55	4,012	45	1,457	100	1,039	71	419	29
Ethnicity												
Hispanic	1,675	100	1,052	63	623	37	271	100	154	57	*117	*43
Non-Hispanic	31,436	100	20,421	65	11,016	35	13,403	100	10,472	78	2,932	22
Race												
White	28,560	100	19,060	67	9,500	33	12,852	100	10,143	79	2,710	21
African American	2,286	100	1,255	55	1,031	45	413	100	*246	*60	*167	*40
Asian American	733	100	318	43	414	57	*27	*100	*15	*54		
All others	1,533	100	839	55	693	45	382	100	223	58	159	42
Annual Household Income												
Less than $20,000	3,266	100	1,808	55	1,458	45	991	100	716	72	275	28
$20,000 to $24,999	1,573	100	893	57	681	43	533	100	334	63	*199	*37
$25,000 to $29,999	1,364	100	674	49	690	51	495	100	355	72	*140	*28
$30,000 to $34,999	1,444	100	1,021	71	423	29	556	100	428	77	128	23
$35,000 to $39,999	1,521	100	885	58	636	42	606	100	481	79	125	21
$40,000 to $49,999	2,721	100	1,792	66	929	34	1,129	100	831	74	298	26
$50,000 to $74,999	5,851	100	3,832	66	2,019	34	2,610	100	2,131	82	480	18
$75,000 to $99,999	4,848	100	3,450	71	1,398	29	2,371	100	1,895	80	477	20
$100,000 to $149,999	4,131	100	3,050	74	1,081	26	1,932	100	1,579	82	352	18
$150,000 or more	2,722	100	1,845	68	877	32	861	100	731	85	130	15
Not reported	3,671	100	2,222	61	1,449	39	1,591	100	1,146	72	445	28
Education												
11 years or less	3,705	100	2,023	55	1,682	45	1,482	100	1,104	74	379	26
12 years	10,503	100	6,621	63	3,882	37	4,975	100	3,839	77	1,136	23
1 to 3 years of college	8,495	100	5,718	67	2,777	33	3,510	100	2,624	75	886	25
4 years of college	6,342	100	4,620	73	1,722	27	2,447	100	2,025	83	422	17
5 years or more of college	4,068	100	2,492	61	1,576	39	1,260	100	1,034	82	226	18
Days of Participation												
1 to 5 days	14,732	100	8,387	57	6,346	43	3,730	100	2,575	69	1,155	31
6 to 10 days	6,168	100	4,012	65	2,156	35	2,721	100	2,128	78	593	22
11 to 25 days	5,971	100	4,361	73	1,610	27	3,457	100	2,760	80	697	20
26 days or more	6,049	100	4,643	77	1,406	23	3,678	100	3,158	86	520	14

* Estimate based on a sample size of 10–29   ... Sample size too small (less than 10) to report data reliably

[1] Includes persons who purchased a license in 2011 in any state Respondents could have been licensed in one state and exempt in another

[2] Includes those persons who did not purchase a license in any state in 2011 and those who did not specify a license purchase in 2011

Table 25. Freshwater Anglers and Days of Fishing by Type of Water: 2011

(Population 16 years old and older. Numbers in thousands. Excludes Great Lakes fishing)

Type of water	Anglers		Days of fishing	
	Number	Percent	Number	Percent
Total, all types of water.	**27,060**	**100**	**443,223**	**100**
Lakes, reservoirs, and ponds	22,791	84	335,732	76
Rivers or streams	11,888	44	148,218	33

Note: Detail does not add to total because of multiple responses and nonresponse

Table 26. Great Lakes Anglers and Days of Fishing by Great Lake: 2011

(Population 16 years old and older. Numbers in thousands)

Great Lake	Anglers		Days of fishing	
	Number	Percent	Number	Percent
Total, all Great Lakes	**1,665**	**100**	**19,661**	**100**
Lake Ontario, including the Niagara River	*143	*9	*2,214	*11
Lake Erie, including the Detroit River	639	38	8,451	43
Lake Huron, including St Mary's River System	*262	*16	*4,410	*22
Lake Michigan	413	25	2,585	13
Lake Superior	*147	*9	*1,527	*8
Lake St Clair, including the St Clair River				
St Lawrence River				
Tributaries to the Great Lakes	*159	*10	*1,254	*6

* Estimate based on a sample size of 10–29   ... Sample size too small (less than 10) to report data reliably

Note: Detail does not add to total because of multiple responses and nonresponse

Table 27. Hunters and Days of Hunting on Public and Private Land by Type of Hunting: 2011

(Population 16 years old and older. Numbers in thousands)

Hunters and days of hunting	Total, all hunting		Big game		Small game		Migratory birds		Other animals	
	Number	Percent	Number	Percent	Number	Percent	Number	Percent	Number	Percent
HUNTERS										
Total, all land	**13,674**	**100**	**11,570**	**100**	**4,506**	**100**	**2,583**	**100**	**2,168**	**100**
Public land, total	**4,918**	**36**	**3,767**	**33**	**1,410**	**31**	**923**	**36**	**523**	**24**
Public land only	1,733	13	1,578	14	606	13	526	20	250	12
Public and private land	3,185	23	2,189	19	805	18	397	15	273	13
Private land, total	**11,537**	**84**	**9,696**	**84**	**3,756**	**83**	**1,999**	**77**	**1,886**	**87**
Private land only	8,352	61	7,507	65	2,951	65	1,602	62	1,614	74
Private and public land	3,185	23	2,189	19	805	18	397	15	273	13
DAYS OF HUNTING										
Total, all land	**281,884**	**100**	**212,116**	**100**	**50,884**	**100**	**23,263**	**100**	**34,434**	**100**
Public land[1]	61,486	22	39,149	18	13,915	27	8,467	36	5,452	16
Private land[2]	218,839	78	167,271	79	36,951	73	13,292	57	27,161	79

[1] Days of hunting on public land include both days spent solely on public land and those spent on public and private land

[2] Days of hunting on private land include both days spent solely on private land and those spent on private and public land

Note: Detail does not add to total because of multiple responses and nonresponse

Table 28. Hunters and Days of Hunting on Public Land by Selected Characteristic: 2011

(Population 16 years old and older. Numbers in thousands)

Characteristic	Total hunters, public and private land	Hunters on public land[1] Number	Percent of total hunters	Percent of hunters using public land	Total days, public and private land	Days on public land[2] Number	Percent of total days	Percent of days on public land
Total persons	**13,674**	**4,918**	**36**	**100**	**281,884**	**61,486**	**22**	**100**
Population Density of Residence								
Urban	5,797	2,390	41	49	97,899	29,594	30	48
Rural	7,877	2,529	32	51	183,986	31,892	17	52
Population Size of Residence								
Metropolitan Statistical Area (MSA)	10,915	3,977	36	81	216,150	50,269	23	82
1,000,000 or more	3,367	1,207	36	25	58,011	13,352	23	22
250,000 to 999,999	2,374	938	39	19	46,830	13,578	29	22
50,000 to 249,999	5,174	1,832	35	37	111,309	23,339	21	38
Outside MSA	2,759	941	34	19	65,734	11,217	17	18
Census Geographic Division								
New England	420	150	36	3	8,416	2,216	26	4
Middle Atlantic	1,558	694	45	14	38,487	7,743	20	13
East North Central	2,688	915	34	19	49,089	9,140	19	15
West North Central	1,661	702	42	14	30,715	7,951	26	13
South Atlantic	1,870	442	24	9	42,430	7,730	18	13
East South Central	1,531	253	17	5	40,701	3,048	7	5
West South Central	1,909	307	16	6	42,409	4,207	10	7
Mountain	1,043	803	77	16	14,723	10,564	72	17
Pacific	996	653	66	13	14,913	8,886	60	14
Age								
16 to 17 years	419	181	43	4	7,379	1,777	24	3
18 to 24 years	1,288	344	27	7	24,253	4,596	19	7
25 to 34 years	2,079	703	34	14	51,074	6,236	12	10
35 to 44 years	2,416	907	38	18	52,209	12,111	23	20
45 to 54 years	3,143	1,202	38	24	59,345	16,771	28	27
55 to 64 years	2,842	1,137	40	23	60,259	13,568	23	22
65 years and older	1,487	445	30	9	27,364	6,428	23	10
65 to 74 years	1,221	356	29	7	23,144	5,240	23	9
75 and older	266	89	33	2	4,220	1,188	28	2
Sex								
Male	12,217	4,523	37	92	263,059	57,722	22	94
Female	1,457	395	27	8	18,826	3,764	20	6
Ethnicity								
Hispanic	271	125	46	3	3,846	1,126	29	2
Non-Hispanic	13,403	4,793	36	97	278,038	60,360	22	98
Race								
White	12,852	4,709	37	96	265,100	58,343	22	95
African American	413				6,368			
Asian American	*27	*21	*79	*(Z)	*680	*449	*66	*1
All others	382	145	38	3	9,737	2,184	22	4
Annual Household Income								
Less than $20,000	991	249	25	5	19,844	3,549	18	6
$20,000 to $24,999	533	133	25	3	6,500	1,260	19	2
$25,000 to $29,999	495	115	23	2	9,289	1,688	18	3
$30,000 to $34,999	556	233	42	5	12,144	3,379	28	5
$35,000 to $39,999	606	182	30	4	11,984	1,732	14	3
$40,000 to $49,999	1,129	393	35	8	24,242	5,455	23	9
$50,000 to $74,999	2,610	1,014	39	21	55,666	13,386	24	22
$75,000 to $99,999	2,371	1,133	48	23	52,926	14,419	27	23
$100,000 to $149,999	1,932	739	38	15	37,706	8,829	23	14
$150,000 or more	861	168	20	3	13,949	1,718	12	3
Not reported	1,591	561	35	11	37,636	6,072	16	10
Education								
11 years or less	1,482	446	30	9	31,409	5,699	18	9
12 years	4,975	1,983	40	40	112,076	27,685	25	45
1 to 3 years of college	3,510	1,274	36	26	75,816	15,799	21	26
4 years of college	2,447	881	36	18	39,414	7,997	20	13
5 years or more of college	1,260	335	27	7	23,169	4,306	19	7

* Estimate based on a sample size of 10–29   ... Sample size too small (less than 10) to report data reliably   (Z) Less than 0 5 percent

[1] Hunters on public land include those who hunted on both public and private land

[2] Days of hunting on public land includes both days spent solely on public land and those spent on public and private land

Note: Percent of total hunters and percent of total days are based on the total hunters and total days columns for each row Percent of hunters using public land and percent of days on public land are based on the total numbers of hunters on public land and total numbers of days on public land, respectively

Table 29. Hunters and Days of Hunting on Private Land by Selected Characteristic: 2011

(Population 16 years old and older. Numbers in thousands)

Characteristic	Hunters				Days of hunting			
	Total hunters, public and private land	Hunters on private land[1]			Total days, public and private land	Days on private land[2]		
		Number	Percent of total hunters	Percent of hunters using private land		Number	Percent of total days	Percent of days on private land
Total persons	13,674	11,537	84	100	281,884	218,839	78	100
Population Density of Residence								
Urban	5,797	4,641	80	40	97,899	68,734	70	31
Rural	7,877	6,896	88	60	183,986	150,105	82	69
Population Size of Residence								
Metropolitan Statistical Area (MSA)	10,915	9,066	83	79	216,150	164,493	76	75
1,000,000 or more	3,367	2,788	83	24	58,011	46,824	81	21
250,000 to 999,999	2,374	1,824	77	16	46,830	32,155	69	15
50,000 to 249,999	5,174	4,454	86	39	111,309	85,513	77	39
Outside MSA	2,759	2,471	90	21	65,734	54,346	83	25
Census Geographic Division								
New England	420	368	88	3	8,416	6,186	74	3
Middle Atlantic	1,558	1,377	88	12	38,487	31,714	82	14
East North Central	2,688	2,432	90	21	49,089	38,347	78	18
West North Central	1,661	1,514	91	13	30,715	22,949	75	10
South Atlantic	1,870	1,699	91	15	42,430	34,591	82	16
East South Central	1,531	1,419	93	12	40,701	35,605	87	16
West South Central	1,909	1,723	90	15	42,409	38,077	90	17
Mountain	1,043	444	43	4	14,723	4,771	32	2
Pacific	996	560	56	5	14,913	6,599	44	3
Age								
16 to 17 years	419	365	87	3	7,379	6,090	83	3
18 to 24 years	1,288	1,142	89	10	24,253	19,266	79	9
25 to 34 years	2,079	1,766	85	15	51,074	42,296	83	19
35 to 44 years	2,416	2,119	88	18	52,209	38,871	74	18
45 to 54 years	3,143	2,568	82	22	59,345	43,001	72	20
55 to 64 years	2,842	2,343	82	20	60,259	48,638	81	22
65 years and older	1,487	1,233	83	11	27,364	20,675	76	9
65 to 74 years	1,221	1,014	83	9	23,144	17,743	77	8
75 and older	266	220	82	2	4,220	2,933	70	1
Sex								
Male	12,217	10,303	84	89	263,059	204,724	78	94
Female	1,457	1,233	85	11	18,826	14,115	75	6
Ethnicity								
Hispanic	271	*168	*62	*1	3,846	*2,524	*66	*1
Non-Hispanic	13,403	11,369	85	99	278,038	216,315	78	99
Race								
White	12,852	10,873	85	94	265,100	205,368	77	94
African American	413	365	88	3	6,368	5,856	92	3
Asian American	*27				*680			
All others	382	288	75	2	9,737	7,377	76	3
Annual Household Income								
Less than $20,000	991	893	90	8	19,844	15,618	79	7
$20,000 to $24,999	533	416	78	4	6,500	5,171	80	2
$25,000 to $29,999	495	460	93	4	9,289	7,869	85	4
$30,000 to $34,999	556	447	80	4	12,144	9,475	78	4
$35,000 to $39,999	606	481	79	4	11,984	9,448	79	4
$40,000 to $49,999	1,129	952	84	8	24,242	18,730	77	9
$50,000 to $74,999	2,610	2,164	83	19	55,666	41,085	74	19
$75,000 to $99,999	2,371	2,051	87	18	52,926	40,929	77	19
$100,000 to $149,999	1,932	1,541	80	13	37,706	28,559	76	13
$150,000 or more	861	768	89	7	13,949	11,593	83	5
Not reported	1,591	1,362	86	12	37,636	30,362	81	14
Education								
11 years or less	1,482	1,306	88	11	31,409	26,387	84	12
12 years	4,975	3,989	80	35	112,076	81,891	73	37
1 to 3 years of college	3,510	3,063	87	27	75,816	60,480	80	28
4 years of college	2,447	2,093	86	18	39,414	30,885	78	14
5 years or more of college	1,260	1,086	86	9	23,169	19,195	83	9

* Estimate based on a sample size of 10–29   ... Sample size too small (less than 10) to report data reliably

[1] Hunters on private land include those who hunted on both private and public land

[2] Days of hunting on private land includes both days spent solely on private land and those spent on private and public land

Note: Percent of total hunters and percent of total days are based on the total hunters and total days columns for each row Percent of hunters using private land and percent of days on private land are based on the total Numbers of hunters on private land and total Numbers of days on private land, respectively

Table 30. Anglers Fishing From Boats and Days of Participation by Type of Fishing: 2011

(Population 16 years old and older. Numbers in thousands)

Participants and days of fishing	Total, all fishing		Freshwater, excludes Great Lakes		Great Lakes		Saltwater	
	Number	Percent	Number	Percent	Number	Percent	Number	Percent
Total anglers	**33,112**	**100**	**27,060**	**100**	**1,665**	**100**	**8,889**	**100**
Anglers fishing from boats	18,017	54	13,683	51	1,141	69	5,814	65
Total days of fishing	**553,841**	**100**	**443,223**	**100**	**19,661**	**100**	**99,474**	**100**
Days fishing from boats	257,444	46	190,518	43	10,799	55	56,127	56

Note: Detail does not add to total because of multiple responses and nonresponse

Table 31. Participation in Ice Fishing and Fly-Fishing: 2011

(Population 16 years old and older. Numbers in thousands)

Anglers and days	Number	Percent
Total anglers	**33,112**	**100**
Ice anglers	1,930	6
Fly-anglers	4,260	13
Total days of fishing	**553,841**	**100**
Days of ice fishing	19,369	3
Days of fly-fishing	37,872	7

Note: Detail does not add to total because of multiple responses

Table 32. Hunters Using Bows and Arrows, Muzzleloaders, or Other Firearms: 2011

(Population 16 years old and older. Numbers in thousands)

Hunters	Number	Percent
Total hunters	**13,674**	**100**
Hunters using bow and arrow	4,472	33
Hunters using muzzleloader	2,981	22
Hunters using other firearm (e g , shotgun, rifle)	12,730	93
Total days of hunting	**281,884**	**100**
With bow and arrow	69,103	25
With muzzleloader	23,167	8
With other firearm (e g , shotgun, rifle)	183,044	65

Note: Detail does not add to total because of multiple responses and nonresponse

Table 33. Hunters Preparing for Hunting by Target Shooting: 2011

(Population 16 years old and older. Numbers in thousands)

Hunters	Total Number	Total Percent
Total hunters	**13,674**	**100**
Target shooting in preparation for hunting	7,178	52
Used shooting ranges	2,943	22
With muzzleloader	420	3
With handgun	1,110	8
With other firearm (e g , shotgun, rifle)	2,322	17
With airgun	406	3
With bow and arrow	*93	*1
With crossbow	564	4

* Estimate based on a sample size of 10–29

Note: Detail does not add to total because of multiple responses

Table 34. Land Owned or Leased for the Primary Purpose of Fishing or Hunting: 2011

(Population 16 years old and older. Numbers in thousands)

Fishing and hunting	Number	Percent
LAND OWNERSHIP		
Sportspersons Owning Land		
Total sportspersons	**1,994**	**100**
Anglers	807	40
Hunters	1,408	71
Acres Owned		
Total acres owned	**180,392**	**100**
Acres for fishing	25,208	14
Acres for hunting	155,184	86
Expenditures for Land Owned		
Total expenditures	**9,155,543**	**100**
For fishing	3,143,921	34
For hunting	6,011,622	66
LAND LEASING		
Sportspersons Leasing Land		
Total sportspersons	**1,451**	**100**
Anglers	207	14
Hunters	1,270	87
Acres Leased		
Total acres leased.	**430,030**	**100**
Acres for fishing	9,984	2
Acres for hunting	420,046	98
Expenditures for Land Leased		
Total expenditures.	**1,407,820**	**100**
For fishing	290,176	21
For hunting	1,117,643	79

Note: Detail does not add to total because of multiple responses

Table 35. Wildlife-Watching Participants by Type of Activity: 2011

(Population 16 years old and older. Numbers in thousands)

Activity	Number	Percent
Total participants	**71,776**	**100**
Away from home	22,496	31
Observe wildlife	19,808	28
Photograph wildlife	12,354	17
Feed wildlife	5,399	8
Around the home	68,598	96
Observe wildlife	45,046	63
Photograph wildlife	25,370	35
Feed wildlife	52,817	74
Visit parks or natural areas[1]	12,311	17
Maintain plantings or natural areas	13,399	19

[1] Includes visits only to parks or natural areas within one mile of home

Note: Detail does not add to total because of multiple responses

Table 36. Participants, Area Visited, Trips, and Days of Participation in Wildlife Watching Away From Home: 2011

(Population 16 years old and older. Numbers in thousands)

Participants, area visited, trips, and days of participation	Number	Percent
PARTICIPANTS		
Total participants	**22,496**	**100**
Observe wildlife	19,808	88
Photograph wildlife	12,354	55
Feed wildlife	5,399	24
AREA VISITED		
Total, all areas	**22,496**	**100**
Public only	12,830	57
Private only	2,105	9
Public and private	5,545	25
Not reported	2,017	9
TRIPS		
Total trips	**242,838**	**100**
Average days per trip	1	(X)
DAYS		
Total days	**335,625**	**100**
Observing wildlife	268,798	80
Photographing wildlife	110,459	33
Feeding wildlife	59,255	18
Average days per participant	**15**	**(X)**
Observing wildlife	14	(X)
Photographing wildlife	9	(X)
Feeding wildlife	11	(X)

(X) Not applicable

Note: Detail does not add to total because of multiple responses

Table 37. Participation in Wildlife-Watching Activities Around the Home: 2011

(Population 16 years old and older. Numbers in thousands)

Activity	Number	Percent	Activity	Number	Percent
Total around the home	**68,598**	100	**PHOTOGRAPH WILDLIFE**		
Observe wildlife	45,046	66			
Photograph wildlife	25,370	37	**Participants photographing:**		
Feed wildlife	52,817	77	Total, 1 day or more	**25,370**	100
Visit parks or natural areas[1]	12,311	18	1 day	4,289	17
Maintain natural areas	8,012	12	2 to 3 days	5,816	23
Maintain plantings	9,214	13	4 to 5 days	3,732	15
			6 to 10 days	4,343	17
OBSERVE WILDLIFE			11 to 20 days	2,961	12
			21 days or more	3,689	15
Participants observing:					
Total, all wildlife	**45,046**	100	**FEED WILDLIFE**		
Birds	41,346	92			
Land mammals, all	35,884	80	**Participants feeding:**		
Large mammals	22,056	49	Total, all wildlife	**52,817**	100
Small mammals	31,629	70	Wild birds	50,217	95
Amphibians or reptiles	14,132	31	Other wildlife	14,820	28
Insects or spiders	16,589	37			
Fish or other wildlife	8,388	19	**MAINTAIN NATURAL AREAS**		
Participants observing:			**Participants maintaining:**		
Total, 1 day or more	**45,046**	100	Total, all acreages	**8,012**	100
1 to 10 days	9,596	21	1 acre or less	4,369	55
11 to 20 days	3,916	9	2 to 10 acres	2,621	33
21 to 50 days	5,791	13	11 to 50 acres	701	9
51 to 100 days	5,091	11	More than 50 acres	271	3
101 to 200 days	6,302	14			
201 days or more	13,123	29	**MAINTAIN PLANTINGS**		
VISIT PARKS OR NATURAL AREAS[1]			Participants maintaining plantings..............	**9,214**	100
Participants visiting:			**Participants spending:**		
Total, 1 day or more	**12,311**	100	Less than $25	3,553	39
1 to 5 days	5,517	45	$25 to $75	1,880	20
6 to 10 days	2,048	17	More than $75	3,385	37
11 days or more	4,438	36	Average expenditure per participant for plantings[2]	239	(X)

(X) Not applicable

[1] Includes visits only to parks or natural areas within one mile of home

[2] Average expenditures are annual estimates

Note: Detail does not add to total because of multiple responses and nonresponse

Table 38. Away-From-Home Wildlife Watchers by Wildlife Observed, Photographed, or Fed and Place: 2011

(Population 16 years old and older. Numbers in thousands)

Wildlife observed, photographed, or fed	Total participants		Participation by place					
			Total		In state of residence		In other states	
	Number	Percent	Number	Percent	Number	Percent	Number	Percent
Total, all wildlife	22,496	100	22,496	100	18,529	82	6,769	30
Total birds	18,924	84	18,924	100	16,037	85	6,257	33
Songbirds (cardinals, robins, etc)	12,120	54	12,120	100	10,616	88	3,356	28
Birds of prey (hawks, eagles, etc)	12,890	57	12,890	100	10,990	85	3,917	30
Waterfowl (ducks, geese, etc)	13,333	59	13,333	100	11,081	83	4,231	32
Other water birds (shorebirds, herons, cranes, etc)	10,606	47	10,606	100	8,509	80	3,483	33
Other birds (pheasants, turkeys, road runners, etc)	6,857	30	6,857	100	5,770	84	1,790	26
Total land mammals	13,653	61	13,653	100	11,743	86	4,180	31
Large land mammals (deer, bear, etc)	10,369	46	10,369	100	8,702	84	3,045	29
Small land mammals (squirrel, prairie dog, etc)	10,299	46	10,299	100	8,758	85	3,299	32
Fish (salmon, shark, etc)	6,358	28	6,358	100	4,964	78	2,075	33
Marine mammals (whales, dolphins, etc)	4,008	18	4,008	100	2,325	58	1,864	47
Other wildlife (turtles, butterflies, etc)	10,113	45	10,113	100	8,602	85	2,865	28

Note: Detail does not add to total because of multiple responses Column showing percent of total participants is based on the "Total, all wildlife" numbers "Participation by place" percent columns are based on the total numbers of participants for each type of wildlife

Table 39. Wild Bird Observers and Days of Observation: 2011

(Population 16 years old and older. Numbers in thousands)

Observers and days of observation	Number	Percent
OBSERVERS		
Total bird observers	46,741	100
Around-the-home observers	41,346	88
Away-from-home observers	17,818	38
DAYS		
Total days observing birds	5,161,909	100
Around the home	4,923,873	95
Away from home	238,036	5

Note: Detail does not add to total because of multiple responses

Table 40. Expenditures for Wildlife Watching: 2011

(Population 16 years old and older)

Expenditure item	Expenditures (thousands of dollars)	Spenders Number (thousands)	Spenders Percent of wildlife-watching participants[1]	Spenders Average per spender (dollars)[2]
Total, all items[3]	54,890,272	55,980	78	981
TRIP-RELATED EXPENDITURES				
Total trip-related..	17,274,675	19,905	88	868
Food and lodging, total...	9,349,439	17,017	76	549
Food	5,465,019	16,740	74	326
Lodging	3,884,420	6,851	30	567
Transportation, total...	6,006,860	18,647	83	322
Public	2,521,247	3,029	13	832
Private	3,485,613	17,768	79	196
Other trip costs, total	1,918,376	9,359	42	205
Guide fees, pack trip or package fees	775,074	2,037	9	380
Public land use fees	239,021	6,212	28	38
Private land use fees	113,207	1,093	5	104
Equipment rental	141,017	1,485	7	95
Boating costs[4]	547,875	1,366	6	401
Heating and cooking fuel	102,182	2,302	10	44
EQUIPMENT AND OTHER EXPENSES				
Total	37,615,597	52,584	73	715
Wildlife-watching equipment, total................................	11,323,179	47,951	67	236
Binoculars, spotting scopes	918,567	5,057	7	182
Cameras, video cameras, special lenses, and other photographic equipment	2,799,579	8,307	12	337
Film and photo processing	528,057	5,742	8	92
Bird food, total	4,068,161	36,956	51	110
Commercially prepared and packaged wild bird food	3,133,968	34,263	48	91
Other bulk foods used to feed wild birds	934,194	13,271	18	70
Feed for other wildlife	1,012,964	9,987	14	101
Nest boxes, bird houses, feeders, baths	969,708	19,181	27	51
Day packs, carrying cases, and special clothing	855,196	6,483	9	132
Other wildlife-watching equipment (such as field guides and maps)	170,946	4,847	7	35
Auxiliary equipment, total..	1,555,374	6,445	9	241
Tents, tarps	289,781	2,964	4	98
Frame packs and backpacking equipment	216,231	1,976	3	109
Other camping equipment	294,173	2,472	3	119
Other auxiliary equipment (such as blinds and GPS devices)	755,188	2,008	3	376
Special equipment, total..	14,272,368	2,219	3	6,433
Off-the-road vehicle	6,475,469	486	1	13,326
Travel or tent trailer, pickup, camper, van, motor home, house trailer, recreational vehicle (RV)	5,868,982	518	1	11,331
Boats, boat accessories	1,703,305	1,175	2	1,449
Cabins				
Other	217,988	246	(Z)	886
Magazines, books, DVDs	420,395	8,480	12	50
Land leasing and ownership	5,676,794	1,233	2	4,603
Membership dues and contributions	2,163,568	10,756	15	201
Plantings	2,203,920	8,818	12	250

... Sample size too small (less than 10) to report data reliably   (Z) Less than 0 5 percent

[1] Percent of wildlife-watching participants column is based on away-from-home participants for trip-related expenditures For equipment and other expenditures the percent of wildlife-watching participants is based on total participants

[2] Average expenditures are annual estimates

[3] Information on trip-related expenditures was collected for away-from-home participants only Equipment and other expenditures are based on information collected from both away-from-home and around-the-home participants

[4] Boating costs include launching, mooring, storage, maintenance, insurance, pumpout fees, and fuel

Note: Detail does not add to total because of multiple responses and nonresponse

Table 41. Selected Characteristics of Participants of Wildlife-Watching Activities Away From Home: 2011

(Population 16 years old and older. Numbers in thousands)

Characteristic	U S population Number	U S population Percent	Total wildlife-watching participants Number	Total wildlife-watching participants Percent who participated	Total wildlife-watching participants Percent	Total away-from-home participants Number	Total away-from-home participants Percent who participated	Total away-from-home participants Percent
Total persons	**239,313**	**100**	**71,776**	**30**	**100**	**22,496**	**9**	**100**
Population Density of Residence								
Urban	180,723	76	46,973	26	65	15,974	9	71
Rural	58,589	24	24,803	42	35	6,523	11	29
Population Size of Residence								
Metropolitan Statistical Area (MSA)	224,025	94	65,664	29	91	20,651	9	92
1,000,000 or more	127,462	53	33,070	26	46	10,672	8	47
250,000 to 999,999	48,157	20	16,436	34	23	4,634	10	21
50,000 to 249,999	48,406	20	16,159	33	23	5,346	11	24
Outside MSA	15,288	6	6,111	40	9	1,845	12	8
Census Geographic Division								
New England	11,593	5	3,954	34	6	1,187	10	5
Middle Atlantic	32,392	14	9,118	28	13	2,561	8	11
East North Central	36,199	15	12,840	35	18	3,168	9	14
West North Central	15,860	7	5,479	35	8	1,783	11	8
South Atlantic	46,417	19	13,315	29	19	4,393	9	20
East South Central	14,206	6	4,663	33	6	1,456	10	6
West South Central	27,195	11	7,164	26	10	1,728	6	8
Mountain	17,013	7	5,189	30	7	2,230	13	10
Pacific	38,438	16	10,054	26	14	3,990	10	18
Age								
16 to 17 years	7,652	3	964	13	1	339	4	2
18 to 24 years	26,517	11	2,580	10	4	773	3	3
25 to 34 years	41,613	17	7,969	19	11	3,117	7	14
35 to 44 years	40,779	17	10,163	25	14	4,326	11	19
45 to 54 years	46,167	19	15,594	34	22	5,768	12	26
55 to 64 years	38,469	16	16,155	42	23	4,740	12	21
65 years and older	38,117	16	18,351	48	26	3,433	9	15
65 to 74 years	22,655	9	12,044	53	17	2,722	12	12
75 and older	15,461	6	6,307	41	9	711	5	3
Sex								
Male, total	114,705	48	33,176	29	46	11,472	10	51
16 to 17 years	3,922	2	535	14	1	*162	*4	*1
18 to 24 years	12,909	5	1,281	10	2	490	4	2
25 to 34 years	20,350	9	3,590	18	5	1,500	7	7
35 to 44 years	19,738	8	5,269	27	7	2,455	12	11
45 to 54 years	22,426	9	7,228	32	10	2,797	12	12
55 to 64 years	18,252	8	7,361	40	10	2,340	13	10
65 years and older	17,108	7	7,912	46	11	1,727	10	8
65 to 74 years	10,832	5	5,406	50	8	1,428	13	6
75 and older	6,276	3	2,505	40	3	299	5	1
Female, total	124,608	52	38,600	31	54	11,025	9	49
16 to 17 years	3,730	2	429	12	1	*176	*5	*1
18 to 24 years	13,608	6	1,299	10	2	284	2	1
25 to 34 years	21,263	9	4,379	21	6	1,617	8	7
35 to 44 years	21,041	9	4,893	23	7	1,871	9	8
45 to 54 years	23,741	10	8,366	35	12	2,971	13	13
55 to 64 years	20,216	8	8,794	44	12	2,400	12	11
65 years and older	21,008	9	10,439	50	15	1,706	8	8
65 to 74 years	11,824	5	6,638	56	9	1,294	11	6
75 and older	9,185	4	3,802	41	5	412	4	2
Ethnicity								
Hispanic	32,557	14	3,723	11	5	1,442	4	6
Non-Hispanic	206,756	86	68,053	33	95	21,054	10	94
Race								
White	182,872	76	65,385	36	91	20,644	11	92
African American	23,402	10	2,590	11	4	610	3	3
Asian American	11,647	5	1,049	9	1	253	2	1
All others	21,392	9	2,752	13	4	989	5	4
Annual Household Income								
Less than $20,000	30,550	13	6,768	22	9	1,622	5	7
$20,000 to $24,999	12,713	5	3,564	28	5	838	7	4
$25,000 to $29,999	10,441	4	2,385	23	3	663	6	3
$30,000 to $34,999	11,504	5	4,046	35	6	756	7	3
$35,000 to $39,999	11,441	5	3,326	29	5	1,018	9	5
$40,000 to $49,999	17,091	7	5,166	30	7	1,691	10	8
$50,000 to $74,999	33,850	14	12,685	37	18	4,773	14	21
$75,000 to $99,999	25,236	11	8,950	35	12	3,769	15	17
$100,000 to $149,999	23,790	10	8,700	37	12	2,775	12	12
$150,000 or more	17,151	7	6,298	37	9	2,088	12	9
Not reported	45,545	19	9,888	22	14	2,502	5	11
Education								
11 years or less	31,574	13	5,575	18	8	1,237	4	5
12 years	81,984	34	21,098	26	29	5,224	6	23
1 to 3 years of college	55,014	23	16,135	29	22	5,337	10	24
4 years of college	42,552	18	16,066	38	22	5,436	13	24
5 years or more of college	28,188	12	12,901	46	18	5,263	19	23

See footnotes at end of table

Table 41. Selected Characteristics of Participants of Wildlife-Watching Activities Away From Home: 2011—Continued

(Population 16 years old and older. Numbers in thousands)

Characteristic	Observe			Photograph			Feed		
	Number	Percent who participated	Percent	Number	Percent who participated	Percent	Number	Percent who participated	Percent
Total persons	**19,808**	**8**	**100**	**12,354**	**5**	**100**	**5,399**	**2**	**100**
Population Density of Residence									
Urban	14,100	8	71	9,302	5	75	3,675	2	68
Rural	5,708	10	29	3,052	5	25	1,724	3	32
Population Size of Residence									
Metropolitan Statistical Area (MSA)	18,335	8	93	11,551	5	93	5,043	2	93
1,000,000 or more	9,523	7	48	6,284	5	51	2,775	2	51
250,000 to 999,999	4,059	8	20	2,646	5	21	782	2	14
50,000 to 249,999	4,753	10	24	2,621	5	21	1,487	3	28
Outside MSA	1,473	10	7	803	5	7	356	2	7
Census Geographic Division									
New England	1,126	10	6	761	7	6	178	2	3
Middle Atlantic	2,200	7	11	1,182	4	10	*379	*1	*7
East North Central	2,644	7	13	1,499	4	12	829	2	15
West North Central	1,589	10	8	999	6	8	411	3	8
South Atlantic	3,962	9	20	2,577	6	21	1,318	3	24
East South Central	1,234	9	6	751	5	6	395	3	7
West South Central	1,615	6	8	874	3	7	888	3	16
Mountain	2,021	12	10	1,415	8	11	384	2	7
Pacific	3,417	9	17	2,295	6	19	616	2	11
Age									
16 to 17 years	*300	*4	*2	*228	*3	*2			
18 to 24 years	522	2	3	388	1	3	*257	*1	*5
25 to 34 years	2,825	7	14	1,704	4	14	960	2	18
35 to 44 years	3,586	9	18	2,045	5	17	900	2	17
45 to 54 years	5,041	11	25	3,641	8	29	1,501	3	28
55 to 64 years	4,363	11	22	2,525	7	20	949	2	18
65 years and older	3,170	8	16	1,822	5	15	693	2	13
65 to 74 years	2,485	11	13	1,482	7	12	634	3	12
75 and older	685	4	3	340	2	3	*60	*(Z)	*1
Sex									
Male, total	9,716	8	49	5,920	5	48	2,602	2	48
16 to 17 years	*126	*3	*1						
18 to 24 years	266	2	1	*228	*2	*2			
25 to 34 years	1,319	6	7	565	3	5	*493	*2	*9
35 to 44 years	2,008	10	10	998	5	8	435	2	8
45 to 54 years	2,337	10	12	1,828	8	15	650	3	12
55 to 64 years	2,121	12	11	1,246	7	10	483	3	9
65 years and older	1,539	9	8	950	6	8	342	2	6
65 to 74 years	1,245	11	6	754	7	6	304	3	6
75 and older	294	5	1	*196	*3	*2			
Female, total	10,092	8	51	6,433	5	52	2,796	2	52
16 to 17 years	*175	*5	*1						
18 to 24 years	256	2	1	*159	*1	*1	*98	*1	*2
25 to 34 years	1,506	7	8	1,139	5	9	467	2	9
35 to 44 years	1,579	8	8	1,046	5	8	465	2	9
45 to 54 years	2,704	11	14	1,814	8	15	851	4	16
55 to 64 years	2,242	11	11	1,279	6	10	466	2	9
65 years and older	1,631	8	8	872	4	7	351	2	7
65 to 74 years	1,240	10	6	728	6	6	330	3	6
75 and older	391	4	2	*144	*2	*1			
Ethnicity									
Hispanic	1,207	4	6	932	3	8	*198	*1	*4
Non-Hispanic	18,602	9	94	11,422	6	92	5,201	3	96
Race									
White	18,318	10	92	11,351	6	92	4,715	3	87
African American	449	2	2	289	1	2	*318	*1	*6
Asian American	193	2	1	*134	*1	*1			
All others	848	4	4	580	3	5	301	1	6
Annual Household Income									
Less than $20,000	1,367	4	7	734	2	6	589	2	11
$20,000 to $24,999	700	6	4	437	3	4	*194	*2	*4
$25,000 to $29,999	630	6	3	508	5	4	*126	*1	*2
$30,000 to $34,999	628	5	3	450	4	4	184	2	3
$35,000 to $39,999	852	7	4	474	4	4	*282	*2	*5
$40,000 to $49,999	1,496	9	8	856	5	7	445	3	8
$50,000 to $74,999	3,994	12	20	2,410	7	20	1,146	3	21
$75,000 to $99,999	3,408	14	17	2,124	8	17	1,130	4	21
$100,000 to $149,999	2,544	11	13	1,644	7	13	395	2	7
$150,000 or more	1,974	12	10	1,331	8	11	392	2	7
Not reported	2,214	5	11	1,386	3	11	516	1	10
Education									
11 years or less	1,065	3	5	581	2	5	564	2	10
12 years	4,149	5	21	2,514	3	20	1,518	2	28
1 to 3 years of college	4,712	9	24	2,753	5	22	1,375	2	25
4 years of college	4,950	12	25	3,369	8	27	1,260	3	23
5 years or more of college	4,933	18	25	3,136	11	25	681	2	13

* Estimate based on a sample size of 10–29   ... Sample size too small (less than 10) to report data reliably   (Z) Less than 0 5 percent

Note: Detail does not add to total because of multiple responses Percent who participated columns show the percent of each row's population who participated in the activity named by the column Percent columns show the percent of each column's participants who are described by the row heading

Table 42. Selected Characteristics of Participants of Wildlife-Watching Activities Around the Home: 2011

(Population 16 years old and older. Numbers in thousands)

Characteristic	U S population		Total wildlife-watching participants			Total around-the-home participants		
	Number	Percent	Number	Percent who participated	Percent	Number	Percent who participated	Percent
Total persons	**239,313**	**100**	**71,776**	**30**	**100**	**68,598**	**29**	**100**
Population Density of Residence								
Urban	180,723	76	46,973	26	65	44,538	25	65
Rural	58,589	24	24,803	42	35	24,060	41	35
Population Size of Residence								
Metropolitan Statistical Area (MSA)	224,025	94	65,664	29	91	62,759	28	91
1,000,000 or more	127,462	53	33,070	26	46	31,459	25	46
250,000 to 999,999	48,157	20	16,436	34	23	15,879	33	23
50,000 to 249,999	48,406	20	16,159	33	23	15,421	32	22
Outside MSA	15,288	6	6,111	40	9	5,839	38	9
Census Geographic Division								
New England	11,593	5	3,954	34	6	3,858	33	6
Middle Atlantic	32,392	14	9,118	28	13	8,744	27	13
East North Central	36,199	15	12,840	35	18	12,492	35	18
West North Central	15,860	7	5,479	35	8	5,201	33	8
South Atlantic	46,417	19	13,315	29	19	12,767	28	19
East South Central	14,206	6	4,663	33	6	4,394	31	6
West South Central	27,195	11	7,164	26	10	7,087	26	10
Mountain	17,013	7	5,189	30	7	4,716	28	7
Pacific	38,438	16	10,054	26	14	9,337	24	14
Age								
16 to 17 years	7,652	3	964	13	1	903	12	1
18 to 24 years	26,517	11	2,580	10	4	2,360	9	3
25 to 34 years	41,613	17	7,969	19	11	7,282	18	11
35 to 44 years	40,779	17	10,163	25	14	9,260	23	13
45 to 54 years	46,167	19	15,594	34	22	14,917	32	22
55 to 64 years	38,469	16	16,155	42	23	15,801	41	23
65 years and older	38,117	16	18,351	48	26	18,074	47	26
65 to 74 years	22,655	9	12,044	53	17	11,914	53	17
75 and older	15,461	6	6,307	41	9	6,161	40	9
Sex								
Male, total	114,705	48	33,176	29	46	31,322	27	46
16 to 17 years	3,922	2	535	14	1	521	13	1
18 to 24 years	12,909	5	1,281	10	2	1,152	9	2
25 to 34 years	20,350	9	3,590	18	5	3,235	16	5
35 to 44 years	19,738	8	5,269	27	7	4,649	24	7
45 to 54 years	22,426	9	7,228	32	10	6,838	30	10
55 to 64 years	18,252	8	7,361	40	10	7,195	39	10
65 years and older	17,108	7	7,912	46	11	7,731	45	11
65 to 74 years	10,832	5	5,406	50	8	5,323	49	8
75 and older	6,276	3	2,505	40	3	2,408	38	4
Female, total	124,608	52	38,600	31	54	37,276	30	54
16 to 17 years	3,730	2	429	12	1	382	10	1
18 to 24 years	13,608	6	1,299	10	2	1,208	9	2
25 to 34 years	21,263	9	4,379	21	6	4,047	19	6
35 to 44 years	21,041	9	4,893	23	7	4,611	22	7
45 to 54 years	23,741	10	8,366	35	12	8,079	34	12
55 to 64 years	20,216	8	8,794	44	12	8,606	43	13
65 years and older	21,008	9	10,439	50	15	10,343	49	15
65 to 74 years	11,824	5	6,638	56	9	6,591	56	10
75 and older	9,185	4	3,802	41	5	3,752	41	5
Ethnicity								
Hispanic	32,557	14	3,723	11	5	3,398	10	5
Non-Hispanic	206,756	86	68,053	33	95	65,200	32	95
Race								
White	182,872	76	65,385	36	91	62,487	34	91
African American	23,402	10	2,590	11	4	2,567	11	4
Asian American	11,647	5	1,049	9	1	951	8	1
All others	21,392	9	2,752	13	4	2,593	12	4
Annual Household Income								
Less than $20,000	30,550	13	6,768	22	9	6,584	22	10
$20,000 to $24,999	12,713	5	3,564	28	5	3,447	27	5
$25,000 to $29,999	10,441	4	2,385	23	3	2,247	22	3
$30,000 to $34,999	11,504	5	4,046	35	6	4,024	35	6
$35,000 to $39,999	11,441	5	3,326	29	5	3,224	28	5
$40,000 to $49,999	17,091	7	5,166	30	7	4,942	29	7
$50,000 to $74,999	33,850	14	12,685	37	18	11,696	35	17
$75,000 to $99,999	25,236	11	8,950	35	12	8,599	34	13
$100,000 to $149,999	23,790	10	8,700	37	12	8,295	35	12
$150,000 or more	17,151	7	6,298	37	9	6,111	36	9
Not reported	45,545	19	9,888	22	14	9,429	21	14
Education								
11 years or less	31,574	13	5,575	18	8	5,418	17	8
12 years	81,984	34	21,098	26	29	20,281	25	30
1 to 3 years of college	55,014	23	16,135	29	22	15,257	28	22
4 years of college	42,552	18	16,066	38	22	15,526	36	23
5 years or more of college	28,188	12	12,901	46	18	12,115	43	18

See footnotes at end of table

(Population 16 years old and older. Numbers in thousands)

Characteristic	Around-the-home participants								
	Observe			Photograph			Feed wild birds		
	Number	Percent who participated	Percent	Number	Percent who participated	Percent	Number	Percent who participated	Percent
Total persons	**45,046**	**19**	**100**	**25,370**	**11**	**100**	**50,217**	**21**	**100**
Population Density of Residence									
Urban	28,670	16	64	16,895	9	67	31,106	17	62
Rural	16,376	28	36	8,475	14	33	19,111	33	38
Population Size of Residence									
Metropolitan Statistical Area (MSA)	41,168	18	91	23,126	10	91	45,739	20	91
1,000,000 or more	20,309	16	45	11,867	9	47	22,417	18	45
250,000 to 999,999	10,220	21	23	5,575	12	22	11,656	24	23
50,000 to 249,999	10,640	22	24	5,684	12	22	11,666	24	23
Outside MSA	3,878	25	9	2,243	15	9	4,478	29	9
Census Geographic Division									
New England	2,630	23	6	1,688	15	7	2,938	25	6
Middle Atlantic	6,231	19	14	3,269	10	13	6,089	19	12
East North Central	7,530	21	17	4,599	13	18	9,874	27	20
West North Central	3,328	21	7	1,848	12	7	3,992	25	8
South Atlantic	7,863	17	17	4,346	9	17	9,493	20	19
East South Central	2,765	19	6	1,292	9	5	3,560	25	7
West South Central	4,979	18	11	2,412	9	10	5,545	20	11
Mountain	3,346	20	7	2,057	12	8	3,049	18	6
Pacific	6,374	17	14	3,858	10	15	5,677	15	11
Age									
16 to 17 years	399	5	1	452	6	2	453	6	1
18 to 24 years	1398	5	3	748	3	3	1287	5	3
25 to 34 years	4087	10	9	3181	8	13	4511	11	9
35 to 44 years	6014	15	13	3969	10	16	5802	14	12
45 to 54 years	9608	21	21	6212	13	24	10642	23	21
55 to 64 years	10757	28	24	6174	16	24	12222	32	24
65 years and older	12783	34	28	4635	12	18	15300	40	30
65 to 74 years	8734	39	19	3714	16	15	9946	44	20
75 and older	4048	26	9	921	6	4	5354	35	11
Sex									
Male, total	19,525	17	43	11,995	10	47	21,404	19	43
16 to 17 years	*250	*6	*1	*273	*7	*1	*204	*5	*(Z)
18 to 24 years	658	5	1	458	4	2	361	3	1
25 to 34 years	1,752	9	4	1,282	6	5	2,002	10	4
35 to 44 years	2,852	14	6	1,851	9	7	2,513	13	5
45 to 54 years	3,947	18	9	3,086	14	12	4,594	20	9
55 to 64 years	4,959	27	11	2,718	15	11	5,374	29	11
65 years and older	5,106	30	11	2,328	14	9	6,356	37	13
65 to 74 years	3,697	34	8	1,826	17	7	4,178	39	8
75 and older	1,409	22	3	502	8	2	2,178	35	4
Female, total	25,521	20	57	13,374	11	53	28,813	23	57
16 to 17 years	*149	*4	*(Z)	*179	*5	*1	*249	*7	*(Z)
18 to 24 years	739	5	2	290	2	1	926	7	2
25 to 34 years	2,336	11	5	1,898	9	7	2,508	12	5
35 to 44 years	3,162	15	7	2,118	10	8	3,289	16	7
45 to 54 years	5,661	24	13	3,126	13	12	6,049	25	12
55 to 64 years	5,798	29	13	3,456	17	14	6,848	34	14
65 years and older	7,677	37	17	2,307	11	9	8,944	43	18
65 to 74 years	5,038	43	11	1,888	16	7	5,767	49	11
75 and older	2,639	29	6	419	5	2	3,176	35	6
Ethnicity									
Hispanic	2,223	7	5	1,276	4	5	2,640	8	5
Non-Hispanic	42,823	21	95	24,094	12	95	47,576	23	95
Race									
White	41,269	23	92	23,396	13	92	46,225	25	92
African American	1,750	7	4	716	3	3	1,518	6	3
Asian American	323	3	1	368	3	1	620	5	1
All others	1,704	8	4	890	4	4	1,854	9	4
Annual Household Income									
Less than $20,000	4,414	14	10	1,656	5	7	4,603	15	9
$20,000 to $24,999	2,113	17	5	1,032	8	4	2,835	22	6
$25,000 to $29,999	1,370	13	3	598	6	2	1,805	17	4
$30,000 to $34,999	2,791	24	6	893	8	4	3,162	27	6
$35,000 to $39,999	2,102	18	5	1,157	10	5	2,293	20	5
$40,000 to $49,999	3,562	21	8	1,916	11	8	3,596	21	7
$50,000 to $74,999	7,544	22	17	5,063	15	20	8,345	25	17
$75,000 to $99,999	5,788	23	13	3,674	15	14	6,362	25	13
$100,000 to $149,999	5,488	23	12	3,728	16	15	5,620	24	11
$150,000 or more	3,683	21	8	2,792	16	11	4,223	25	8
Not reported	6,192	14	14	2,862	6	11	7,374	16	15
Education									
11 years or less	3,414	11	8	1,228	4	5	4,011	13	8
12 years	12,933	16	29	6,225	8	25	16,061	20	32
1 to 3 years of college	10,026	18	22	6,002	11	24	10,963	20	22
4 years of college	10,211	24	23	6,345	15	25	11,479	27	23
5 years or more of college	8,462	30	19	5,569	20	22	7,701	27	15

* Estimate based on a sample size of 10–29   (Z) Less than 0 5 percent

Note: Detail does not add to total because of multiple responses and nonresponse Percent who participated columns show the percent of each row's population who participated in the activity named by the column Percent columns show the percent of each column's participants who are described by the row heading

Table 43. Land Owned or Leased for the Primary Purpose of Wildlife Watching: 2011

(Population 16 years old and older. Numbers in thousands)

Wildlife watching	Number	Average per person[1]
Land Ownership for Wildlife Watching		
Participants owning land	1,206	(X)
Acres owned	39,420	33
Expenditures for owned land	5,573,697	4,623
Land Leasing for Wildlife Watching		
Participants leasing land	*124	(X)
Acres leased	*3,618	*29
Expenditures for leased land	*103,097	*832

* Estimate based on a sample size of 10–29   (X) Not Applicable

[1] Average expenditures are annual estimates

Note: Detail does not add to total because of multiple responses and nonresponse

Table 44. Participation of Wildlife-Watching Participants in Fishing and Hunting: 2011

(Population 16 years old and older. Numbers in thousands)

Type of fishing and hunting	Total		Away from home		Around the home	
	Number	Percent	Number	Percent	Number	Percent
Total participants	**71,776**	**100**	**22,496**	**100**	**68,598**	**100**
Nonsportspersons	52,459	73	13,909	62	51,310	75
Sportspersons	19,317	27	8,587	38	17,288	25
Anglers	17,029	24	7,549	34	15,211	22
Hunters	7,805	11	3,656	16	6,989	10

Note: Detail does not add to total because of multiple responses and nonresponse

Table 45. Participation of Sportspersons in Wildlife-Watching Activities: 2011

(Population 16 years old and older. Numbers in thousands)

Wildlife-watching activity	Sportspersons		Anglers		Hunters	
	Number	Percent	Number	Percent	Number	Percent
Total sportspersons	**37,397**	**100**	**33,112**	**100**	**13,674**	**100**
Sportspersons who:						
Did not engage in wildlife-watching activities	18,079	48	16,082	49	5,869	43
Engaged in wildlife-watching activities	19,317	52	17,029	51	7,805	57
Away from home	8,587	23	7,549	23	3,656	27
Around the home	17,288	46	15,211	46	6,989	51

Note: Detail does not add to total because of multiple responses and nonresponse

Table 46. Participation in Wildlife-Related Recreation by State Residents Both Inside and Outside Their Resident State: 2011

(Population 16 years old and older. Numbers in thousands)

Participant's state of residence	Population	Total participants		Sportspersons		Wildlife-watching participation	
		Number	Percent of population	Number	Percent of population	Number	Percent of population
United States, total	**239,313**	**90,108**	**38**	**37,397**	**16**	**71,776**	**30**
Alabama	3,664	1,490	41	744	20	1,079	29
Alaska	526	337	64	235	45	247	47
Arizona	5,084	1,660	33	721	14	1,281	25
Arkansas	2,238	1,119	50	572	26	828	37
California	28,562	7,360	26	1,898	7	6,475	23
Colorado	3,946	1,854	47	727	18	1,456	37
Connecticut	2,781	1,204	43	347	12	1,093	39
Delaware	699	260	37	101	14	209	30
Florida	14,855	4,652	31	2,068	14	3,598	24
Georgia	7,459	2,752	37	981	13	2,206	30
Hawaii	995	222	22	108	11	161	16
Idaho	1,172	638	54	331	28	464	40
Illinois	9,988	3,493	35	1,487	15	2,784	28
Indiana	4,965	2,131	43	842	17	1,681	34
Iowa	2,363	1,097	46	586	25	780	33
Kansas	2,163	1,011	47	453	21	776	36
Kentucky	3,376	1,470	44	643	19	1,221	36
Louisiana	3,449	1,380	40	802	23	840	24
Maine	1,066	520	49	233	22	401	38
Maryland	4,480	1,396	31	426	9	1,224	27
Massachusetts	5,320	1,779	33	464	9	1,530	29
Michigan	7,787	3,709	48	1,636	21	3,067	39
Minnesota	4,133	2,107	51	1,400	34	1,498	36
Mississippi	2,220	1,017	46	700	32	630	28
Missouri	4,667	2,105	45	1,001	21	1,645	35
Montana	777	334	43	223	29	258	33
Nebraska	1,387	499	36	258	19	362	26
Nevada	2,024	594	29	171	8	504	25
New Hampshire	1,066	470	44	168	16	388	36
New Jersey	6,852	2,057	30	709	10	1,708	25
New Mexico	1,551	592	38	252	16	486	31
New York	15,503	5,143	33	1,980	13	4,081	26
North Carolina	7,264	2,717	37	1,394	19	2,124	29
North Dakota	(NA)	(NA)	(NA)	(NA)	(NA)	(NA)	(NA)
Ohio	8,999	4,078	45	1,603	18	3,155	35
Oklahoma	2,828	1,549	55	770	27	1,233	44
Oregon	3,061	1,396	46	444	15	1,239	40
Pennsylvania	10,036	4,063	40	1,277	13	3,329	33
Rhode Island	848	309	36	94	11	270	32
South Carolina	3,555	1,299	37	615	17	944	27
South Dakota	631	371	59	190	30	267	42
Tennessee	4,945	2,121	43	923	19	1,733	35
Texas	18,681	5,888	32	2,711	15	4,263	23
Utah	2,036	784	39	406	20	558	27
Vermont	512	316	62	134	26	273	53
Virginia	6,136	2,580	42	842	14	2,212	36
Washington	5,293	2,311	44	968	18	1,932	37
West Virginia	1,464	868	59	322	22	751	51
Wisconsin	4,460	2,499	56	1,198	27	2,152	48
Wyoming	424	250	59	145	34	182	43

(NA) Not available

Note: Detail does not add to total because of multiple responses U S totals include responses from participants residing in the District of Columbia, as described in Appendix D

Table 47. Participation in Wildlife-Related Recreation in Each State by Both Residents and Nonresidents of the State: 2011

(Population 16 years old and older. Numbers in thousands)

State where activity took place	Total participants		Sportspersons		Wildlife-watching participants	
	Number	Percent	Number	Percent	Number	Percent
United States, total	**90,108**	**100**	**37,397**	**42**	**71,776**	**80**
Alabama	1,732	100	948	55	1,114	64
Alaska	1,014	100	563	55	640	63
Arizona	2,136	100	786	37	1,566	73
Arkansas	1,323	100	696	53	852	64
California	7,849	100	1,820	23	6,733	86
Colorado	2,315	100	919	40	1,782	77
Connecticut	1,361	100	350	26	1,178	87
Delaware	344	100	177	52	243	71
Florida	6,354	100	3,152	50	4,308	68
Georgia	3,058	100	1,059	35	2,393	78
Hawaii	465	100	158	34	358	77
Idaho	838	100	534	64	558	67
Illinois	3,799	100	1,309	34	3,019	79
Indiana	2,308	100	867	38	1,719	74
Iowa	1,255	100	598	48	837	67
Kansas	1,156	100	527	46	792	69
Kentucky	1,710	100	713	42	1,319	77
Louisiana	1,709	100	904	53	1,010	59
Maine	1,117	100	413	37	838	75
Maryland	1,613	100	445	28	1,362	84
Massachusetts	2,199	100	538	24	1,828	83
Michigan	4,397	100	1,938	44	3,199	73
Minnesota	2,518	100	1,649	65	1,577	63
Mississippi	1,350	100	782	58	781	58
Missouri	2,494	100	1,277	51	1,716	69
Montana	570	100	335	59	402	71
Nebraska	558	100	289	52	384	69
Nevada	734	100	163	22	643	88
New Hampshire	786	100	247	31	630	80
New Jersey	2,438	100	794	33	1,875	77
New Mexico	783	100	304	39	566	72
New York	5,536	100	2,109	38	4,239	77
North Carolina	3,497	100	1,631	47	2,432	70
North Dakota	(NA)	(NA)	(NA)	(NA)	(NA)	(NA)
Ohio	4,344	100	1,561	36	3,197	74
Oklahoma	1,727	100	779	45	1,263	73
Oregon	1,786	100	703	39	1,440	81
Pennsylvania	4,564	100	1,424	31	3,598	79
Rhode Island	402	100	179	45	308	77
South Carolina	1,729	100	847	49	1,103	64
South Dakota	662	100	430	65	384	58
Tennessee	2,584	100	994	38	1,955	76
Texas	6,305	100	2,713	43	4,376	69
Utah	1,015	100	493	49	717	71
Vermont	512	100	254	50	370	72
Virginia	3,269	100	1,068	33	2,509	77
Washington	2,756	100	1,005	36	2,168	79
West Virginia	1,176	100	447	38	850	72
Wisconsin	3,500	100	1,554	44	2,359	67
Wyoming	775	100	390	50	518	67

* Estimate based on a sample size of 10–29   (NA) Not available

Note: Detail does not add to total because of multiple responses U S totals include responses from participants residing in the District of Columbia, as described in Appendix D

Table 48. Expenditures for Wildlife-Related Recreation by State Where Spending Took Place: 2011

(Population 16 years old and older. Expenditures in thousands of dollars)

State where spending took place	Total, wildlife-related expenditures				Fishing and hunting expenditures			
	Total	Trip-related	Equipment	Other	Total	Trip-related	Equipment	Other
United States, total	**144,651,796**	**49,485,328**	**80,843,000**	**24,788,145**	**89,761,524**	**32,210,653**	**43,227,403**	**14,323,468**
Alabama	2,665,172	763,220	1,711,316	190,636	1,930,968	722,029	1,043,040	165,898
Alaska	3,339,913	2,666,145	630,715	43,053	1,281,558	695,800	551,230	34,528
Arizona	2,367,995	897,293	1,144,520	326,181	1,432,115	506,095	808,438	117,582
Arkansas	1,775,635	691,310	810,190	274,135	1,559,561	656,790	653,616	249,155
California	7,496,449	3,903,886	2,917,174	675,389	3,718,773	2,122,206	1,431,197	165,370
Colorado	2,975,305	1,239,959	1,549,645	185,701	1,543,221	624,323	827,397	91,501
Connecticut	1,701,961	514,304	833,076	354,581	767,258	286,924	345,695	134,639
Delaware	325,374	90,245	146,729	88,400	155,586	54,176	43,460	57,950
Florida	9,036,766	4,815,253	2,733,398	1,488,115	5,995,434	3,082,600	1,944,968	967,865
Georgia	4,556,286	1,727,674	2,558,603	270,009	2,753,862	888,638	1,669,103	196,122
Hawaii	993,025	752,407	212,240	28,378	324,522	124,708	197,638	2,177
Idaho	1,582,416	628,991	780,265	173,161	1,150,375	546,512	488,083	115,780
Illinois	3,829,506	812,263	1,871,628	1,145,615	2,523,249	646,140	1,086,006	791,103
Indiana	1,692,628	698,567	785,849	208,212	941,286	492,210	307,649	141,427
Iowa	1,540,021	286,130	982,005	271,886	828,853	222,073	446,164	160,616
Kansas	906,039	293,551	236,355	376,132	697,624	247,952	179,430	270,242
Kentucky	2,946,272	626,124	1,546,698	773,451	2,173,052	500,766	1,379,622	292,663
Louisiana	2,238,502	1,000,985	1,014,000	223,516	1,695,750	778,840	736,916	179,993
Maine	1,417,258	830,869	416,881	169,508	618,404	316,723	244,768	56,912
Maryland	1,303,595	350,179	806,654	146,762	820,174	245,757	472,892	101,525
Massachusetts	1,961,405	556,738	709,183	695,484	683,507	270,646	383,216	29,646
Michigan	6,090,451	1,780,639	3,193,893	1,115,919	4,869,636	1,364,077	2,531,190	974,369
Minnesota	3,885,325	1,387,813	2,132,200	365,311	3,264,034	1,159,597	1,962,218	142,219
Mississippi	2,629,194	650,396	1,710,722	268,076	2,286,772	559,903	1,472,411	254,458
Missouri	2,681,426	893,867	1,398,330	389,229	1,740,608	682,933	791,728	265,947
Montana	1,408,180	666,395	568,822	172,963	1,007,383	374,484	464,613	168,286
Nebraska	1,309,521	233,081	867,358	209,082	796,225	146,362	457,559	192,304
Nevada	1,182,878	284,367	511,929	386,583	500,850	170,000	236,043	94,807
New Hampshire	553,507	287,092	188,907	77,508	272,317	185,279	77,587	9,451
New Jersey	2,294,691	749,520	864,754	680,417	1,308,413	521,397	457,200	329,816
New Mexico	936,549	446,916	410,204	79,429	609,433	299,979	273,607	35,847
New York	9,166,012	2,527,906	5,098,727	1,539,380	5,014,223	1,868,034	2,674,940	471,249
North Carolina	3,294,423	1,612,019	1,418,915	263,489	2,364,762	1,244,710	969,655	150,397
North Dakota	(NA)	(NA)	(NA)	(NA)	(NA)	(NA)	(NA)	(NA)
Ohio	3,510,736	1,002,362	1,412,777	1,095,597	2,771,930	915,296	955,751	900,883
Oklahoma	1,775,835	392,794	903,428	479,613	1,301,173	284,875	622,201	394,097
Oregon	2,653,246	924,413	1,460,670	268,163	956,024	442,172	441,703	72,149
Pennsylvania	2,793,977	667,890	1,599,038	527,050	1,523,089	401,221	810,451	311,417
Rhode Island	360,420	167,465	156,775	36,180	159,940	88,545	64,637	6,757
South Carolina	2,019,749	850,232	1,046,902	122,615	1,552,496	589,394	855,615	107,487
South Dakota	1,230,541	605,390	472,350	152,801	1,063,546	471,308	441,898	150,340
Tennessee	2,868,103	991,489	1,701,509	175,106	1,925,532	493,049	1,310,767	121,716
Texas	6,222,843	2,360,889	2,867,946	994,008	4,399,085	1,882,809	1,947,975	568,300
Utah	1,749,270	708,740	879,698	160,833	1,163,865	413,017	641,686	109,162
Vermont	744,040	179,223	360,957	203,860	455,533	129,717	247,540	78,275
Virginia	3,542,179	1,066,100	1,718,530	757,549	2,583,572	766,337	1,225,209	592,025
Washington	4,894,639	1,209,116	3,306,250	379,274	1,721,268	702,458	919,896	98,914
West Virginia	1,200,485	495,132	617,953	87,400	874,707	394,806	434,257	45,644
Wisconsin	5,522,195	1,200,307	3,081,200	1,240,688	4,033,338	965,547	2,000,568	1,067,223
Wyoming	1,137,200	874,268	180,927	82,005	786,944	553,099	158,761	75,085

See footnotes at end of table

U.S. Fish and Wildlife Service and U.S. Census Bureau

Table 48. Expenditures for Wildlife-Related Recreation by State Where Spending Took Place: 2011—Continued

(Population 16 years old and older. Numbers in thousands)

State where spending took place	Wildlife-watching expenditures			
	Total	Trip-related	Equipment	Other
United States, total	**54,890,272**	**17,274,675**	**27,150,921**	**10,464,677**
Alabama	734,204	*41,191	668,276	*24,738
Alaska	2,058,355	1,970,345	79,485	*8,524
Arizona	935,880	391,198	336,081	208,600
Arkansas	216,074	*34,520	156,574	
California	3,777,677	1,781,680	1,485,977	510,019
Colorado	1,432,084	615,636	722,249	94,199
Connecticut	934,703	227,380	487,381	219,942
Delaware	169,788	36,069	103,269	30,450
Florida	3,041,333	1,732,652	788,430	520,250
Georgia	1,802,423	839,036	889,500	*73,887
Hawaii	668,504	627,700	14,603	26,201
Idaho	432,041	82,479	292,182	*57,380
Illinois	1,306,258	166,123	785,622	354,513
Indiana	751,343	*206,357	478,201	66,785
Iowa	711,168	64,058	535,840	111,270
Kansas	208,415	*45,599	56,925	105,891
Kentucky	773,221	125,358	167,075	480,788
Louisiana	542,752	*222,145	277,084	*43,523
Maine	798,854	514,145	172,113	112,596
Maryland	483,421	104,421	333,762	45,237
Massachusetts	1,277,898	286,092	325,967	665,838
Michigan	1,220,815	416,562	662,703	141,550
Minnesota	621,290	228,217	169,982	223,092
Mississippi	342,422	*90,493	238,311	*13,617
Missouri	940,818	210,934	606,603	123,282
Montana	400,797	291,910	104,210	*4,677
Nebraska	513,297	86,719	409,799	16,778
Nevada	682,028	114,366	275,886	291,776
New Hampshire	281,190	101,813	111,320	68,057
New Jersey	986,278	228,123	407,554	350,601
New Mexico	327,117	146,937	136,597	43,583
New York	4,151,789	659,871	2,423,787	1,068,131
North Carolina	929,661	367,309	449,260	113,092
North Dakota	(NA)	(NA)	(NA)	(NA)
Ohio	738,806	87,066	457,027	194,714
Oklahoma	474,662	*107,919	281,227	*85,516
Oregon	1,697,222	482,241	1,018,967	196,014
Pennsylvania	1,270,888	266,669	788,587	215,632
Rhode Island	200,480	78,920	92,137	29,423
South Carolina	467,253	260,838	191,288	*15,127
South Dakota	166,995	134,082	30,452	*2,461
Tennessee	942,572	498,440	390,742	53,390
Texas	1,823,758	478,080	919,971	425,708
Utah	585,405	295,723	238,012	*51,671
Vermont	288,507	49,506	113,416	125,585
Virginia	958,607	299,762	493,321	165,524
Washington	3,173,371	506,658	2,386,353	280,360
West Virginia	325,778	100,326	183,696	*41,756
Wisconsin	1,488,857	234,760	1,080,632	173,464
Wyoming	350,256	321,169	22,166	*6,920

* Estimate based on a sample size of 10–29   ... Sample size too small (less than 10) to report data reliably   (NA) Not available

Note: U S totals include responses from participants residing in the District of Columbia, as described in Appendix D

Table 49. Expenditures for Wildlife-Related Recreation in the United States by State Residents Both Inside and Outside Their Resident State: 2011

(Population 16 years old and older. Numbers in thousands)

Participant's state of residence	Total, wildlife-related expenditures				Fishing and hunting expenditures			
	Total	Trip-related	Equipment	Other	Total	Trip-related	Equipment	Other
United States, total	**144,651,796**	**49,485,328**	**80,843,000**	**24,788,145**	**89,761,524**	**32,210,653**	**43,227,403**	**14,323,468**
Alabama	2,580,330	710,864	1,692,392	177,074	1,767,160	617,679	998,359	151,122
Alaska	1,014,001	365,578	621,150	27,273	869,773	313,999	536,453	19,321
Arizona	2,553,755	941,641	1,283,558	328,556	1,546,497	507,957	937,457	101,083
Arkansas	1,717,671	638,207	824,044	255,420	1,498,616	613,342	662,679	222,596
California	8,904,405	4,928,288	3,189,756	786,361	4,427,335	2,596,721	1,596,696	233,918
Colorado	2,444,637	1,019,057	1,281,295	144,285	1,441,355	512,345	866,761	62,250
Connecticut	2,385,182	986,943	960,807	437,432	1,059,979	492,315	426,145	141,518
Delaware	511,995	142,197	296,620	73,177	151,054	46,336	62,050	42,667
Florida	8,091,232	3,820,030	2,697,940	1,573,261	5,476,780	2,613,804	1,846,212	1,016,764
Georgia	5,060,457	2,462,015	2,354,755	243,687	2,482,983	856,617	1,462,415	163,950
Hawaii	442,305	154,484	221,880	65,940	309,694	102,723	204,591	2,380
Idaho	1,035,849	278,400	669,734	87,716	610,771	196,598	385,618	28,555
Illinois	5,091,826	1,445,339	2,229,211	1,417,276	3,133,455	918,369	1,162,720	1,052,366
Indiana	1,966,673	935,484	800,178	231,011	963,370	531,352	304,547	127,471
Iowa	1,882,200	616,181	992,194	273,824	1,013,538	388,268	460,246	165,024
Kansas	900,397	262,694	276,533	361,169	643,300	214,658	211,820	216,823
Kentucky	2,924,946	579,125	1,627,013	718,808	2,112,626	485,558	1,394,306	232,761
Louisiana	2,470,997	1,198,064	984,961	287,972	1,699,110	755,747	699,953	243,410
Maine	622,529	217,143	328,944	76,442	387,872	168,129	173,050	46,693
Maryland	1,730,084	652,348	854,361	223,375	1,106,794	358,666	610,726	137,401
Massachusetts	1,939,377	607,740	827,332	504,306	774,231	335,517	371,711	67,004
Michigan	6,150,417	1,742,178	3,284,436	1,123,803	4,919,017	1,351,218	2,578,221	989,578
Minnesota	4,371,217	1,761,329	1,990,741	619,147	3,499,788	1,293,168	1,817,156	389,463
Mississippi	2,524,916	556,106	1,713,495	255,315	2,173,769	487,354	1,447,246	239,169
Missouri	2,765,273	1,034,244	1,306,487	424,541	1,582,437	606,378	698,530	277,528
Montana	1,277,677	577,844	545,920	153,913	1,051,377	434,401	467,035	149,941
Nebraska	1,445,193	323,928	796,405	324,860	858,584	178,484	394,386	285,714
Nevada	1,282,868	407,053	535,633	340,182	485,601	233,524	204,670	47,407
New Hampshire	506,690	256,534	201,908	48,248	341,541	197,176	132,719	11,646
New Jersey	2,992,311	1,256,192	915,432	820,687	1,648,405	679,364	527,251	441,790
New Mexico	906,190	392,074	427,509	86,608	585,688	260,497	285,114	40,076
New York	10,665,327	3,600,610	5,130,402	1,934,315	5,309,319	2,086,496	2,668,628	554,194
North Carolina	3,742,754	1,863,117	1,545,115	334,522	2,496,929	1,247,168	1,040,438	209,323
North Dakota	(NA)	(NA)	(NA)	(NA)	(NA)	(NA)	(NA)	(NA)
Ohio	4,086,277	1,525,835	1,448,588	1,111,854	3,242,586	1,337,160	990,466	914,960
Oklahoma	1,905,525	512,273	914,697	478,554	1,414,920	391,940	631,095	391,885
Oregon	2,445,732	764,576	1,433,103	248,053	733,240	256,927	411,066	65,248
Pennsylvania	2,475,374	507,790	1,530,270	437,314	1,472,760	421,023	793,380	258,357
Rhode Island	330,687	151,989	140,715	37,982	168,733	63,931	98,201	6,601
South Carolina	2,149,460	767,251	1,261,311	120,898	1,838,305	621,493	1,113,809	103,003
South Dakota	722,526	237,321	436,656	48,549	660,736	201,487	413,928	45,321
Tennessee	2,871,608	897,275	1,821,155	153,178	2,137,741	590,473	1,448,405	98,862
Texas	6,237,199	2,414,822	2,838,198	984,180	4,559,419	2,079,809	1,925,507	554,103
Utah	1,326,803	452,085	776,883	97,835	946,736	322,728	575,859	48,149
Vermont	624,724	150,041	374,085	100,598	443,690	125,292	250,839	67,559
Virginia	3,467,271	1,108,672	1,575,251	783,347	2,418,819	754,336	1,074,714	589,768
Washington	5,275,143	1,332,774	3,477,820	464,549	2,195,318	916,795	1,085,454	193,068
West Virginia	1,285,342	550,452	665,620	69,270	953,839	417,965	484,767	51,107
Wisconsin	4,906,805	1,078,953	3,026,952	800,900	3,415,396	810,087	1,980,609	624,699
Wyoming	462,645	186,799	229,934	45,912	334,306	134,941	159,516	39,849

See footnotes at end of table

Table 49. Expenditures for Wildlife-Related Recreation in the United States by State Residents Both Inside and Outside Their Resident State: 2011—Continued

(Population 16 years old and older. Numbers in thousands)

Participant's state of residence	Wildlife-watching expenditures			
	Total	Trip-related	Equipment	Other
United States, total	**54,890,272**	**17,274,675**	**27,150,921**	**10,464,677**
Alabama	813,170	*93,185	694,033	*25,952
Alaska	144,228	51,579	84,697	*7,952
Arizona	1,007,258	433,685	346,100	227,474
Arkansas	219,055	*24,866	161,365	*32,824
California	4,477,069	2,331,567	1,593,060	552,443
Colorado	1,003,282	506,713	414,534	82,035
Connecticut	1,325,203	494,628	534,661	295,914
Delaware	360,941	95,861	234,570	30,510
Florida	2,614,452	1,206,226	851,728	556,497
Georgia	2,577,474	*1,605,397	892,339	*79,737
Hawaii	132,611	51,761	17,289	63,560
Idaho	425,078	*81,801	284,115	*59,161
Illinois	1,958,371	526,970	1,066,491	364,911
Indiana	1,003,303	*404,132	495,630	103,540
Iowa	868,662	227,914	531,948	108,800
Kansas	257,096	48,036	64,713	144,347
Kentucky	812,320	*93,567	232,707	486,047
Louisiana	771,887	*442,317	285,008	*44,562
Maine	234,657	*49,014	155,894	29,749
Maryland	623,290	293,681	243,635	85,974
Massachusetts	1,165,146	272,223	455,621	437,302
Michigan	1,231,400	*390,960	706,215	134,225
Minnesota	871,430	*468,161	173,584	229,684
Mississippi	351,147	*68,752	266,249	*16,146
Missouri	1,182,836	427,866	607,957	147,013
Montana	226,300	*143,443	78,885	*3,972
Nebraska	586,609	145,444	402,020	39,146
Nevada	797,267	173,529	330,964	292,775
New Hampshire	165,149	59,358	69,189	36,602
New Jersey	1,343,906	576,828	388,181	378,897
New Mexico	320,502	131,576	142,394	46,531
New York	5,356,008	1,514,114	2,461,773	1,380,121
North Carolina	1,245,825	615,949	504,677	125,199
North Dakota	(NA)	(NA)	(NA)	(NA)
Ohio	843,691	188,675	458,123	196,894
Oklahoma	490,605	*120,334	283,602	*86,669
Oregon	1,712,492	507,648	1,022,037	182,806
Pennsylvania	1,002,614	*86,767	736,890	178,957
Rhode Island	161,954	88,059	42,514	31,381
South Carolina	311,155	*145,758	147,503	*17,895
South Dakota	61,790	*35,834	22,728	*3,228
Tennessee	733,867	306,802	372,750	54,315
Texas	1,677,780	*335,013	912,691	430,076
Utah	380,067	129,357	201,024	*49,686
Vermont	181,034	24,749	123,247	33,039
Virginia	1,048,452	354,336	500,537	193,579
Washington	3,079,826	415,979	2,392,366	271,481
West Virginia	331,503	*132,487	180,852	*18,163
Wisconsin	1,491,409	*268,866	1,046,342	176,201
Wyoming	128,338	51,858	70,417	*6,062

* Estimate based on a sample size of 10–29   (NA) Not available

Note: U S totals include responses from participants residing in the District of Columbia, as described in Appendix D

Table 50. Anglers and Hunters by Sportsperson's State of Residence: 2011

(Population 16 years old and older. Numbers in thousands)

Sportsperson's state of residence	Population	Fished or hunted		Fished only		Hunted only		Fished and hunted	
		Number	Percent of population	Number	Percent of population	Number	Percent of population	Number	Percent of population
United States, total	**239,313**	**37,397**	**16**	**23,714**	**10**	**4,285**	**2**	**9,389**	**4**
Alabama	3,664	744	20	252	7	*228	*6	264	7
Alaska	526	235	45	129	25	*24	*5	82	16
Arizona	5,084	721	14	462	9	*135	*3	*124	*2
Arkansas	2,238	572	26	252	11	*105	*5	214	10
California	28,562	1,898	7	1,431	5	198	1	269	1
Colorado	3,946	727	18	567	14	*60	*2	99	3
Connecticut	2,781	347	12	265	10			76	3
Delaware	699	101	14	78	11	*9	*1	*14	*2
Florida	14,855	2,068	14	1,731	12	*78	*1	252	2
Georgia	7,459	981	13	672	9	*138	*2	171	2
Hawaii	995	108	11	85	9			*21	*2
Idaho	1,172	331	28	169	14			*119	*10
Illinois	9,988	1,487	15	976	10	*252	*3	260	3
Indiana	4,965	842	17	465	9	*56	*1	322	6
Iowa	2,363	586	25	369	16	*64	*3	152	6
Kansas	2,163	453	21	275	13	*18	*1	159	7
Kentucky	3,376	643	19	327	10	*151	*4	165	5
Louisiana	3,449	802	23	511	15	*69	*2	222	6
Maine	1,066	233	22	92	9	*37	*3	104	10
Maryland	4,480	426	9	337	8			*72	*2
Massachusetts	5,320	464	9	398	7			59	1
Michigan	7,787	1,636	21	1,128	14	*170	*2	337	4
Minnesota	4,133	1,400	34	925	22	*71	*2	403	10
Mississippi	2,220	700	32	263	12	*96	*4	340	15
Missouri	4,667	1,001	21	507	11	132	3	363	8
Montana	777	223	29	114	15	*30	*4	78	10
Nebraska	1,387	258	19	143	10	*61	*4	54	4
Nevada	2,024	171	8	122	6	*15	*1	*34	*2
New Hampshire	1,066	168	16	125	12			*39	*4
New Jersey	6,852	709	10	593	9	*30	*(Z)	86	1
New Mexico	1,551	252	16	185	12	*21	*1	*47	*3
New York	15,503	1,980	13	1,241	8	*172	*1	567	4
North Carolina	7,264	1,394	19	1,077	15	*88	*1	230	3
North Dakota	(NA)	(NA)	(NA)	(NA)	(NA)	(NA)	(NA)	(NA)	(NA)
Ohio	8,999	1,603	18	1,075	12	*168	*2	360	4
Oklahoma	2,828	770	27	551	19			*193	*7
Oregon	3,061	444	15	263	9	*58	*2	*123	*4
Pennsylvania	10,036	1,277	13	574	6	269	3	434	4
Rhode Island	848	94	11	77	9			16	2
South Carolina	3,555	615	17	377	11	*42	*1	196	6
South Dakota	631	190	30	*58	*9	*27	*4	106	17
Tennessee	4,945	923	19	637	13	*91	*2	196	4
Texas	18,681	2,711	15	1,631	9	*356	*2	724	4
Utah	2,036	406	20	245	12	*55	*3	106	5
Vermont	512	134	26	64	12	30	6	41	8
Virginia	6,136	842	14	488	8	135	2	219	4
Washington	5,293	968	18	749	14	*54	*1	165	3
West Virginia	1,464	322	22	111	8	*83	*6	128	9
Wisconsin	4,460	1,198	27	434	10	*260	*6	504	11
Wyoming	424	145	34	69	16	*30	*7	46	11

* Estimate based on a sample size of 10–29   ... Sample size too small (less than 10) to report data reliably   (NA) Not available   (Z) Less than 0 5 percent

Note: U S totals include responses from participants residing in the District of Columbia, as described in Appendix D

Table 51. Anglers and Hunters by State Where Fishing or Hunting Took Place: 2011

(Population 16 years old and older. Numbers in thousands)

State where fishing or hunting took place	Anglers						Hunters					
	Total anglers, residents and nonresidents		State residents		Nonresidents		Total hunters, residents and nonresidents		State residents		Nonresidents	
	Number	Percent	Number	Percent	Number	Percent	Number	Percent	Number	Percent	Number	Percent
United States, total	33,112	100	30,037	91	6,964	21	13,674	100	12,890	94	1,942	14
Alabama	683	100	473	69	210	31	535	100	492	92	*44	*8
Alaska	538	100	211	39	327	61	125	100	104	83		
Arizona	637	100	533	84	*104	*16	269	100	225	83	*45	*17
Arkansas	555	100	458	83	*97	*17	363	100	316	87		
California	1,674	100	1,576	94	98	6	394	100	377	96		
Colorado	767	100	593	77	175	23	259	100	144	55	*115	*45
Connecticut	342	100	277	81	*65	*19	50	100	46	93		
Delaware	166	100	59	36	*107	*64	23	100	19	84		
Florida	3,092	100	1,895	61	1,197	39	242	100	215	89		
Georgia	829	100	764	92	*65	*8	392	100	293	75	*98	*25
Hawaii	157	100	104	66			*23	*100	*23	*100		
Idaho	447	100	238	53	208	47	246	100	*162	*66	*85	*34
Illinois	1,044	100	955	92	*88	*8	512	100	459	90		
Indiana	801	100	720	90	*81	*10	392	100	377	96		
Iowa	473	100	416	88	*58	*12	253	100	200	79		
Kansas	400	100	372	93	*28	*7	283	100	170	60	*112	*40
Kentucky	554	100	451	81	*103	*19	347	100	316	91		
Louisiana	825	100	700	85	*125	*15	277	100	253	91		
Maine	341	100	193	56	149	44	181	100	141	78	*40	*22
Maryland	426	100	347	81	80	19	88	100	*69	*78	*19	*22
Massachusetts	532	100	377	71	155	29	56	100	52	93		
Michigan	1,744	100	1,397	80	347	20	529	100	501	95		
Minnesota	1,562	100	1,303	83	259	17	477	100	457	96		
Mississippi	651	100	600	92			483	100	436	90		
Missouri	1,071	100	827	77	244	23	576	100	477	83	*100	*17
Montana	267	100	185	69	82	31	150	100	104	70	*46	*30
Nebraska	207	100	177	85			128	100	110	86		
Nevada	147	100	114	78			43	100	39	91		
New Hampshire	228	100	153	67	75	33	56	100	42	74	*14	*26
New Jersey	766	100	509	66	*257	*34	94	100	93	99		
New Mexico	278	100	213	77	*65	*23	69	100	64	93		
New York	1,882	100	1,585	84	297	16	823	100	739	90	*84	*10
North Carolina	1,525	100	1,196	78	329	22	335	100	259	77	*76	*23
North Dakota	(NA)	(NA)	(NA)	(NA)	(NA)	(NA)	(NA)	(NA)	(NA)	(NA)	(NA)	(NA)
Ohio	1,342	100	1,257	94	*85	*6	553	100	516	93	*37	*7
Oklahoma	729	100	680	93	*49	*7	244	100	219	90		
Oregon	638	100	373	59	264	41	196	100	181	92		
Pennsylvania	1,101	100	891	81	210	19	775	100	699	90	*76	*10
Rhode Island	175	100	79	45	96	55	20	100	15	77		
South Carolina	744	100	561	75	*182	*25	254	100	180	71	*74	*29
South Dakota	268	100	156	58	*112	*42	270	100	127	47	144	53
Tennessee	826	100	709	86	*117	*14	375	100	276	74		
Texas	2,246	100	2,133	95	*114	*5	1,147	100	1,080	94	*67	*6
Utah	414	100	343	83	*70	*17	193	100	158	82	*35	*18
Vermont	207	100	95	46	112	54	90	100	66	74		
Virginia	833	100	649	78	184	22	432	100	326	75	*106	*25
Washington	938	100	835	89	*103	*11	219	100	200	92		
West Virginia	305	100	222	73	*84	*27	247	100	184	74		
Wisconsin	1,247	100	910	73	337	27	895	100	763	85	*131	*15
Wyoming	303	100	110	36	*193	*64	140	100	76	54	*64	*46

* Estimate based on a sample size of 10–29   ... Sample size too small (less than 10) to report data reliably   (NA) Not available

Note: For the U S row, detail does not add to total because of multiple responses U S totals include responses from participants residing in the District of Columbia, as described in Appendix D

Table 52. Hunters by Type of Hunting and State Where Hunting Took Place: 2011

(Population 16 years old and older. Numbers in thousands)

State where hunting took place	Total, all hunting		Big game		Small game		Migratory birds		Other animals	
	Number	Percent	Number	Percent	Number	Percent	Number	Percent	Number	Percent
United States, total	**13,674**	**100**	**11,570**	**85**	**4,506**	**33**	**2,583**	**19**	**2,168**	**16**
Alabama	535	100	477	89	*126	*24			*68	*13
Alaska	125	100	110	88	*25	*20				
Arizona	269	100	*127	*47	*105	*39	*75	*28		
Arkansas	363	100	318	88	*83	*23	*97	*27	*96	*27
California	394	100	154	39	201	51	221	56	*62	*16
Colorado	259	100	178	69	*101	*39			*37	*14
Connecticut	50	100	*30	*60	*31	*62				
Delaware	23	100	*18	*80			*9	*39		
Florida	242	100	187	77					*77	*32
Georgia	392	100	349	89	*117	*30			*65	*17
Hawaii	*23	*100	*22	*96						
Idaho	246	100	177	72						
Illinois	512	100	351	69	*237	*46	*156	*30	*153	*30
Indiana	392	100	266	68	*126	*32				
Iowa	253	100	199	79	*131	*52				
Kansas	283	100	162	57	189	67	*68	*24		
Kentucky	347	100	315	91	*134	*39				
Louisiana	277	100	217	78	*95	*34	*110	*40		
Maine	181	100	143	79	*60	*33			*21	*12
Maryland	88	100	*73	*83	*35	*40	*29	*32		
Massachusetts	56	100	*41	*72	*26	*46				
Michigan	529	100	488	92	*114	*22				
Minnesota	477	100	412	86	*160	*34	*68	*14		
Mississippi	483	100	469	97	*106	*22	*39	*8		
Missouri	576	100	464	80	146	25	*99	*17	*45	*8
Montana	150	100	128	86	*55	*36				
Nebraska	128	100	93	72	*45	*35	*29	*22		
Nevada	43	100	*30	*70	*20	*46				
New Hampshire	56	100	46	82	*17	*31				
New Jersey	94	100	89	95	*23	*24	*18	*19		
New Mexico	69	100	*44	*64						
New York	823	100	777	94	*380	*46				
North Carolina	335	100	281	84	*59	*17	*89	*27		
North Dakota	(NA)	(NA)	(NA)	(NA)	(NA)	(NA)	(NA)	(NA)	(NA)	(NA)
Ohio	553	100	515	93	*193	*35			*72	*13
Oklahoma	244	100	*144	*59	*123	*50			*37	*15
Oregon	196	100	189	96						
Pennsylvania	775	100	755	97	*204	*26				
Rhode Island	20	100	*9	*47	*13	*64	*8	*39		
South Carolina	254	100	224	88	*63	*25	*63	*25		
South Dakota	270	100	122	45	212	78	*58	*21		
Tennessee	375	100	337	90	*122	*33	*114	*30		
Texas	1,147	100	937	82	*247	*22	*391	*34	432	38
Utah	193	100	149	77	*63	*33	*30	*16		
Vermont	90	100	84	93	*22	*24	*5	*6	*18	*20
Virginia	432	100	405	94	85	20	*85	*20		
Washington	219	100	189	86						
West Virginia	247	100	244	99	*86	*35				
Wisconsin	895	100	785	88	*219	*24	*105	*12		
Wyoming	140	100	130	93						

* Estimate based on a sample size of 10–29   … Sample size too small (less than 10) to report data reliably   (NA) Not available

Note: Detail does not add to total because of multiple responses U S totals include responses from participants residing in the District of Columbia, as described in Appendix D

Table 53. Days of Hunting by State Where Hunting Took Place and Hunter's State of Residence: 2011

(Population 16 years old and older. Numbers in thousands)

State	Days of hunting in state						Days of hunting by state residents					
	Total days, residents and nonresidents		Days by state residents		Days by nonresidents		Total days, in state of residence and other states		Days in state of residence		Days in other states	
	Number	Percent	Number	Percent	Number	Percent	Number	Percent	Number	Percent	Number	Percent
United States, total	281,884	100	263,038	93	20,291	7	281,884	100	263,038	93	20,291	7
Alabama	10,548	100	10,285	98	*263	*2	10,393	100	10,285	99		
Alaska	1,336	100	1,044	78			1,096	100	1,044	95		
Arizona	2,634	100	2,363	90	*271	*10	3,164	100	2,363	75		
Arkansas	10,967	100	10,006	91			10,712	100	10,006	93		
California	6,731	100	6,585	98			8,036	100	6,585	82	*1,451	*18
Colorado	2,184	100	1,553	71	*630	*29	1,806	100	1,553	86		
Connecticut	1,011	100	947	94			1,348	100	947	70	*401	*30
Delaware	380	100	343	90			453	100	343	76	*110	*24
Florida	5,252	100	4,969	95			6,693	100	4,969	74	*1,724	*26
Georgia	8,920	100	7,742	87	*1,177	*13	8,318	100	7,742	93		
Hawaii	774	100	*774	*100			786	100	*774	*99		
Idaho	3,227	100	*1,983	*61	*1,243	*39	2,009	100	*1,983	*99		
Illinois	7,836	100	7,354	94			7,786	100	7,354	94	*432	*6
Indiana	10,863	100	10,814	100			10,926	100	10,814	99		
Iowa	4,240	100	3,988	94			4,163	100	3,988	96		
Kansas	5,209	100	4,075	78	*1,134	*22	4,193	100	4,075	97		
Kentucky	12,222	100	11,402	93			11,979	100	11,402	95		
Louisiana	5,222	100	5,044	97			6,738	100	5,044	75	*1,694	*25
Maine	2,523	100	2,240	89	*283	*11	2,410	100	2,240	93		
Maryland	1,032	100	*919	*89	*112	*11	1,418	100	*919	*65		
Massachusetts	1,062	100	1,041	98			1,403	100	1,041	74	*363	*26
Michigan	11,020	100	10,840	98			11,358	100	10,840	95		
Minnesota	5,589	100	5,502	98			8,053	100	5,502	68	*2,551	*32
Mississippi	9,105	100	8,537	94			8,755	100	8,537	98		
Missouri	10,087	100	9,154	91	*932	*9	9,716	100	9,154	94	*562	*6
Montana	2,493	100	2,002	80	*491	*20	2,158	100	2,002	93		
Nebraska	1,554	100	1,490	96			1,584	100	1,490	94		
Nevada	748	100	699	93			897	100	699	78	*198	*22
New Hampshire	1,359	100	1,207	89	*153	*11	1,330	100	1,207	91		
New Jersey	2,400	100	2,380	99			2,928	100	2,380	81	*547	*19
New Mexico	927	100	851	92			911	100	851	93		
New York	18,433	100	17,673	96	*760	*4	17,741	100	17,673	100		
North Carolina	7,608	100	7,314	96	*293	*4	8,177	100	7,314	89		
North Dakota	(NA)	(NA)	(NA)	(NA)	(NA)	(NA)	(NA)	(NA)	(NA)	(NA)	(NA)	(NA)
Ohio	8,967	100	8,688	97	*278	*3	9,066	100	8,688	96		
Oklahoma	4,968	100	4,790	96			5,201	100	4,790	92		
Oregon	2,205	100	2,133	97			2,264	100	2,133	94		
Pennsylvania	18,247	100	17,648	97	*598	*3	17,826	100	17,648	99		
Rhode Island	419	100	248	59			318	100	248	78	*70	*22
South Carolina	4,353	100	3,882	89	*471	*11	4,255	100	3,882	91		
South Dakota	3,742	100	2,811	75	930	25	2,901	100	2,811	97		
Tennessee	9,846	100	9,507	97			9,603	100	9,507	99		
Texas	20,372	100	19,778	97	*594	*3	19,905	100	19,778	99		
Utah	2,720	100	2,482	91	*238	*9	2,643	100	2,482	94		
Vermont	1,584	100	1,403	89			1,618	100	1,403	87	*215	*13
Virginia	10,060	100	9,302	92	*758	*8	10,306	100	9,302	90	*1,004	*10
Washington	2,547	100	2,445	96			2,756	100	2,445	89	*311	*11
West Virginia	3,166	100	3,035	96			3,254	100	3,035	93		
Wisconsin	12,177	100	10,085	83	*2,092	*17	10,219	100	10,085	99		
Wyoming	1,726	100	1,103	64	*623	*36	1,171	100	1,103	94	*68	*6

* Estimate based on a sample size of 10–29   ... Sample size too small (less than 10) to report data reliably   (NA) Not available

Note: U S totals include responses from participants residing in the District of Columbia, as described in Appendix D

Table 54. Days of Hunting by Type of Hunting and State Where Hunting Took Place: 2011

(Population 16 years old and older. Numbers in thousands)

State where hunting took place	Total, all hunting		Big game		Small game		Migratory birds		Other animals	
	Number	Percent	Number	Percent	Number	Percent	Number	Percent	Number	Percent
United States, total	**281,884**	**100**	**212,116**	**75**	**50,884**	**18**	**23,263**	**8**	**34,434**	**12**
Alabama	10,548	100	8,790	83	*1,282	*12			*862	*8
Alaska	1,336	100	1,211	91	*124	*9				
Arizona	2,634	100	*774	*29	*1,443	*55	*324	*12		
Arkansas	10,967	100	9,401	86	*1,253	*11	*2,018	*18	*1,214	*11
California	6,731	100	1,824	27	2,045	30	2,860	42	*1,058	*16
Colorado	2,184	100	1,327	61	*730	*33			*508	*23
Connecticut	1,011	100	*481	*48	*457	*45				
Delaware	380	100	*322	*85			*83	*22		
Florida	5,252	100	4,051	77					*1,538	*29
Georgia	8,920	100	8,268	93	*1,966	*22			*1,907	*21
Hawaii	*774	*100	*688	*89						
Idaho	3,227	100	2,664	83						
Illinois	7,836	100	4,915	63	*1,220	*16	*1,075	*14	*1,174	*15
Indiana	10,863	100	6,261	58	*1,666	*15				
Iowa	4,240	100	3,106	73	*1,169	*28				
Kansas	5,209	100	3,486	67	1,644	32	*357	*7		
Kentucky	12,222	100	9,720	80	*1,742	*14				
Louisiana	5,222	100	3,697	71	*950	*18	*1,085	*21		
Maine	2,523	100	1,827	72	*802	*32			*237	*9
Maryland	1,032	100	*786	*76	*136	*13	*152	*15		
Massachusetts	1,062	100	*769	*72	*268	*25				
Michigan	11,020	100	9,584	87	*1,208	*11				
Minnesota	5,589	100	3,573	64	*2,014	*36	*1,238	*22		
Mississippi	9,105	100	7,410	81	*1,445	*16	*231	*3		
Missouri	10,087	100	8,386	83	1,298	13	*848	*8	*629	*6
Montana	2,493	100	2,040	82	*678	*27				
Nebraska	1,554	100	1,081	70	*332	*21	*255	*16		
Nevada	748	100	*343	*46	*316	*42				
New Hampshire	1,359	100	1,057	78	*185	*14				
New Jersey	2,400	100	2,078	87	*270	*11	*225	*9		
New Mexico	927	100	*569	*61						
New York	18,433	100	15,649	85	*3,620	*20				
North Carolina	7,608	100	5,059	67	*1,343	*18	*1,665	*22		
North Dakota	(NA)	(NA)	(NA)	(NA)	(NA)	(NA)	(NA)	(NA)	(NA)	(NA)
Ohio	8,967	100	6,747	75	*1,884	*21			*1,297	*14
Oklahoma	4,968	100	*2,776	*56	*1,399	*28			*1,679	*34
Oregon	2,205	100	1,918	87						
Pennsylvania	18,247	100	17,389	95	*1,152	*6				
Rhode Island	419	100	*234	*56	*147	*35	*71	*17		
South Carolina	4,353	100	3,559	82	*438	*10	*333	*8		
South Dakota	3,742	100	982	26	1,660	44	*342	*9		
Tennessee	9,846	100	7,622	77	*3,061	*31	*593	*6		
Texas	20,372	100	12,651	62	*3,238	*16	*1,672	*8	7,882	39
Utah	2,720	100	1,962	72	*452	*17	*597	*22		
Vermont	1,584	100	1,406	89	*225	*14	*35	*2	*92	*6
Virginia	10,060	100	9,396	93	*699	*7	*262	*3		
Washington	2,547	100	2,210	87						
West Virginia	3,166	100	2,580	81	*851	*27				
Wisconsin	12,177	100	8,575	70	*2,640	*22	*1,276	*10		
Wyoming	1,726	100	1,487	86						

* Estimate based on a sample size of 10–29   ... Sample size too small (less than 10) to report data reliably   (NA) Not available

Note: Detail does not add to total because of multiple responses U S totals include responses from participants residing in the District of Columbia, as described in Appendix D

Table 55. Expenditures for Hunting by State Where Spending Took Place: 2011

(Population 16 years old and older. Expenditures in thousands of dollars)

State where spending took place	Total expenditures	Trip-related expenditures				Expenditures for equipment				Expenditures for other items[2]
		Total trip-related	Food and lodging	Trans-portation	Other trip costs	Total equipment	Hunting equipment[1]	Auxiliary equipment[1]	Special equipment[1]	
United States, total	**33,702,017**	**10,421,189**	**3,881,304**	**4,767,915**	**1,771,970**	**13,972,490**	**7,738,324**	**1,844,880**	**4,389,286**	**9,308,340**
Alabama	913,387	404,966	151,664	160,803	*92,498	357,045	173,693	*63,734		151,376
Alaska	424,803	167,664	68,265	63,078	36,321	244,032	113,578	*12,745		13,107
Arizona	337,759	148,623	57,806	74,731	*16,085	133,703	80,563	*17,195		55,433
Arkansas	1,018,793	317,150	133,327	152,564	*31,259	466,793	409,109	*50,371		234,850
California	964,054	501,877	114,203	227,036	160,638	382,590	224,800	*88,376		79,588
Colorado	460,914	220,754	86,645	81,818	52,290	185,179	142,127	*25,522		54,981
Connecticut	301,988	28,253	*7,577	15,353	*5,323	159,642	108,687	*15,039		114,093
Delaware	40,771	*5,426	*2,851	*2,185		12,475	*8,430			*22,870
Florida	715,733	280,965	75,876	125,965	*79,124	219,590	185,070	*22,630		215,178
Georgia	964,887	486,854	241,218	155,601	*90,036	328,558	299,661	*21,874		149,475
Hawaii	*50,962	*22,634	*7,981	*14,099	*554	*27,374	*26,445			*954
Idaho	477,548	285,440	77,409	114,160	*93,870	131,968	73,694	*16,137		60,140
Illinois	1,216,281	273,779	139,784	106,027	*27,967	369,894	235,424	*67,077		572,608
Indiana	222,310	64,900	25,507	35,471		105,008	86,825	*15,676		52,402
Iowa	405,451	121,534	58,278	59,244		151,252	108,302	*36,960		132,665
Kansas	401,452	149,787	50,646	72,731	*26,410	71,835	61,867	*9,968		179,829
Kentucky	797,766	241,639	62,367	106,402	*72,869	350,029	272,967	*56,892		206,098
Louisiana	564,385	244,997	100,546	111,188	*33,263	177,639	142,761	*20,136		141,749
Maine	202,639	102,037	64,615	33,273	*4,149	60,394	46,748	*4,946		40,208
Maryland	264,119	50,221	*20,853	14,058	*15,310	127,600	105,922	*21,678		*86,297
Massachusetts	87,483	*16,941	*7,064	*8,640		62,893	*45,364	*16,349		7,649
Michigan	2,338,684	271,341	105,419	143,776	*22,146	1,317,004	407,636	*76,709		750,339
Minnesota	725,407	235,024	113,805	95,062	*26,158	400,397	336,690	54,429		89,986
Mississippi	914,889	244,140	114,436	98,317	*31,386	428,296	299,769	52,450		242,453
Missouri	906,888	308,718	124,111	142,245	42,362	355,911	265,218	38,051		242,259
Montana	627,298	232,599	90,862	132,275	*9,461	284,624	164,708	*88,982		110,075
Nebraska	526,527	89,522	40,072	44,014	*5,436	258,741	148,017	51,066		178,263
Nevada	204,137	86,725	25,465	29,484	*31,776	79,937	45,804	*20,582		37,475
New Hampshire	60,578	33,890	9,463	23,614		23,426	19,467	*3,959		3,262
New Jersey	115,797	34,419	*11,665	18,664		67,032	33,483	*7,214		14,345
New Mexico	139,264	*65,792	*24,371	*35,197	*6,225	*54,420	*43,569	*7,257		19,051
New York	1,564,205	810,119	237,046	528,953	*44,120	483,719	397,260	*51,249		270,368
North Carolina	525,281	224,555	78,189	96,908	*49,457	181,501	146,819	*34,293		119,225
North Dakota	(NA)	(NA)	(NA)	(NA)	(NA)	(NA)	(NA)	(NA)	(NA)	(NA)
Ohio	752,996	320,777	57,043	163,800		274,391	220,095	*54,296		157,828
Oklahoma	355,680	109,173	*38,010	*37,246	*33,918	*182,698	*170,187	*10,882		*63,809
Oregon	238,696	83,492	35,895	42,322	*5,274	134,260	*36,835	*24,709		20,944
Pennsylvania	970,598	172,710	61,534	98,835	*12,342	563,664	319,457	100,525		234,223
Rhode Island	18,308	4,610	1,585	2,914		12,119	*9,583	*863		1,578
South Carolina	505,311	229,561	95,412	96,014	*38,134	191,589	81,911	*22,483		84,161
South Dakota	596,824	338,230	154,811	139,036	*44,382	115,496	65,594	*24,101		143,098
Tennessee	494,005	210,025	95,404	99,196	*15,425	216,306	158,388	*57,918		67,674
Texas	1,835,098	837,479	332,375	379,419	*125,685	537,597	343,969	*154,067		460,022
Utah	499,141	186,765	50,622	101,917	*34,226	261,972	148,128	*46,555		50,403
Vermont	292,328	39,469	14,096	21,883	*3,490	190,433	129,785	13,467		62,426
Virginia	877,038	297,241	73,309	93,747	130,185	286,072	227,495	53,040		293,725
Washington	356,251	163,423	75,198	77,154	*11,070	156,398	109,555	*38,486		36,431
West Virginia	409,219	68,531	37,185	28,376		307,999	79,373	*43,866		32,689
Wisconsin	2,544,591	358,080	160,687	156,022	*41,371	1,464,520	137,004	*64,793		721,991
Wyoming	288,736	159,115	40,461	67,319	*51,334	80,980	48,959	*25,881		48,642

* Estimate based on a sample size of 10–29   ... Sample size too small (less than 10) to report data reliably   (NA) Not available

[1] See Table 17 for a detailed listing of hunting, auxiliary, and special equipment items

[2] Includes expenditures for magazine subscriptions, membership dues and contributions, land leasing and ownership, licenses, stamps, tags, and permits, and plantings

Note: U S totals include responses from participants residing in the District of Columbia, as described in Appendix D

Table 56. Freshwater (Except Great Lakes) Anglers and Days of Fishing by State Where Fishing Took Place: 2011

(Population 16 years old and older. Numbers in thousands)

State where fishing took place	Anglers						Days of fishing					
	Total anglers, residents and nonresidents		State residents		Nonresidents		Total days, residents and nonresidents		Days by state residents		Days by nonresidents	
	Number	Percent	Number	Percent	Number	Percent	Number	Percent	Number	Percent	Number	Percent
United States, total	27,060	100	24,914	92	4,540	17	443,223	100	403,207	91	42,801	10
Alabama	598	100	451	75	*147	*25	9,746	100	8,999	92	*746	*8
Alaska	302	100	166	55	*136	*45	2,995	100	2,139	71	*857	*29
Arizona	637	100	533	84	*104	*16	4,825	100	4,141	86	*684	*14
Arkansas	555	100	458	83	*97	*17	15,662	100	15,055	96	*607	*4
California	1,352	100	1,304	96	48	4	17,382	100	17,086	98	296	2
Colorado	767	100	593	77	175	23	8,433	100	7,490	89	943	11
Connecticut	243	100	211	87	*33	*13	3,518	100	3,416	97	*102	*3
Delaware	55	100	28	51			655	100	567	87		
Florida	1,214	100	956	79	258	21	25,729	100	21,001	82	4,728	18
Georgia	763	100	725	95			8,106	100	7,932	98		
Hawaii												
Idaho	447	100	238	53	208	47	5,507	100	2,165	39	3,342	61
Illinois	937	100	861	92	*76	*8	12,312	100	11,959	97	*353	*3
Indiana	716	100	636	89	*81	*11	19,324	100	18,787	97	*537	*3
Iowa	473	100	416	88	*58	*12	5,978	100	5,790	97	*187	*3
Kansas	400	100	372	93	*28	*7	4,163	100	4,088	98	*75	*2
Kentucky	554	100	451	81	*103	*19	10,245	100	9,385	92	*860	*8
Louisiana	720	100	642	89			16,665	100	16,437	99		
Maine	283	100	173	61	111	39	3,223	100	2,403	75	820	25
Maryland	227	100	192	84	*36	*16	3,160	100	2,809	89	*351	*11
Massachusetts	294	100	232	79	*62	*21	4,499	100	4,211	94	*288	*6
Michigan	1,361	100	1,054	77	307	23	20,961	100	19,006	91	1,955	9
Minnesota	1,413	100	1,159	82	254	18	20,768	100	19,086	92	1,682	8
Mississippi	609	100	562	92			7,751	100	7,086	91		
Missouri	1,071	100	827	77	244	23	14,865	100	13,263	89	1,603	11
Montana	267	100	185	69	82	31	2,450	100	2,091	85	358	15
Nebraska	207	100	177	85			2,595	100	2,493	96		
Nevada	147	100	114	78			1,400	100	1,295	93		
New Hampshire	209	100	140	67	69	33	3,606	100	3,121	87	485	13
New Jersey	258	100	251	97			2,680	100	2,597	97		
New Mexico	278	100	213	77	*65	*23	3,899	100	3,622	93	*278	*7
New York	1,212	100	1,056	87	156	13	19,200	100	18,257	95	942	5
North Carolina	1,054	100	948	90	*106	*10	15,764	100	15,446	98	*317	*2
North Dakota	(NA)	(NA)	(NA)	(NA)	(NA)	(NA)	(NA)	(NA)	(NA)	(NA)	(NA)	(NA)
Ohio	1,161	100	1,099	95	*62	*5	14,040	100	13,523	96	*517	*4
Oklahoma	729	100	680	93	*49	*7	8,499	100	7,943	93	*556	*7
Oregon	516	100	347	67	169	33	5,201	100	4,173	80	1,029	20
Pennsylvania	874	100	695	80	179	20	8,906	100	7,335	82	1,572	18
Rhode Island	42	100	34	80			739	100	690	93		
South Carolina	537	100	437	81	*100	*19	9,221	100	8,843	96	*378	*4
South Dakota	268	100	156	58	*112	*42	4,069	100	3,525	87	*544	*13
Tennessee	826	100	709	86	*117	*14	16,957	100	16,041	95	*916	*5
Texas	1,758	100	1,666	95	*92	*5	22,616	100	22,099	98	*518	*2
Utah	414	100	343	83	*70	*17	5,979	100	5,373	90	*606	*10
Vermont	207	100	95	46	112	54	2,215	100	1,751	79	464	21
Virginia	551	100	455	82	*97	*18	7,904	100	7,422	94	*481	*6
Washington	743	100	660	89	*84	*11	10,940	100	10,650	97	*290	*3
West Virginia	305	100	222	73	*84	*27	4,521	100	4,271	94	*250	*6
Wisconsin	1,107	100	808	73	299	27	19,950	100	13,514	68	6,436	32
Wyoming	303	100	110	36	*193	*64	3,123	100	2,009	64	*1,114	*36

* Estimate based on a sample size of 10–29   ... Sample size too small (less than 10) to report data reliably   (NA) Not available

Note: For the U S row, detail does not add to total because of multiple responses U S totals include responses from participants residing in the District of Columbia, as described in Appendix D

Table 57. Great Lakes Anglers and Days of Great Lakes Fishing by State Where Fishing Took Place: 2011

(Population 16 years old and older. Numbers in thousands)

State where fishing took place	Anglers						Days of fishing					
	Total anglers, residents and nonresidents		State residents		Nonresidents		Total days, residents and nonresidents		Days by state residents		Days by nonresidents	
	Number	Percent	Number	Percent	Number	Percent	Number	Percent	Number	Percent	Number	Percent
United States, total	1,665	100	1,525	92	224	13	19,661	100	18,231	93	1,503	8
Illinois												
Indiana												
Michigan	650	100	558	86	*92	*14	10,987	100	10,373	94	*614	*6
Minnesota												
New York	332	100	*290	*87	*42	*13	4,485	100	*4,062	*91	*422	*9
Ohio	344	100	*315	*92			2,161	100	*2,068	*96		
Pennsylvania												
Wisconsin	*178	*100	*138	*77	*40	*23	*1,246	*100	*977	*78	*269	*22

* Estimate based on a sample size of 10–29   ... Sample size too small (less than 10) to report data reliably

Note: For the U S row, detail does not add to total because of multiple responses

Table 58. Saltwater Anglers and Days of Saltwater Fishing by State Where Fishing Took Place: 2011

(Population 16 years old and older. Numbers in thousands)

State where fishing took place	Anglers						Days of fishing					
	Total anglers, residents and nonresidents		State residents		Nonresidents		Total days, residents and nonresidents		Days by state residents		Days by nonresidents	
	Number	Percent	Number	Percent	Number	Percent	Number	Percent	Number	Percent	Number	Percent
United States, total	8,889	100	6,600	74	2,764	31	99,474	100	86,027	86	13,681	14
Alabama	134	100	*69	*52	*65	*48	1,490	100	*1,215	*82	*275	*18
Alaska	334	100	102	30	*232	*70	1,446	100	923	64	*523	*36
California	775	100	721	93	*54	*7	7,193	100	6,998	97	*195	*3
Connecticut	165	100	126	76	*39	*24	1,291	100	1,086	84	*206	*16
Delaware	138	100	43	31	*95	*69	1,339	100	778	58	*561	*42
Florida	2,398	100	1,390	58	1,007	42	36,348	100	31,592	87	4,756	13
Georgia	*139	*100	*123	*88			*728	*100	*639	*88		
Hawaii	155	100	102	66			1,794	100	1,617	90		
Louisiana	196	100	*124	*63			1,533	100	*1,267	*83		
Maine	133	100	*71	*54	*62	*46	756	100	*547	*72	*209	*28
Maryland	224	100	177	79	*47	*21	1,533	100	1,330	87	*204	*13
Massachusetts	323	100	216	67	107	33	4,049	100	3,551	88	497	12
Mississippi	*120	*100	*116	*97			*2,293	*100	*2,284	*100		
New Hampshire	*49	*100	*40	*82			*730	*100	*669	*92		
New Jersey	604	100	354	59	*250	*41	7,020	100	5,736	82	*1,284	*18
New York	801	100	*673	*84	*128	*16	7,684	100	*6,861	*89	*822	*11
North Carolina	632	100	426	67	207	33	4,504	100	3,340	74	1,163	26
Oregon	177	100	*77	*44	*100	*56	608	100	*344	*57	*263	*43
Rhode Island	151	100	62	41	89	59	1,430	100	977	68	453	32
South Carolina	305	100	213	70	*92	*30	2,318	100	1,994	86	*324	*14
Texas	751	100	685	91	*66	*9	8,157	100	7,562	93	*595	*7
Virginia	429	100	331	77	97	23	2,772	100	2,092	75	680	25
Washington	401	100	359	89			2,700	100	2,625	97		

* Estimate based on a sample size of 10–29   ... Sample size too small (less than 10) to report data reliably

Note: For the U S row, detail does not add to total because of multiple responses U S totals include responses from participants residing in the District of Columbia, as described in Appendix D

Table 59. Days of Fishing by State Where Fishing Took Place and Angler's State of Residence: 2011

(Population 16 years old and older. Numbers in thousands)

State	Days of fishing in state						Days of fishing by state residents					
	Total days, residents and nonresidents		Days by state residents		Days by nonresidents		Total days, in state of residence and other states		Days in state of residence		Days in other states	
	Number	Percent	Number	Percent	Number	Percent	Number	Percent	Number	Percent	Number	Percent
United States, total	**553,841**	**100**	**502,008**	**91**	**57,499**	**10**	**553,841**	**100**	**502,008**	**91**	**57,499**	**10**
Alabama	10,878	100	9,905	91	974	9	10,176	100	9,905	97	272	3
Alaska	4,360	100	3,073	70	1,287	30	3,121	100	3,073	98	48	2
Arizona	4,825	100	4,141	86	*684	*14	5,283	100	4,141	78	1,143	22
Arkansas	15,662	100	15,055	96	*607	*4	15,141	100	15,055	99	86	1
California	23,754	100	23,267	98	487	2	25,662	100	23,267	91	2,395	9
Colorado	8,433	100	7,490	89	943	11	8,726	100	7,490	86	1,236	14
Connecticut	4,705	100	4,395	93	*310	*7	5,713	100	4,395	77	1,318	23
Delaware	2,052	100	1,328	65	*724	*35	1,681	100	1,328	79	353	21
Florida	57,594	100	48,050	83	9,544	17	49,500	100	48,050	97	1,450	3
Georgia	8,729	100	8,456	97	*273	*3	9,061	100	8,456	93	605	7
Hawaii	1,882	100	1,705	91			1,739	100	1,705	98	34	2
Idaho	5,507	100	2,165	39	3,342	61	2,424	100	2,165	89	259	11
Illinois	13,343	100	12,946	97	*397	*3	15,614	100	12,946	83	2,667	17
Indiana	20,775	100	20,238	97	*537	*3	21,542	100	20,238	94	1,304	6
Iowa	5,978	100	5,790	97	*187	*3	6,909	100	5,790	84	1,119	16
Kansas	4,163	100	4,088	98	*75	*2	4,694	100	4,088	87	605	13
Kentucky	10,245	100	9,385	92	*860	*8	10,245	100	9,385	92	860	8
Louisiana	18,079	100	17,586	97	*494	*3	18,351	100	17,586	96	765	4
Maine	3,873	100	2,897	75	976	25	2,915	100	2,897	99	18	1
Maryland	4,711	100	4,160	88	550	12	5,676	100	4,160	73	1,516	27
Massachusetts	8,367	100	7,589	91	779	9	9,166	100	7,589	83	1,578	17
Michigan	28,177	100	26,014	92	2,164	8	26,744	100	26,014	97	730	3
Minnesota	21,702	100	19,959	92	1,743	8	24,903	100	19,959	80	4,944	20
Mississippi	9,176	100	8,501	93			8,700	100	8,501	98	199	2
Missouri	14,865	100	13,263	89	1,603	11	14,448	100	13,263	92	1,185	8
Montana	2,450	100	2,091	85	358	15	3,263	100	2,091	64	1,172	36
Nebraska	2,595	100	2,493	96			2,924	100	2,493	85	432	15
Nevada	1,400	100	1,295	93			2,044	100	1,295	63	749	37
New Hampshire	4,370	100	3,870	89	499	11	4,155	100	3,870	93	284	7
New Jersey	9,454	100	8,087	86	*1,367	*14	9,578	100	8,087	84	1,491	16
New Mexico	3,899	100	3,622	93	*278	*7	3,868	100	3,622	94	247	6
New York	29,874	100	27,804	93	2,071	7	29,112	100	27,804	96	1,309	4
North Carolina	23,472	100	21,939	93	1,532	7	23,491	100	21,939	93	1,552	7
North Dakota	(NA)	(NA)	(NA)	(NA)	(NA)	(NA)	(NA)	(NA)	(NA)	(NA)	(NA)	(NA)
Ohio	16,874	100	16,264	96	*609	*4	19,116	100	16,264	85	2,851	15
Oklahoma	8,499	100	7,943	93	*556	*7	8,661	100	7,943	92	718	8
Oregon	5,658	100	4,396	78	1,263	22	4,673	100	4,396	94	277	6
Pennsylvania	10,136	100	8,364	83	1,772	17	9,926	100	8,364	84	1,562	16
Rhode Island	2,080	100	1,579	76	501	24	1,764	100	1,579	90	184	10
South Carolina	11,189	100	10,487	94	*702	*6	11,459	100	10,487	92	973	8
South Dakota	4,069	100	3,525	87	*544	*13	3,649	100	3,525	97	124	3
Tennessee	16,957	100	16,041	95	*916	*5	17,834	100	16,041	90	1,793	10
Texas	30,667	100	29,572	96	*1,095	*4	34,735	100	29,572	85	5,163	15
Utah	5,979	100	5,373	90	*606	*10	5,612	100	5,373	96	239	4
Vermont	2,215	100	1,751	79	464	21	1,885	100	1,751	93	134	7
Virginia	10,521	100	9,367	89	1,153	11	10,342	100	9,367	91	975	9
Washington	13,449	100	13,107	97	*341	*3	17,818	100	13,107	74	4,711	26
West Virginia	4,521	100	4,271	94	*250	*6	4,767	100	4,271	90	495	10
Wisconsin	21,284	100	14,576	68	6,708	32	15,320	100	14,576	95	744	5
Wyoming	3,123	100	2,009	64	*1,114	*36	2,170	100	2,009	93	161	7

* Estimate based on a sample size of 10–29   ... Sample size too small (less than 10) to report data reliably   (NA) Not available

Note: U S totals include responses from participants residing in the District of Columbia, as described in Appendix D

Table 60. Expenditures for Fishing by State Where Spending Took Place: 2011

(Population 16 years old and older. Expenditures in thousands of dollars)

State where spending took place	Total expenditures	Trip-related expenditures				Expenditures for equipment				Expenditures for other items[2]
		Total trip-related	Food and lodging	Trans-portation	Other trip costs	Total equipment	Fishing equipment[1]	Auxiliary equipment[1]	Special equipment[1]	
United States, total	**41,788,936**	**21,789,465**	**7,711,318**	**6,261,536**	**7,816,610**	**15,506,433**	**6,141,895**	**1,106,865**	**8,257,673**	**4,493,037**
Alabama	456,442	317,064	121,973	78,970	116,120	127,616	107,492	*16,676		11,762
Alaska	639,356	528,135	227,663	164,152	136,321	91,228	56,246	20,338		19,992
Arizona	755,478	357,472	123,342	95,693	138,437	337,188	62,790	*9,343	*265,056	60,818
Arkansas	495,584	339,640	153,245	117,488	68,907	142,292	45,750			13,651
California	2,268,610	1,620,329	576,406	462,576	581,347	577,356	320,577	141,384	*115,394	70,925
Colorado	648,563	403,569	134,342	193,604	75,624	213,528	121,723	*32,643		31,466
Connecticut	436,473	258,671	66,355	46,676	145,640	163,275	58,289	32,986		14,526
Delaware	104,370	48,750	20,765	12,069	15,915	21,411	12,965	*1,100		34,209
Florida	4,629,202	2,801,636	900,222	563,990	1,337,423	1,085,576	600,093	76,817	*408,666	741,990
Georgia	872,550	401,784	166,506	152,932	82,346	430,234	111,651			40,532
Hawaii	203,492	102,074	24,985	30,283	46,806	100,236	48,734	*2,525		*1,182
Idaho	422,120	261,072	96,171	123,836	41,065	105,933	78,610	*6,297		55,115
Illinois	972,729	372,361	124,642	98,210	149,509	387,439	100,569	*15,611	*271,258	212,929
Indiana	671,840	427,310	140,320	136,879	150,110	164,516	92,066	*12,805		80,015
Iowa	277,999	100,539	34,913	33,101	32,525	159,732	48,500	*7,180	*104,052	17,728
Kansas	210,303	98,165	28,249	35,760	34,156	68,046	24,341			44,092
Kentucky	807,293	259,128	92,732	93,334	73,062	463,240	51,282		*399,129	84,925
Louisiana	807,033	533,843	217,851	126,429	189,563	242,032	88,745			31,158
Maine	371,829	214,686	89,002	52,979	72,705	141,385	34,117	*11,210	*96,057	15,758
Maryland	535,232	195,536	60,387	37,093	98,056	332,279	77,882			7,417
Massachusetts	455,403	253,705	62,852	52,098	138,754	188,541	77,827	*4,947	*105,767	13,157
Michigan	2,427,110	1,092,735	373,964	344,495	374,276	1,117,911	259,043	*84,705	*774,162	216,464
Minnesota	2,414,257	924,573	372,819	269,690	282,064	1,448,648	375,809	*25,336	*1,047,503	41,036
Mississippi	527,740	315,763	101,802	93,213	120,748	200,790	164,977			11,187
Missouri	657,024	374,215	146,842	146,217	81,157	262,939	143,930	*8,061	*110,948	19,869
Montana	339,383	141,885	54,909	57,950	29,027	140,728	83,447			56,770
Nebraska	182,679	56,840	20,029	24,374	12,437	112,780	65,105	*7,839	*39,836	13,059
Nevada	138,800	83,275	34,026	32,323	16,926	49,130	22,165	*5,180		6,395
New Hampshire	208,524	151,389	39,031	38,369	73,989	51,872	30,551	*4,093		5,263
New Jersey	1,120,236	486,978	129,828	103,695	253,455	319,118	151,784	41,474	*125,860	314,139
New Mexico	418,249	234,187	93,272	114,565	26,351	169,541	42,787	*11,780	*114,974	14,521
New York	1,962,538	1,057,916	333,483	306,506	417,927	758,530	395,723	75,814	*286,993	146,092
North Carolina	1,523,131	1,020,156	443,338	239,146	337,672	480,065	269,784	*25,767	*184,514	22,910
North Dakota	(NA)	(NA)	(NA)	(NA)	(NA)	(NA)	(NA)	(NA)	(NA)	(NA)
Ohio	1,794,642	594,519	171,728	165,782	257,009	460,353	220,277	*39,299	*200,776	739,770
Oklahoma	730,503	175,701	69,820	71,458	34,423	227,980	70,531	*69,769		326,822
Oregon	640,855	358,680	148,761	95,820	114,099	235,384	68,013	*14,338	*153,032	46,791
Pennsylvania	485,490	228,510	76,705	83,154	68,651	193,879	114,099	*12,696		63,100
Rhode Island	130,046	83,935	22,082	17,062	44,791	41,804	14,985	*813	*26,006	4,307
South Carolina	686,328	359,834	116,079	89,606	154,149	319,015	231,271	*9,818		7,479
South Dakota	202,797	133,078	44,159	64,968	23,951	64,834	45,547	*8,359		4,885
Tennessee	1,137,104	283,024	78,345	112,279	92,401	803,472	210,219	*20,154		50,608
Texas	1,540,434	1,045,330	422,885	297,817	324,629	471,190	203,698	*27,174		23,914
Utah	451,259	226,251	93,714	77,555	54,983	211,585	52,178	*10,909		13,423
Vermont	131,317	90,248	40,684	26,215	23,350	26,007	15,437	*819		15,062
Virginia	1,142,099	469,096	215,544	113,859	139,693	379,123	133,986	*6,264	*238,872	293,880
Washington	1,030,036	539,035	160,994	170,219	207,823	435,580	214,677	48,657	*172,245	55,421
West Virginia	428,646	326,275	158,734	77,728	89,813	97,553	56,130			4,819
Wisconsin	1,418,591	607,467	232,140	220,905	154,422	480,273	93,996		*380,740	330,851
Wyoming	463,814	393,984	34,547	91,201	268,236	44,907	30,752			24,923

* Estimate based on a sample size of 10–29   ... Sample size too small (less than 10) to report data reliably   (NA) Not available

[1] See Table 12 for a detailed listing of fishing, auxiliary, and special equipment items

[2] Includes expenditures for magazine subscriptions, membership dues and contributions, land leasing and ownership, and licenses, stamps, tags, and permits

Note: U S totals include responses from participants residing in the District of Columbia, as described in Appendix D
   The Texas Parks and Wildlife Department has expressed concerns regarding the fishing expenditure estimates from the USFWS National Survey Please contact them at *inld@tpwd.state.gov* or *cfish@tpwd.state.gov* for department statistics

Table 61. Participation in Wildlife-Watching Activities by State Residents Both Inside and Outside Their Resident State: 2011

(Population 16 years old and older. Numbers in thousands)

Participant's state of residence	Population	Total participants		Away from home		Around the home	
		Number	Percent of population	Number	Percent of population	Number	Percent of population
United States, total	**239,313**	**71,776**	**30**	**22,496**	**9**	**68,598**	**29**
Alabama	3,664	1,079	29	*340	*9	1,073	29
Alaska	526	247	47	118	22	229	43
Arizona	5,084	1,281	25	534	11	1,222	24
Arkansas	2,238	828	37	*120	*5	820	37
California	28,562	6,475	23	2,675	9	5,939	21
Colorado	3,946	1,456	37	621	16	1,299	33
Connecticut	2,781	1,093	39	385	14	1,053	38
Delaware	699	209	30	71	10	200	29
Florida	14,855	3,598	24	1,363	9	3,312	22
Georgia	7,459	2,206	30	*1,008	*14	2,054	28
Hawaii	995	161	16	103	10	115	12
Idaho	1,172	464	40	*220	*19	439	37
Illinois	9,988	2,784	28	652	7	2,752	28
Indiana	4,965	1,681	34	477	10	1,657	33
Iowa	2,363	780	33	215	9	758	32
Kansas	2,163	776	36	168	8	751	35
Kentucky	3,376	1,221	36	298	9	1,117	33
Louisiana	3,449	840	24	*221	*6	794	23
Maine	1,066	401	38	*110	*10	399	37
Maryland	4,480	1,224	27	392	9	1,203	27
Massachusetts	5,320	1,530	29	453	9	1,490	28
Michigan	7,787	3,067	39	855	11	2,865	37
Minnesota	4,133	1,498	36	483	12	1,419	34
Mississippi	2,220	630	28	*135	*6	620	28
Missouri	4,667	1,645	35	622	13	1,538	33
Montana	777	258	33	*96	*12	235	30
Nebraska	1,387	362	26	150	11	325	23
Nevada	2,024	504	25	191	9	465	23
New Hampshire	1,066	388	36	89	8	387	36
New Jersey	6,852	1,708	25	564	8	1,661	24
New Mexico	1,551	486	31	200	13	465	30
New York	15,503	4,081	26	1,263	8	3,856	25
North Carolina	7,264	2,124	29	505	7	2,110	29
North Dakota	(NA)	(NA)	(NA)	(NA)	(NA)	(NA)	(NA)
Ohio	8,999	3,155	35	730	8	3,142	35
Oklahoma	2,828	1,233	44	*411	*15	1,225	43
Oregon	3,061	1,239	40	401	13	1,206	39
Pennsylvania	10,036	3,329	33	734	7	3,228	32
Rhode Island	848	270	32	66	8	260	31
South Carolina	3,555	944	27	*219	*6	915	26
South Dakota	631	267	42	*108	*17	267	42
Tennessee	4,945	1,733	35	682	14	1,584	32
Texas	18,681	4,263	23	*977	*5	4,249	23
Utah	2,036	558	27	263	13	430	21
Vermont	512	273	53	85	17	270	53
Virginia	6,136	2,212	36	553	9	2,185	36
Washington	5,293	1,932	37	693	13	1,849	35
West Virginia	1,464	751	51	*255	*17	743	51
Wisconsin	4,460	2,152	48	453	10	2,076	47
Wyoming	424	182	43	104	25	161	38

* Estimate based on a sample size of 10–29   (NA) Not available

Note: Detail does not add to total because of multiple responses U S totals include responses from participants residing in the District of Columbia, as described in Appendix D

Table 62. Participation in Wildlife-Watching Activities by State Where Activity Took Place: 2011

(Population 16 years old and older. Numbers in thousands)

State where activity took place	Total participants Number	Total participants Percent	Away from home Number	Away from home Percent	Around the home Number	Around the home Percent
United States, total	**71,776**	**100**	**22,496**	**31**	**68,598**	**96**
Alabama	1,114	100	*336	*30	1,073	96
Alaska	640	100	498	78	229	36
Arizona	1,566	100	732	47	1,222	78
Arkansas	852	100	*137	*16	820	96
California	6,733	100	2,790	41	5,939	88
Colorado	1,782	100	902	51	1,299	73
Connecticut	1,178	100	441	37	1,053	89
Delaware	243	100	89	37	200	82
Florida	4,308	100	1,902	44	3,312	77
Georgia	2,393	100	1,129	47	2,054	86
Hawaii	358	100	295	82	115	32
Idaho	558	100	281	50	439	79
Illinois	3,019	100	704	23	2,752	91
Indiana	1,719	100	*413	*24	1,657	96
Iowa	837	100	212	25	758	91
Kansas	792	100	169	21	751	95
Kentucky	1,319	100	348	26	1,117	85
Louisiana	1,010	100	*371	*37	794	79
Maine	838	100	538	64	399	48
Maryland	1,362	100	421	31	1,203	88
Massachusetts	1,828	100	662	36	1,490	81
Michigan	3,199	100	958	30	2,865	90
Minnesota	1,577	100	509	32	1,419	90
Mississippi	781	100	*262	*34	620	79
Missouri	1,716	100	579	34	1,538	90
Montana	402	100	230	57	235	58
Nebraska	384	100	155	40	325	85
Nevada	643	100	287	45	465	72
New Hampshire	630	100	311	49	387	61
New Jersey	1,875	100	605	32	1,661	89
New Mexico	566	100	261	46	465	82
New York	4,239	100	1,157	27	3,856	91
North Carolina	2,432	100	703	29	2,110	87
North Dakota	(NA)	(NA)	(NA)	(NA)	(NA)	(NA)
Ohio	3,197	100	744	23	3,142	98
Oklahoma	1,263	100	*411	*33	1,225	97
Oregon	1,440	100	537	37	1,206	84
Pennsylvania	3,598	100	809	22	3,228	90
Rhode Island	308	100	82	27	260	84
South Carolina	1,103	100	378	34	915	83
South Dakota	384	100	221	58	267	70
Tennessee	1,955	100	787	40	1,584	81
Texas	4,376	100	1,026	23	4,249	97
Utah	717	100	402	56	430	60
Vermont	370	100	177	48	270	73
Virginia	2,509	100	759	30	2,185	87
Washington	2,168	100	891	41	1,849	85
West Virginia	850	100	348	41	743	87
Wisconsin	2,359	100	499	21	2,076	88
Wyoming	518	100	435	84	161	31

* Estimate based on a sample size of 10–29   (NA) Not available

Note: Detail does not add to total because of multiple responses U S totals include responses from participants residing in the District of Columbia, as described in Appendix D

Table 63. Participation in Away-From-Home Wildlife Watching by State Where Activity Took Place: 2011

(Population 16 years old and older. Numbers in thousands)

State where activity took place	Total participants		State residents		Nonresidents	
	Number	Percent	Number	Percent	Number	Percent
United States, total	**22,496**	**100**	**18,529**	**82**	**6,769**	**30**
Alabama	*336	*100	*301	*90		
Alaska	498	100	104	21	395	79
Arizona	732	100	443	61	289	39
Arkansas	*137	*100	*112	*82		
California	2,790	100	2,407	86	383	14
Colorado	902	100	558	62	343	38
Connecticut	441	100	339	77	*102	*23
Delaware	89	100	48	55		
Florida	1,902	100	1,076	57	825	43
Georgia	1,129	100	*870	*77	*258	*23
Hawaii	295	100	88	30	*207	*70
Idaho	281	100	*184	*66	*96	*34
Illinois	704	100	444	63	*259	*37
Indiana	*413	*100	*375	*91		
Iowa	212	100	145	69	*67	*31
Kansas	169	100	135	80		
Kentucky	348	100	*232	*67	*116	*33
Louisiana	*371	*100	*167	*45		
Maine	538	100	*101	*19	437	81
Maryland	421	100	271	64	*150	*36
Massachusetts	662	100	342	52	320	48
Michigan	958	100	*790	*82	*168	*18
Minnesota	509	100	*430	*84	*79	*16
Mississippi	*262	*100	*111	*43		
Missouri	579	100	465	80	*114	*20
Montana	230	100	*71	*31	160	69
Nebraska	155	100	126	81		
Nevada	287	100	132	46	*154	*54
New Hampshire	311	100	*69	*22	242	78
New Jersey	605	100	436	72	*169	*28
New Mexico	261	100	170	65	*91	*35
New York	1,157	100	913	79	244	21
North Carolina	703	100	386	55	317	45
North Dakota	(NA)	(NA)	(NA)	(NA)	(NA)	(NA)
Ohio	744	100	696	94		
Oklahoma	*411	*100	*381	*93		
Oregon	537	100	336	63	*201	*37
Pennsylvania	809	100	*502	*62	307	38
Rhode Island	82	100	35	43	*47	*57
South Carolina	378	100	*211	*56	*167	*44
South Dakota	221	100	*104	*47	117	53
Tennessee	787	100	485	62	*303	*38
Texas	1,026	100	*899	*88	*127	*12
Utah	402	100	224	56	178	44
Vermont	177	100	80	45	*97	*55
Virginia	759	100	460	61	299	39
Washington	891	100	607	68	284	32
West Virginia	348	100	*249	*71	*99	*29
Wisconsin	499	100	*282	*56	*217	*44
Wyoming	435	100	100	23	336	77

* Estimate based on a sample size of 10–29   ... Sample size too small (less than 10) to report data reliably   (NA) Not available

Note: Detail does not add to total because of multiple responses U S totals include responses from participants residing in the District of Columbia, as described in
  Appendix D

Table 64. Days of Wildlife Watching Away From Home by State Where Activity Took Place and Participant's State of Residence: 2011

(Population 16 years old and older. Numbers in thousands)

State	Days of activity in state						Days of activity by state residents					
	Total days, residents and nonresidents		Days by residents		Days by nonresidents		Total days, in state of residence and other states		Days in state of residence		Days in other states	
	Number	Percent	Number	Percent	Number	Percent	Number	Percent	Number	Percent	Number	Percent
United States, total	335,625	100	268,412	80	67,213	20	335,625	100	268,412	80	67,213	20
Alabama	*1,525	*100	*1,269	*83			*1,831	*100	*1,269	*69		
Alaska	5,159	100	1,739	34	3,420	66	1,783	100	1,739	98		
Arizona	11,907	100	7,696	65	4,210	35	9,637	100	7,696	80	*1,941	*20
Arkansas	*1,427	*100	*1,326	*93			*1,411	*100	*1,326	*94		
California	27,352	100	24,683	90	2,668	10	28,574	100	24,683	86	3,890	14
Colorado	6,937	100	4,790	69	2,147	31	5,865	100	4,790	82	*1,075	*18
Connecticut	8,964	100	8,085	90	*880	*10	10,930	100	8,085	74	2,845	26
Delaware	1,573	100	1,330	85			1,924	100	1,330	69	595	31
Florida	16,786	100	8,307	49	8,478	51	11,866	100	8,307	70	*3,558	*30
Georgia	34,309	100	*33,442	*97	*866	*3	*34,530	*100	*33,442	*97		
Hawaii	4,660	100	2,675	57	*1,985	*43	2,830	100	2,675	95	*155	*5
Idaho	3,757	100	*3,248	*86	*509	*14	*3,639	*100	*3,248	*89		
Illinois	6,434	100	4,098	64	*2,336	*36	6,898	100	4,098	59	*2,800	*41
Indiana	*2,924	*100	*2,743	*94			*3,552	*100	*2,743	*77	*809	*23
Iowa	2,547	100	2,235	88	*312	*12	3,391	100	2,235	66	*1,155	*34
Kansas	1,019	100	780	77			1,258	100	780	62	*478	*38
Kentucky	2,890	100	*1,868	*65	*1,021	*35	2,974	100	*1,868	*63	*1,106	*37
Louisiana	*4,916	*100	*4,248	*86			*5,540	*100	*4,248	*77		
Maine	7,334	100	*4,675	*64	2,659	36	*4,824	*100	*4,675	*97		
Maryland	4,458	100	3,708	83	*750	*17	4,578	100	3,708	81	*870	*19
Massachusetts	10,546	100	7,797	74	2,750	26	9,554	100	7,797	82	1,758	18
Michigan	10,343	100	*9,498	*92	*845	*8	10,418	100	*9,498	*91		
Minnesota	6,974	100	*6,684	*96	*290	*4	*7,780	*100	*6,684	*86	*1,097	*14
Mississippi	*3,946	*100	*3,608	*91			*4,411	*100	*3,608	*82		
Missouri	8,200	100	7,835	96	*365	*4	9,573	100	7,835	82	*1,737	*18
Montana	1,395	100	*625	*45	770	55	*1,412	*100	*625	*44		
Nebraska	2,361	100	2,243	95			2,732	100	2,243	82	*489	*18
Nevada	1,619	100	1,177	73	*442	*27	2,631	100	1,177	45	1,454	55
New Hampshire	1,896	100	*1,074	*57	822	43	1,382	100	*1,074	*78	*308	*22
New Jersey	6,210	100	5,608	90	*602	*10	8,207	100	5,608	68	2,600	32
New Mexico	5,962	100	4,371	73	*1,590	*27	4,733	100	4,371	92	*361	*8
New York	22,814	100	21,631	95	1,182	5	29,118	100	21,631	74	*7,487	*26
North Carolina	9,275	100	6,768	73	2,507	27	9,463	100	6,768	72	*2,695	*28
North Dakota	(NA)	(NA)	(NA)	(NA)	(NA)	(NA)	(NA)	(NA)	(NA)	(NA)	(NA)	(NA)
Ohio	6,251	100	6,174	99			7,285	100	6,174	85		
Oklahoma	*3,084	*100	*2,964	*96			*3,128	*100	*2,964	*95		
Oregon	7,268	100	5,294	73	*1,974	*27	6,673	100	5,294	79	*1,379	*21
Pennsylvania	9,554	100	*7,217	*76	2,337	24	*7,863	*100	*7,217	*92		
Rhode Island	1,230	100	815	66	*416	*34	1,094	100	815	74	279	26
South Carolina	4,254	100	*2,650	*62	*1,604	*38	*3,361	*100	*2,650	*79		
South Dakota	1,559	100	*1,090	*70	*469	*30	*1,170	*100	*1,090	*93		
Tennessee	6,424	100	4,443	69	*1,981	*31	6,521	100	4,443	68	*2,078	*32
Texas	11,840	100	*10,441	*88	*1,399	*12	*11,193	*100	*10,441	*93		
Utah	5,169	100	2,642	51	2,527	49	3,127	100	2,642	84	*485	*16
Vermont	2,602	100	1,908	73	*693	*27	2,092	100	1,908	91	*184	*9
Virginia	4,552	100	2,697	59	1,855	41	5,848	100	2,697	46	3,150	54
Washington	9,641	100	8,311	86	1,330	14	13,740	100	8,311	60	*5,429	*40
West Virginia	3,648	100	*3,254	*89	*394	*11	*4,995	*100	*3,254	*65		
Wisconsin	6,080	100	*4,999	*82	*1,082	*18	*5,773	*100	*4,999	*87		
Wyoming	3,125	100	1,119	36	2,006	64	1,676	100	1,119	67	*557	*33

* Estimate based on a sample size of 10–29   ... Sample size too small (less than 10) to report data reliably   (NA) Not available

Note: Detail does not add to total because of nonresponse U S totals include responses from participants residing in the District of Columbia, as described in Appendix D

(Population 16 years old and older. Expenditures in thousands of dollars)

State where spending took place	Total expenditures	Trip-related expenditures				Expenditures for equipment				Expenditures for other items[2]
		Total trip-related	Food and lodging	Trans-portation	Other trip costs	Total equipment	Wildlife-watching equipment[1]	Auxiliary equipment[1]	Special equipment[1]	
United States, total	54,890,272	17,274,675	9,349,439	6,006,860	1,918,376	27,150,920	11,323,179	1,555,374	14,272,368	10,464,677
Alabama	734,204	*41,191	*12,168	*27,359		668,276	205,102			*24,738
Alaska	2,058,355	1,970,345	1,052,372	559,450	358,522	79,485	42,200	*30,249		*8,524
Arizona	935,880	391,198	194,925	176,576	19,697	336,081	153,714	*9,624		208,600
Arkansas	216,074	*34,520	*21,808	*12,384		156,574	130,345			
California	3,777,677	1,781,680	933,483	663,484	184,713	1,485,977	689,999	203,591	*592,386	510,019
Colorado	1,432,084	615,636	353,088	232,716	29,832	722,249	173,569	*27,294		94,199
Connecticut	934,703	227,380	110,505	67,546	49,328	487,381	194,705	*42,576	*250,100	219,942
Delaware	169,788	36,069	17,873	15,646	*2,550	103,269	41,391	*3,583		30,450
Florida	3,041,333	1,732,652	890,458	619,555	222,639	788,430	475,771	*31,088	*281,572	520,250
Georgia	1,802,423	839,036	499,054	325,328	*14,654	889,500	552,517			*73,887
Hawaii	668,504	627,700	291,313	161,888	*174,500	14,603	13,150			26,201
Idaho	432,041	82,479	*29,524	*52,108		292,182	111,633			*57,380
Illinois	1,306,258	166,123	69,757	73,868	*22,497	785,622	279,555	*16,412		354,513
Indiana	751,343	*206,357	*75,968	*105,843	*24,546	478,201	311,413	*151,057		66,785
Iowa	711,168	64,058	*21,563	38,820	*3,675	535,840	136,695	*12,723		111,270
Kansas	208,415	*45,599	*31,572	*13,199		56,925	50,966	*5,855		105,891
Kentucky	773,221	125,358	62,455	40,780	*22,122	167,075	127,922			480,788
Louisiana	542,752	*222,145	*124,839	*57,122		277,084	205,180			*43,523
Maine	798,854	514,145	347,602	122,931	43,612	172,113	102,630	*4,980		112,596
Maryland	483,421	104,421	52,292	47,525	*4,605	333,762	203,752	*8,655		45,237
Massachusetts	1,277,898	286,092	199,653	72,675	13,765	325,967	252,447	*22,159		665,838
Michigan	1,220,815	416,562	233,162	151,611	*31,789	662,703	428,804			141,550
Minnesota	621,290	228,217	*93,443	114,518	*20,255	169,982	133,721	*8,882		223,092
Mississippi	342,422	*90,493	*37,648	*43,128		238,311	109,337			*13,617
Missouri	940,818	210,934	102,373	104,728	*3,833	606,603	385,224	*11,392		123,282
Montana	400,797	291,910	78,188	72,284	*141,438	104,210	57,216			*4,677
Nebraska	513,297	86,719	37,379	26,323	*23,017	409,799	74,551			16,778
Nevada	682,028	114,366	62,091	47,764	*4,511	275,886	52,938	*3,594		291,776
New Hampshire	281,190	101,813	63,685	31,262	*6,866	111,320	71,447	*7,845		68,057
New Jersey	986,278	228,123	119,222	96,801	*12,100	407,554	255,080	*36,352		350,601
New Mexico	327,117	146,937	106,077	38,740	2,120	136,597	77,186	*7,940		43,583
New York	4,151,789	659,871	357,330	190,566	*111,976	2,423,787	1,072,128	*129,447		1,068,131
North Carolina	929,661	367,309	202,953	151,292	*13,064	449,260	366,507	*30,245		113,092
North Dakota	(NA)	(NA)	(NA)	(NA)	(NA)	(NA)	(NA)	(NA)	(NA)	(NA)
Ohio	738,806	87,066	37,548	45,488		457,027	326,560			194,714
Oklahoma	474,662	*107,919	*36,629	*43,151		281,227	198,315			*85,516
Oregon	1,697,222	482,241	275,422	196,880	*9,939	1,018,967	253,194	*28,155		196,014
Pennsylvania	1,270,888	266,669	203,405	58,372		788,587	314,038	*67,809		215,632
Rhode Island	200,480	78,920	23,731	20,728	*34,460	92,137	28,841	*1,746		29,423
South Carolina	467,253	260,838	196,463	54,740	*9,635	191,288	132,988			*15,127
South Dakota	166,995	134,082	70,135	54,421	*9,526	30,452	22,878			*2,461
Tennessee	942,572	498,440	397,766	85,791	*14,883	390,742	225,362	*32,497		53,390
Texas	1,823,758	478,080	253,565	196,653	*27,862	919,971	590,272	*25,487		425,708
Utah	585,405	295,723	125,937	92,783	*77,003	238,012	92,629	*10,627		*51,671
Vermont	288,507	49,506	19,845	26,257	*3,403	113,416	37,509	*4,457	*71,451	125,585
Virginia	958,607	299,762	157,750	129,698	12,313	493,321	349,008	*27,800		165,524
Washington	3,173,371	506,658	310,010	157,634	39,014	2,386,353	248,525	*77,929		280,360
West Virginia	325,778	100,326	*47,295	*42,747		183,696	126,116	*41,168		*41,756
Wisconsin	1,488,857	234,760	144,379	81,894	*8,488	1,080,632	419,479			173,464
Wyoming	350,256	321,169	157,429	155,218	8,522	22,166	21,261			*6,920

* Estimate based on a sample size of 10–29   ... Sample size too small (less than 10) to report data reliably   (NA) Not available

[1] See Table 40 for a detailed listing of wildlife-watching, auxiliary, and special equipment items

[2] Includes expenditures for magazine subscriptions, membership dues and contributions, and land leasing and ownership

Note: U S totals include responses from participants residing in the District of Columbia, as described in Appendix D

Appendix A

Appendix A.
Definitions

Annual household income—Total 2011 income of household members before taxes and other deductions.

Around-the-home wildlife watching—Activity within 1 mile of home with one of six primary purposes: (1) taking special interest in or trying to identify birds or other wildlife; (2) photographing wildlife; (3) feeding birds or other wildlife; (4) maintaining natural areas of at least one-quarter acre for the benefit of wildlife; (5) maintaining plantings (such as shrubs and agricultural crops) for the benefit of wildlife; and (6) visiting parks and natural areas to observe, photograph, or feed wildlife.

Auxiliary equipment—Equipment owned primarily for wildlife-associated recreation. For the sportspersons section, these include sleeping bags, packs, duffel bags, tents, binoculars and field glasses, special fishing and hunting clothing, foul weather gear, boots and waders, maintenance and repair of equipment, and processing and taxidermy costs. For the wildlife-watching section, these include tents, tarps, frame packs, backpacking and other camping equipment, and blinds. For both sportspersons and wildlife watchers, it also includes electronic auxiliary equipment such as Global Positioning Systems.

Away-from-home wildlife watching—Trips or outings at least 1 mile from home for the primary purpose of observing, photographing, or feeding wildlife. Trips to zoos, circuses, aquariums, and museums are not included.

Big game—Bear, deer, elk, moose, wild turkey, and similar large animals that are hunted.

Census Divisions

East North Central
Illinois
Indiana
Michigan
Ohio
Wisconsin

East South Central
Alabama
Kentucky
Mississippi
Tennessee

Middle Atlantic
New Jersey
New York
Pennsylvania

Mountain
Arizona
Colorado
Idaho
Montana
Nevada
New Mexico
Utah
Wyoming

New England
Connecticut
Maine
Massachusetts
New Hampshire
Rhode Island
Vermont

Pacific
Alaska
California
Hawaii
Oregon
Washington

South Atlantic
Delaware
District of Columbia
Florida
Georgia
Maryland
North Carolina
South Carolina
Virginia
West Virginia

West North Central
Kansas
Iowa
Minnesota
Missouri
Nebraska
North Dakota
South Dakota

West South Central
Arkansas
Louisiana
Oklahoma
Texas

Day—Any part of a day spent participating in a given activity. For example, if someone hunted two hours one day and three hours another day, it would be reported as two days of hunting. If someone hunted two hours in the morning and three hours in the afternoon of the same day, it would be considered one day of hunting.

Education—The highest completed grade of school or year of college.

Expenditures—Money spent in 2011 for wildlife-related recreation trips in the United States, wildlife-related recreational equipment purchased in the United States, and other items. The "other items" were books, magazines, and DVDs; membership dues and contributions, land leasing or owning; hunting and fishing licenses; and plantings, all for the purpose of wildlife-related recreation. Expenditures included both money spent by participants for themselves and the value of gifts they received.

Fishing—The sport of catching or attempting to catch fish with a hook and line, bow and arrow, or spear; it also includes catching or gathering shellfish (clams, crabs, etc.); and the noncommercial seining or netting of fish, unless the fish are for use as bait. For example, seining for smelt is fishing, but seining for bait minnows is not included as fishing.

Fishing equipment—Items owned primarily for fishing:

  Rods, reels, poles, and rodmaking components

  Lines and leaders

  Artificial lures, flies, baits, and dressing for flies or lines

  Hooks, sinkers, swivels, and other items attached to a line, except lures and baits

  Tackle boxes

  Creels, stringers, fish bags, landing nets, and gaff hooks

  Minnow traps, seines, and bait containers

  Depth finders, fish finders, and other electronic fishing devices

  Ice fishing equipment

  Other fishing equipment

Freshwater—Reservoirs, lakes, ponds, and the nontidal portions of rivers and streams.

Great Lakes fishing—Fishing in Lakes Superior, Michigan, Huron, St. Clair, Erie, and Ontario, their connecting waters such as the St. Mary's River system, Detroit River, St. Clair River, and the Niagara River, and the St. Lawrence River south of the bridge at Cornwall, New York. Great Lakes fishing includes fishing in tributaries of the Great Lakes for smelt, steelhead, and salmon.

Home—The starting point of a wildlife-related recreational trip. It may be a permanent residence or a temporary or seasonal residence such as a cabin.

Hunting—The sport of shooting or attempting to shoot wildlife with firearms or archery equipment.

Hunting equipment—Items owned primarily for hunting:

Rifles, shotguns, muzzleloaders, and handguns

Archery equipment

Telescopic sights

Decoys and game calls

Ammunition

Hand loading equipment

Hunting dogs and associated costs

Other hunting equipment

Land leasing and owning—Leasing or owning land either singly or in cooperation with others for the primary purpose of fishing, hunting, or wildlife watching on it.

Maintain natural areas—To set aside 1/4 acre or more of natural environment, such as wood lots or open fields, for the primary purpose of benefiting wildlife.

Maintain plantings—To introduce or encourage the growth of food and cover plants for the primary purpose of benefiting wildlife.

Metropolitan Statistical Area (MSA)—A Metropolitan Statistical Area is a grouping of one or more counties or equivalent entities that contain at least one urbanized area of 50,000 or more inhabitants. The "Outside MSA" classification include census-defined Micropolitan Statistical Areas (or Micro areas). A Micro area is defined as a grouping of one or more counties or equivalent entities that contain at least one urban cluster of at least 10,000 but less than 50,000 inhabitants. Refer to <www.census.gov /population/metro/about/>, for a more detailed definition of the Metropolitan Statistical Area.

Migratory birds—Birds that regularly migrate from one region or climate to another such as ducks, geese, and doves and other birds that may be hunted.

Multiple responses—The term used to reflect the fact that individuals or their characteristics fall into more than one reporting category. An example of a big game hunter who hunted for deer and elk demonstrates the effect of multiple responses. In this case, adding the number of deer hunters (one) and elk hunters (one) would overstate the number of big game hunters (one) because deer and elk hunters are not

mutually exclusive categories. In contrast, for example, total participants is the sum of male and female participants, because "male" and "female" are mutually exclusive categories.

Nonresidents—Individuals who do not live in the State being reported. For example, a person living in Texas who watches whales in California is a nonresidential wildlife-watcher in California.

Nonresponse—A term used to reflect the fact that some Survey respondents provide incomplete sets of information. For example, a Survey respondent may have been unable to identify the primary type of hunting for which a gun was bought. Total hunting expenditure estimates will include the gun purchase, but it will not appear as spending for big game or any other type of hunting. Nonresponses result in reported totals that are greater than the sum of their parts.

Observe—To take special interest in or try to identify birds, fish or other wildlife.

Other animals—Coyotes, crows, foxes, groundhogs, prairie dogs, raccoons, alligators, and similar animals that can be legally hunted and are not classified as big game, small game, or migratory birds. They may be classified as unprotected or predatory animals by the State in which they are hunted. Feral pigs are classified as "other animals" in all States except Hawaii, where they are considered big game.

Participants—Individuals who engage in fishing, hunting, or a wildlife-watching activity. Unless otherwise stated, a person has to have hunted, fished, or wildlife watched in 2011 to be considered a participant.

Plantings—See "Maintain plantings."

Primary purpose—The principal motivation for an activity, trip, or expenditure.

Private land—Land owned by a business, nongovernmental organization, private individual, or a group of individuals such as an association or club.

Public land—Land that is owned by local governments (such as county parks and municipal watersheds),

State governments (such as State parks and wildlife management areas), or the federal government (such as National Forests, Recreational Areas, and Wildlife Refuges).

Residents—Individuals who lived in the State being reported. For example, a person who lives in California and watches whales in California is a residential wildlife watcher in California.

Rural—All territory, population, and housing units located outside of urbanized areas and urban clusters, as determined by the U.S. Census Bureau.

Saltwater—Oceans, tidal bays and sounds, and the tidal portions of rivers and streams.

Screening interviews—The first Survey contact with a sample household. Screening interviews are conducted with a household representative to identify respondents who are eligible for in-depth interviews. Screening interviews gather data such as age and sex about individuals in the households. Further information on screening interviews is available on page vii in the "Survey Background and Method" section of this report.

Small game—Grouse, pheasants, quail, rabbits, squirrels, and similar small animals for which States have small game seasons and bag limits.

Special equipment—Big-ticket equipment items that are owned primarily for wildlife-related recreation:

Bass boats

Other types of motor boats

Canoes and other types of nonmotor boats

Boat motors, boat trailer/hitches, and other boat accessories

Pickups, campers, vans, travel or tent trailers, motor homes, house trailers, recreational vehicles (RVs)

Cabins

Off-the-road vehicles such as trail bikes, all terrain vehicles (ATVs), dune buggies, four-wheelers, 4x4 vehicles, and snowmobiles

Other special equipment

Spenders—Individuals who spent money on fishing, hunting, or wildlife-watching activities or equipment and also participated in those activities.

Sportspersons—Individuals who engaged in fishing, hunting, or both.

Trip—An outing involving fishing, hunting, or wildlife watching. A trip may begin from an individual's principal residence or from another place, such as a vacation home or the home of a relative. A trip may last an hour, a day, or many days.

Type of fishing—There are three types of fishing: (1) freshwater except Great Lakes, (2) Great Lakes, and (3) saltwater.

Type of hunting—There are four types of hunting: (1) big game, (2) small game, (3) migratory bird, and (4) other animal.

Unspecified expenditure—An item that was purchased for use in both fishing and hunting, rather than primarily one or the other. Auxiliary equipment, special equipment, magazines and books, and membership dues and contributions are the items for which a purchase could be categorized as "unspecified."

Urban—All territory, population, and housing units located within boundaries that encompass densely settled territory, consisting of core census block groups or blocks that have a population density of at least 1,000 people per square mile and surrounding census blocks that have an overall density of at least 500 people per square mile. Under certain conditions, less densely settled territory may be included, as determined by the Census Bureau.

Visit parks or natural areas—A visit to places accessible to the public and that are owned or leased by a governmental entity, nongovernmental organization, business, or a private individual or group such as an association or club.

Wildlife—Animals such as birds, fish, insects, mammals, amphibians, and reptiles that are living in natural or wild environments. Wildlife does not include animals living in aquariums, zoos, and other artificial surroundings or domestic animals such as farm animals or pets.

Wildlife observed, photographed, or fed—Examples of species that wildlife watchers observe, photograph, and/or feed are (1) *Wild birds*—songbirds such as cardinals, robins, warblers, jays, buntings, and sparrows; birds of prey such as hawks, owls, eagles, and falcons; waterfowl such as ducks, geese, and swans; other water birds such as shorebirds, herons, pelicans, and cranes; and other birds such as pheasants, turkeys, road runners, and woodpeckers; (2) *Land mammals*—large land mammals such as bears, bison, deer, moose, and elk; small land mammals such as squirrels, foxes, prairie dogs, and rabbits; (3) *Fish* such as salmon, sharks, and groupers; (4) *Marine mammals* such as whales, dolphins, and manatees; and (5) *Other wildlife* such as butterflies, turtles, spiders, and snakes.

Wildlife-related recreation—Recreational fishing, hunting, and wildlife watching.

Wildlife watching—There are six types of wildlife watching: (1) closely observing, (2) photographing, (3) feeding, (4) visiting parks or natural areas, (5) maintaining plantings, and (6) maintaining natural areas. These activities must be the primary purpose of the trip or the around-the-home undertaking.

Wildlife-watching equipment—Items owned primarily for observing, photographing, or feeding wildlife:

Binoculars and spotting scopes

Cameras, video cameras, special lenses, and other photographic equipment

Film and developing

Commercially prepared and packaged wild bird food

Other bulk food used to feed wild birds

Food for other wildlife

Nest boxes, bird houses, feeders, and baths

Day packs, carrying cases, and special clothing

Other items such as field guides and maps

Appendix B

Appendix B.
2010 Participation of 6- to 15-Year-Olds and Historical Participation of Sportspersons: Data From Screening Interviews

The 2011 National Survey of Fishing, Hunting, and Wildlife-Associated Recreation was carried out in two phases. The first (or screening) phase began in April 2011. The main purpose of this phase was to collect information about all persons 16 years old and older in order to develop a sample of potential sportspersons and wildlife watchers for the second (or detailed) phase. However, information was also collected on the number of persons 6 to 15 years old who participated in wildlife-related recreation activities in 2010.

It is important to emphasize that the information reported from the 2011 screen relates to activity only up to and including 2010. Also, these data are reported by one household respondent speaking for all household members rather than the actual participants. In addition, these data are based on long-term recall (at least a 12-month recall), which has been found in Survey research (see *Investigation of Possible Recall/Reference Period Bias in National Surveys of Fishing, Hunting and Wildlife-Associated Recreation, December 1989, Westat, Inc.*) to add bias to the resulting estimates. In many cases, longer recall periods result in overestimating participation and expenditures for wildlife-related recreation.

Tables B-1 through B-4 report data on first-time participation and the most recent year of hunting and fishing for participants 6 years of age and older. Tables B-5 through B-8 report data specifically on 6- to 15-year-old participants in 2010. Detailed expenditures and recreational activity data were not gathered for the 6- to 15-year-old participants. Table B-9 lists the trend data for 6- to 15-year-old participants.

Because of differences in methodologies of the screening and the detailed phases of the 2011 Survey, the estimates of the two phases are not comparable. Only participants 16 years old and older were eligible for the detailed phase. The screening phase covered activity for 2010 or earlier; the detailed phase has estimates for only 2011. The detailed phase was a series of interviews of the actual participants conducted at 4- and 8-month intervals. The screening phase was a single interview of one household respondent who reported household events with one year or more recall. The shorter recall period of the detailed phase enabled better data accuracy.

Table B-1. Anglers and Hunters Participating for the First Time in 2010 by Age Group

(Population 6 years old and older. Numbers in thousands)

Age group	Total anglers in 2010	Fishing for first time		Total hunters in 2010	Hunting for first time	
		Number	Percent of anglers in age group		Number	Percent of hunters in age group
Total, all ages............................	55,792	4,261	8	17,060	1,365	8
6 to 8 years	3,103	938	30	174	108	62
9 to 11 years	3,825	646	17	533	154	29
12 to 15 years	4,451	492	11	1,319	366	28
16 to 17 years	1,750	167	10	571	*68	*12
18 to 24 years	5,106	227	4	1,820	186	10
25 to 34 years	8,525	633	7	2,578	160	6
35 to 44 years	8,792	597	7	2,699	*156	*6
45 to 54 years	9,467	323	3	3,482	*127	*4
55 to 64 years	6,337	109	2	2,424		
65 years or older	4,435	129	3	1,460		

* Estimate based on a sample size of 10–29   Sample size too small (less than 10) to report data reliably

Note: Data reported on this table are from screening interviews in which one adult household member responded for all household members The screening interview required the respondent to recall 12 months worth of activity

Table B-2. Anglers and Hunters Participating in 2009 but Not in 2010 by Age Group

(Population 6 years old and older. Numbers in thousands)

Age group	Anglers		Hunters	
	Number	Percent	Number	Percent
Total, all ages............................	12,084	100	2,930	100
6 to 8 years	572	5		
9 to 11 years	589	5	*86	*3
12 to 15 years	1,052	9	*92	*3
16 to 17 years	452	4	*102	*3
18 to 24 years	1,274	11	289	10
25 to 34 years	1,771	15	546	19
35 to 44 years	1,913	16	537	18
45 to 54 years	2,093	17	550	19
55 to 64 years	1,425	12	429	15
65 years or older	944	8	292	10

* Estimate based on a sample size of 10–29   Sample size too small (less than 10) to report data reliably

Note: Data reported on this table are from screening interviews in which one adult household member responded for all household members The screening interview required the respondent to recall 12 months worth of activity

Table B-3. Most Recent Year of Hunting by Age Group

(Population 6 years old and older. Numbers in thousands)

Age group	Total, all persons who hunted in 2010 or earlier year		Most recent year of hunting					
			2010		2009		2008	
	Number	Percent	Number	Percent	Number	Percent	Number	Percent
Total, all ages............................	48,941	100	17,060	35	2,945	6	1,665	3
6 to 11 years	867	100	707	82	*93	*11		
12 to 15 years	1,550	100	1,319	85	*92	*6		
16 to 17 years	800	100	571	71	*102	*13	*88	*11
18 to 24 years	3,357	100	1,820	54	293	9	177	5
25 to 34 years	6,469	100	2,578	40	546	8	298	5
35 to 44 years	7,291	100	2,699	37	539	7	305	4
45 to 54 years	10,215	100	3,482	34	553	5	439	4
55 to 64 years	9,113	100	2,424	27	435	5	170	2
65 years or older	9,279	100	1,460	16	293	3	157	2

Age group	Most recent year of hunting							
	2007		2006		2005		Before 2005	
	Number	Percent	Number	Percent	Number	Percent	Number	Percent
Total, all ages............................	1,084	2	1,048	2	818	2	23,945	49
6 to 11 years								
12 to 15 years								
16 to 17 years								
18 to 24 years	*152	*5	121	4	*89	*3	680	20
25 to 34 years	225	3	145	2	152	2	2,496	39
35 to 44 years	216	3	133	2	*132	*2	3,201	44
45 to 54 years	226	2	288	3	116	1	4,970	49
55 to 64 years	97	1	93	1	189	2	5,667	62
65 years or older	132	1	226	2	104	1	6,869	74

* Estimate based on a sample size of 10–29   Sample size too small (less than 10) to report data reliably

Note: Data reported on this table are from screening interviews in which one adult household member responded for all household members The screening interview required the respondent to recall 12 months worth of activity

Table B-4. Most Recent Year of Fishing by Age Group

(Population 6 years old and older. Numbers in thousands)

Age group	Total, all persons who fished in 2010 or earlier year		Most recent year of fishing					
			2010		2009		2008	
	Number	Percent	Number	Percent	Number	Percent	Number	Percent
Total, all ages............................	126,710	100	55,804	44	12,224	10	5,925	5
6 to 11 years	9,021	100	6,928	77	1,163	13	372	4
12 to 15 years	7,327	100	4,451	61	1,052	14	553	8
16 to 17 years	3,082	100	1,750	57	457	15	194	6
18 to 24 years	10,982	100	5,106	46	1,327	12	737	7
25 to 34 years	18,236	100	8,525	47	1,793	10	955	5
35 to 44 years	18,799	100	8,793	47	1,923	10	764	4
45 to 54 years	22,840	100	9,467	41	2,121	9	1,102	5
55 to 64 years	19,247	100	6,346	33	1,441	7	705	4
65 years or older	17,177	100	4,438	26	947	6	542	3

Age group	Most recent year of fishing							
	2007		2006		2005		Before 2005	
	Number	Percent	Number	Percent	Number	Percent	Number	Percent
Total, all ages............................	3,672	3	4,174	3	2,557	2	40,869	32
6 to 11 years	159	2	*157	*2	*37	*(Z)	188	2
12 to 15 years	140	2	446	6	174	2	475	6
16 to 17 years	136	4	*97	*3	115	4	300	10
18 to 24 years	483	4	628	6	254	2	2,104	19
25 to 34 years	704	4	678	4	422	2	4,769	26
35 to 44 years	575	3	645	3	398	2	5,521	29
45 to 54 years	700	3	655	3	521	2	8,077	35
55 to 64 years	412	2	420	2	375	2	9,401	49
65 years or older	362	2	448	3	263	2	10,036	58

* Estimate based on a sample size of 10–29   (Z) Less than 0 5 percent

Note: Data reported on this table are from screening interviews in which one adult household member responded for all household members The screening interview required the respondent to recall 12 months worth of activity

Table B-5. Anglers and Hunters 6 to 15 Years Old: 2010

(Population 6 to 15 years old. Numbers in thousands)

Sportspersons	Total, 6 to 15 years old		12 to 15 years old		9 to 11 years old		6 to 8 years old	
	Number	Percent	Number	Percent	Number	Percent	Number	Percent
Total sportspersons, fished or hunted.........	11,673	100	4,702	100	3,861	100	3,109	100
Total anglers	11,379	97	4,451	95	3,825	99	3,103	100
Fished only	9,647	83	3,384	72	3,328	86	2,935	94
Fished and hunted	1,732	15	1,067	23	497	13	168	5
Total hunters	2,026	17	1,319	28	533	14	174	6
Hunted only	293	3	251	5	*36	*1		
Hunted and fished	1,732	15	1,067	23	497	13	168	5

* Estimate based on a sample size of 10–29   Sample size too small (less than 10) to report data reliably

Note: Detail does not add to total because of multiple responses Data reported on this table are from screening interviews in which one adult household member responded for all household members 6 to 15 years old The screening interview required the respondent to recall 12 months worth of activity Includes persons who fished or hunted only in other countries

Table B-6. Wildlife-Watching Participants 6 to 15 Years Old by Wildlife-Watching Activity: 2010

(Population 6 to 15 years old. Numbers in thousands)

Activity	Total, 6 to 15 years old			12 to 15 years old			9 to 11 years old			6 to 8 years old		
	Number	Percent of participants	Percent of population	Number	Percent of participants	Percent of population	Number	Percent of participants	Percent of population	Number	Percent of participants	Percent of population
Total participants	12,654	100	31	4,611	100	28	4,688	100	38	3,356	100	28
Away from home	5,287	42	13	2,001	43	12	1,793	38	14	1,492	44	13
Around the home	11,130	88	27	4,002	87	24	4,182	89	33	2,947	88	25
Observe wildlife	9,621	76	24	3,310	72	20	3,741	80	30	2,571	77	22
Photograph wildlife	2,246	18	6	846	18	5	954	20	8	446	13	4
Feed wild birds or other wildlife	4,436	35	11	1,412	31	9	1,744	37	14	1,279	38	11
Maintain plantings or natural areas	1,718	14	4	517	11	3	813	17	7	389	12	3

Note: Detail does not add to total because of multiple responses Columns showing percent of participants are based on the first row of each column Columns showing percent of population in age group are based on the U S population in each age category, including those who did not participate in wildlife-watching activities Data reported on this table are from screening interviews in which one adult household member responded for all household members 6 to 15 years old The screening interview required the respondent to recall 12 months worth of activity Includes persons who participated only in other countries

Table B-7. Selected Characteristics of Anglers and Hunters 6 to 15 Years Old: 2010

(Population 6 to 15 years old. Numbers in thousands)

Characteristic	U S population Number	U S population Percent	Sportspersons, fished or hunted Number	Sportspersons, fished or hunted Percent who participated	Sportspersons, fished or hunted Percent	Fished only Number	Fished only Percent who participated	Fished only Percent
Total persons	**40,735**	**100**	**11,673**	**29**	**100**	**9,647**	**24**	**100**
Population Density of Residence								
Urban	30,138	74	7,329	24	63	6,444	21	67
Rural	10,596	26	4,344	41	37	3,203	30	33
Population Size of Residence								
Metropolitan Statistical Area (MSA)	38,520	95	10,666	28	91	8,968	23	93
1,000,000 or more	21,283	52	4,786	22	41	4,272	20	44
250,000 to 999,999	8,804	22	2,521	29	22	2,102	24	22
50,000 to 249,999	8,433	21	3,358	40	29	2,595	31	27
Outside MSA	2,214	5	1,007	45	9	679	31	7
Census Geographic Division								
New England	1,726	4	465	27	4	441	26	5
Middle Atlantic	5,034	12	1,146	23	10	1,042	21	11
East North Central	6,072	15	2,315	38	20	1,842	30	19
West North Central	2,645	6	1,242	47	11	924	35	10
South Atlantic	7,606	19	2,212	29	19	1,875	25	19
East South Central	2,407	6	850	35	7	635	26	7
West South Central	5,365	13	1,133	21	10	842	16	9
Mountain	3,168	8	1,001	32	9	870	27	9
Pacific	6,711	16	1,308	19	11	1,176	18	12
Age								
6 to 8 years	11,866	29	3,109	26	27	2,935	25	30
9 to 11 years	12,488	31	3,861	31	33	3,328	27	35
12 to 15 years	16,380	40	4,702	29	40	3,384	21	35
Sex								
Male, total	21,420	53	7,202	34	62	5,634	26	58
6 to 8 years	5,925	15	1,731	29	15	1,589	27	16
9 to 11 years	6,818	17	2,413	35	21	2,001	29	21
12 to 15 years	8,678	21	3,058	35	26	2,044	24	21
Female, total	19,315	47	4,470	23	38	4,013	21	42
6 to 8 years	5,942	15	1,378	23	12	1,346	23	14
9 to 11 years	5,670	14	1,448	26	12	1,327	23	14
12 to 15 years	7,702	19	1,645	21	14	1,340	17	14
Ethnicity								
Hispanic	7,846	19	1,173	15	10	1,137	14	12
Non-Hispanic	32,889	81	10,500	32	90	8,510	26	88
Race								
White	28,458	70	9,889	35	85	8,037	28	83
African American	5,116	13	557	11	5	482	9	5
Asian American	2,055	5	227	11	2	209	10	2
All others	5,105	13	1,000	20	9	919	18	10
Annual Household Income								
Less than $20,000	4,686	12	917	20	8	796	17	8
$20,000 to $24,999	2,236	5	364	16	3	326	15	3
$25,000 to $29,999	2,073	5	364	18	3	316	15	3
$30,000 to $34,999	1,777	4	391	22	3	294	17	3
$35,000 to $39,999	2,045	5	660	32	6	519	25	5
$40,000 to $49,999	2,939	7	842	29	7	725	25	8
$50,000 to $74,999	7,146	18	2,009	28	17	1,661	23	17
$75,000 to $99,999	4,599	11	1,973	43	17	1,457	32	15
$100,000 to $149,999	4,452	11	2,077	47	18	1,737	39	18
$150,000 or more	3,281	8	1,058	32	9	905	28	9
Not reported	5,501	14	1,019	19	9	911	17	9

See footnotes at end of table

(Population 6 to 15 years old. Numbers in thousands)

Characteristic	Hunted only			Fished and hunted		
	Number	Percent who participated	Percent	Number	Percent who participated	Percent
Total persons	293	1	100	1,732	4	100
Population Density of Residence						
Urban	*118	*(Z)	*40	767	3	44
Rural	176	2	60	965	9	56
Population Size of Residence						
Metropolitan Statistical Area (MSA)	242	1	82	1,456	4	84
1,000,000 or more	*53	*(Z)	*18	462	2	27
250,000 to 999,999				386	4	22
50,000 to 249,999	*155	*2	*53	609	7	35
Outside MSA	*52	*2	*18	276	12	16
Census Geographic Division						
New England				*23	*1	*1
Middle Atlantic				*61	*1	*4
East North Central	*99	*2	*34	374	6	22
West North Central				295	11	17
South Atlantic	*73	*1	*25	264	3	15
East South Central				200	8	12
West South Central				274	5	16
Mountain				122	4	7
Pacific				119	2	7
Age						
6 to 8 years				168	1	10
9 to 11 years	*36	*(Z)	*12	497	4	29
12 to 15 years	251	2	86	1,067	7	62
Sex						
Male, total	170	1	58	1,399	7	81
6 to 8 years				138	2	8
9 to 11 years				398	6	23
12 to 15 years	151	2	51	863	10	50
Female, total	*124	*1	*42	333	2	19
6 to 8 years						
9 to 11 years				99	2	6
12 to 15 years	*101	*1	*34	204	3	12
Ethnicity						
Hispanic				*36	*(Z)	*2
Non-Hispanic	293	1	100	1,697	5	98
Race						
White	292	1	100	1,560	5	90
African American				*75	*1	*4
Asian American						
All others				*79	*2	*5
Annual Household Income						
Less than $20,000				*110	*2	*6
$20,000 to $24,999						
$25,000 to $29,999				*40	*2	*2
$30,000 to $34,999				*72	*4	*4
$35,000 to $39,999				*134	*7	*8
$40,000 to $49,999				112	4	6
$50,000 to $74,999				310	4	18
$75,000 to $99,999	*91	*2	*31	425	9	25
$100,000 to $149,999	*40	*1	*14	300	7	17
$150,000 or more	*45	*1	*15	*108	*3	*6
Not reported				93	2	5

* Estimate based on a sample size of 10–29   Sample size too small (less than 10) to report data reliably   (Z) Less than 0 5 percent

Note: Percent who participated columns show the percent of each row's population who participated in the activity named by the column (the percent of those living in urban areas who fished only, etc) Percent columns show the percent of each column's participants who are described by the row heading (the percent of those who fished only who lived in urban areas, etc) Data reported on this table are from screening interviews in which one adult household member responded for all household members The screening interview required the respondent to recall 12 months worth of activity

Table B-8. Selected Characteristics of Wildlife-Watching Participants 6 to 15 Years Old: 2010

(Population 6 to 15 years old. Numbers in thousands)

Characteristic	U S population		Participants								
			Total			Away from home			Around the home		
	Number	Percent	Number	Percent who participated	Percent	Number	Percent who participated	Percent	Number	Percent who participated	Percent
Total persons	**40,735**	**100**	**12,654**	**31**	**100**	**5,287**	**13**	**100**	**11,130**	**27**	**100**
Population Density of Residence											
Urban	30,138	74	8,458	28	67	3,682	12	70	7,294	24	66
Rural	10,596	26	4,196	40	33	1,605	15	30	3,836	36	34
Population Size of Residence											
Metropolitan Statistical Area (MSA)	38,520	95	11,953	31	94	5,002	13	95	10,509	27	94
1,000,000 or more	21,283	52	6,085	29	48	2,437	11	46	5,372	25	48
250,000 to 999,999	8,804	22	2,856	32	23	1,223	14	23	2,431	28	22
50,000 to 249,999	8,433	21	3,012	36	24	1,342	16	25	2,707	32	24
Outside MSA	2,214	5	701	32	6	285	13	5	621	28	6
Census Geographic Division											
New England	1,726	4	593	34	5	274	16	5	521	30	5
Middle Atlantic	5,034	12	1,434	28	11	430	9	8	1,309	26	12
East North Central	6,072	15	2,204	36	17	904	15	17	2,004	33	18
West North Central	2,645	6	1,003	38	8	455	17	9	846	32	8
South Atlantic	7,606	19	2,392	31	19	1,012	13	19	2,079	27	19
East South Central	2,407	6	590	24	5	299	12	6	565	23	5
West South Central	5,365	13	1,451	27	11	420	8	8	1,282	24	12
Mountain	3,168	8	999	32	8	541	17	10	822	26	7
Pacific	6,711	16	1,989	30	16	953	14	18	1,701	25	15
Age											
6 to 8 years	11,866	29	3,356	28	27	1,492	13	28	2,947	25	26
9 to 11 years	12,488	31	4,688	38	37	1,793	14	34	4,182	33	38
12 to 15 years	16,380	40	4,611	28	36	2,001	12	38	4,002	24	36
Sex											
Male, total	21,420	53	6,690	31	53	2,808	13	53	5,819	27	52
6 to 8 years	5,925	15	1,601	27	13	676	11	13	1,405	24	13
9 to 11 years	6,818	17	2,571	38	20	1,006	15	19	2,230	33	20
12 to 15 years	8,678	21	2,518	29	20	1,126	13	21	2,184	25	20
Female, total	19,315	47	5,964	31	47	2,479	13	47	5,312	28	48
6 to 8 years	5,942	15	1,755	30	14	816	14	15	1,542	26	14
9 to 11 years	5,670	14	2,117	37	17	787	14	15	1,952	34	18
12 to 15 years	7,702	19	2,092	27	17	876	11	17	1,818	24	16
Ethnicity											
Hispanic	7,846	19	1,430	18	11	510	6	10	1,278	16	11
Non-Hispanic	32,889	81	11,224	34	89	4,777	15	90	9,852	30	89
Race											
White	28,458	70	10,346	36	82	4,226	15	80	9,178	32	82
African American	5,116	13	768	15	6	324	6	6	704	14	6
Asian American	2,055	5	460	22	4	258	13	5	388	19	3
All others	5,105	13	1,081	21	9	480	9	9	861	17	8
Annual Household Income											
Less than $20,000	4,686	12	998	21	8	392	8	7	825	18	7
$20,000 to $24,999	2,236	5	516	23	4	248	11	5	425	19	4
$25,000 to $29,999	2,073	5	574	28	5	208	10	4	518	25	5
$30,000 to $34,999	1,777	4	538	30	4	115	6	2	534	30	5
$35,000 to $39,999	2,045	5	384	19	3	198	10	4	375	18	3
$40,000 to $49,999	2,939	7	1,076	37	9	504	17	10	952	32	9
$50,000 to $74,999	7,146	18	2,687	38	21	1,046	15	20	2,316	32	21
$75,000 to $99,999	4,599	11	1,824	40	14	730	16	14	1,617	35	15
$100,000 to $149,999	4,452	11	1,809	41	14	816	18	15	1,567	35	14
$150,000 or more	3,281	8	1,301	40	10	663	20	13	1,140	35	10
Not reported	5,501	14	947	17	7	367	7	7	861	16	8

Note: Percent who participated columns show the percent of each row's population who participated in the activity named by the column (the percent of those living in urban areas who fished only, etc.) Percent columns show the percent of each column's participants who are described by the row heading (the percent of those who fished only who lived in urban areas, etc.) Data reported on this table are from screening interviews in which one adult household member responded for all household members The screening interview required the respondent to recall 12 months worth of activity

Table B-9. Participants in Wildlife-Related Recreation 6 to 15 Years Old by State Residents Both Inside and Outside Their Resident State: 2010

(Population 16 years old and older. Numbers in thousands)

Participant's state of residence	Population	Total participants		Sportspersons		Wildlife-watching participants	
		Number	Percent of population	Number	Percent of population	Number	Percent of population
United States, total	**40,735**	**17,956**	**44**	**11,673**	**29**	**12,654**	**31**
Alabama	621	219	35	182	29	134	22
Alaska	97	60	61	48	49	42	43
Arizona	955	328	34	221	23	206	22
Arkansas	393	174	44	*155	*39	*112	*29
California	5,127	1,886	37	902	18	1,431	28
Colorado	674	303	45	200	30	219	32
Connecticut	446	209	47	120	27	150	34
Delaware	112	49	44	38	34	26	24
Florida	2,213	990	45	672	30	646	29
Georgia	1,425	601	42	297	21	390	27
Hawaii	155	50	32	25	16	41	26
Idaho	227	172	76	130	57	*113	*50
Illinois	1,737	763	44	605	35	549	32
Indiana	870	540	62	424	49	344	40
Iowa	385	217	56	191	50	127	33
Kansas	384	214	56	161	42	131	34
Kentucky	554	222	40	206	37	116	21
Louisiana	620	183	29	*97	*16	*140	*23
Maine	145	86	59	67	46	70	48
Maryland	738	271	37	161	22	217	29
Massachusetts	789	320	41	172	22	249	32
Michigan	1,279	600	47	449	35	413	32
Minnesota	677	414	61	345	51	*264	*39
Mississippi	414	199	48	191	46	*71	*17
Missouri	776	466	60	363	47	339	44
Montana	116	90	78	80	69	*65	*56
Nebraska	243	117	48	94	39	66	27
Nevada	367	156	43	71	19	130	35
New Hampshire	156	74	47	52	33	52	34
New Jersey	1,132	470	42	213	19	377	33
New Mexico	283	110	39	79	28	59	21
New York	2,399	722	30	523	22	479	20
North Carolina	1,249	721	58	490	39	513	41
North Dakota	(NA)	(NA)	(NA)	(NA)	(NA)	(NA)	(NA)
Ohio	1,479	648	44	483	33	479	32
Oklahoma	505	226	45	209	41	87	17
Oregon	476	201	42	119	25	164	35
Pennsylvania	1,504	810	54	410	27	578	38
Rhode Island	123	43	35	26	21	31	25
South Carolina	589	290	49	191	32	192	33
South Dakota	106	72	68	62	59	*55	*52
Tennessee	817	333	41	271	33	268	33
Texas	3,846	1,446	38	672	17	1,112	29
Utah	476	266	56	179	38	167	35
Vermont	67	49	72	29	43	41	61
Virginia	1,009	432	43	205	20	332	33
Washington	857	391	46	214	25	311	36
West Virginia	214	157	73	*150	*70	*45	*21
Wisconsin	707	483	68	353	50	419	59
Wyoming	69	57	83	*41	*59	41	59

(NA) Not available

Note: Detail does not add to total because of multiple responses U S totals include responses from participants residing in the District of Columbia, as described in Appendix D Data reported on this table are from screening interviews in which one adult household member responded for all household members 6 to 15 years old The screening interview required the respondent to recall 12 months worth of activity Includes persons who fished or hunted only in other countries

Table B-10. Anglers and Hunters 6 to 15 Years Old by State Residents Participating Both Inside and Outside Their Resident State: 2010

(Population 6 to 15 years old. Numbers in thousands)

Sportsperson's state of residence	Population	Fished or hunted		Fished only		Hunted only		Fished and hunted	
		Number	Percent of population	Number	Percent of population	Number	Percent of population	Number	Percent of population
United States, total	**40,735**	**11,673**	**29**	**9,647**	**24**	**293**	**1**	**1,732**	**4**
Alabama	621	182	29	*127	*20			*55	*9
Alaska	97	48	49	44	45				
Arizona	955	221	23	196	20				
Arkansas	393	*155	*39	*94	*24			*60	*15
California	5,127	902	18	825	16			*77	*2
Colorado	674	200	30	193	29				
Connecticut	446	120	27	118	27				
Delaware	112	38	34	35	31				
Florida	2,213	672	30	614	28			*47	*2
Georgia	1,425	297	21	*262	*18			*30	*2
Hawaii	155	25	16	22	14				
Idaho	227	130	57	125	55				
Illinois	1,737	605	35	574	33				
Indiana	870	424	49	387	44				
Iowa	385	191	50	167	43			*22	*6
Kansas	384	161	42	105	27			*49	*13
Kentucky	554	206	37	138	25			*54	*10
Louisiana	620	*97	*16					*34	*5
Maine	145	67	46	*56	*39				
Maryland	738	161	22	155	21				
Massachusetts	789	172	22	169	21				
Michigan	1,279	449	35	*281	*22				
Minnesota	677	345	51	*221	*33			*121	*18
Mississippi	414	191	46	*148	*36			*42	*10
Missouri	776	363	47	293	38			68	9
Montana	116	80	69	*45	*38				
Nebraska	243	94	39	77	32				
Nevada	367	71	19	66	18				
New Hampshire	156	52	33	46	30				
New Jersey	1,132	213	19	210	19				
New Mexico	283	79	28	67	24			*12	*4
New York	2,399	523	22	489	20				
North Carolina	1,249	490	39	396	32				
North Dakota	(NA)	(NA)	(NA)	(NA)	(NA)	(NA)	(NA)	(NA)	(NA)
Ohio	1,479	483	33	375	25				
Oklahoma	505	209	41	190	38				
Oregon	476	119	25	101	21				
Pennsylvania	1,504	410	27	343	23				
Rhode Island	123	26	21	26	21				
South Carolina	589	191	32	*133	*23			*36	*6
South Dakota	106	62	59	*39	*36				
Tennessee	817	271	33	222	27			*48	*6
Texas	3,846	672	17	504	13			*161	*4
Utah	476	179	38	149	31			*30	*6
Vermont	67	29	43	25	37				
Virginia	1,009	205	20	160	16			*31	*3
Washington	857	214	25	184	21				
West Virginia	214	*150	*70	*111	*52				
Wisconsin	707	353	50	*226	*32				
Wyoming	69	*41	*59	*30	*44				

* Estimate based on a sample size of 10–29   Sample size too small (less than 10) to report data reliably   (NA) Not available

Note: U S totals include responses from participants residing in the District of Columbia, as described in Appendix D Data reported on this table are from screening interviews in which one adult household member responded for all household members 6 to 15 years old The screening interview required the respondent to recall 12 months worth of activity Includes persons who fished or hunted only in other countries

Table B-11. Participants in Wildlife-Watching Activities 6 to 15 Years Old by State Residents Participating Both Inside and Outside Their Resident State: 2010

(Population 6 to 15 years old. Numbers in thousands)

Participant's state of residence	Population	Participants					
		Total		Away from home		Around the home	
		Number	Percent of population	Number	Percent of population	Number	Percent of population
United States, total	**40,735**	**12,654**	**31**	**5,287**	**13**	**11,130**	**27**
Alabama	621	134	22	*44	*7	132	21
Alaska	97	42	43	*15	*15	37	38
Arizona	955	206	22	103	11	178	19
Arkansas	393	*112	*29			*88	*22
California	5,127	1,431	28	661	13	1,232	24
Colorado	674	219	32	94	14	182	27
Connecticut	446	150	34	66	15	129	29
Delaware	112	26	24	*12	*10	21	19
Florida	2,213	646	29	271	12	520	24
Georgia	1,425	390	27	*144	*10	374	26
Hawaii	155	41	26	*27	*18	36	23
Idaho	227	*113	*50	*99	*44	*90	*40
Illinois	1,737	549	32	244	14	484	28
Indiana	870	344	40	*96	*11	332	38
Iowa	385	127	33	65	17	104	27
Kansas	384	131	34	*49	*13	113	29
Kentucky	554	116	21	*57	*10	105	19
Louisiana	620	*140	*23			*136	*22
Maine	145	70	48	*33	*22	61	42
Maryland	738	217	29	123	17	197	27
Massachusetts	789	249	32	114	14	219	28
Michigan	1,279	413	32	*198	*15	375	29
Minnesota	677	*264	*39	*149	*22	*199	*29
Mississippi	414	*71	*17			*70	*17
Missouri	776	339	44	114	15	317	41
Montana	116	*65	*56	*42	*36	*63	*54
Nebraska	243	66	27	*36	*15	*48	*20
Nevada	367	130	35	*81	*22	81	22
New Hampshire	156	52	34	*28	*18	50	32
New Jersey	1,132	377	33	110	10	356	31
New Mexico	283	59	21	33	12	50	18
New York	2,399	479	20	*234	*10	375	16
North Carolina	1,249	513	41	*287	*23	390	31
North Dakota	(NA)	(NA)	(NA)	(NA)	(NA)	(NA)	(NA)
Ohio	1,479	479	32	231	16	394	27
Oklahoma	505	87	17	*48	*9	*70	*14
Oregon	476	164	35	*60	*13	155	33
Pennsylvania	1,504	578	38	*86	*6	578	38
Rhode Island	123	31	25	13	11	27	22
South Carolina	589	192	33	*30	*5	189	32
South Dakota	106	*55	*52	*40	*37	*44	*41
Tennessee	817	268	33	*187	*23	258	32
Texas	3,846	1,112	29	*318	*8	989	26
Utah	476	167	35	*60	*13	145	30
Vermont	67	41	61	*20	*30	35	52
Virginia	1,009	332	33	118	12	313	31
Washington	857	311	36	190	22	241	28
West Virginia	214	*45	*21			*45	*21
Wisconsin	707	419	59	*135	*19	419	59
Wyoming	69	41	59	*29	*42	*33	*48

* Estimate based on a sample size of 10–29   Sample size too small (less than 10) to report data reliably   (NA) Not available

Note: Detail does not add to total because of multiple responses U S totals include responses from participants residing in the District of Columbia, as described in
    Appendix D Data reported on this table are from screening interviews in which one adult household member responded for all household members 6 to 15 years old
    The screening interview required the respondent to recall 12 months worth of activity Includes persons who fished or hunted only in other countries

Table B-12. Participation by 6-to-15-Year-Olds in 1980, 1985, 1990, 1995, 2000, 2005, and 2010

(Numbers in thousands)

Participant	1980			1985			1990		
	Number of participants	Percent change from previous survey	Percent of 6-to-15-year-old population	Number of participants	Percent change from previous survey	Percent of 6-to-15-year-old population	Number of participants	Percent change from previous survey	Percent of 6-to-15-year-old population
Total sportspersons.....................	**12,141**	**(NA)**	34	**12,558**	3	36	**14,011**	12	39
Anglers	11,787	(NA)	33	12,243	4	35	13,790	13	39
Hunters	1,962	(NA)	6	1,799	–8	5	1,730	–4	5
Total wildlife watchers	**(NA)**	**(NA)**	**(NA)**	**17,789**	**(NA)**	51	**17,136**	–4	48
Around the home	(NA)	(NA)	(NA)	16,151	(NA)	46	15,406	–5	43
Away from home	(NA)	(NA)	(NA)	6,615	(NA)	19	7,311	11	21
	1995			2000			2005		
	Number of participants	Percent change from previous survey	Percent of 6-to-15-year-old population	Number of participants	Percent change from previous survey	Percent of 6-to-15-year-old population	Number of participants	Percent change from previous survey	Percent of 6-to-15-year-old population
Total sportspersons.....................	**15,019**	7	39	**13,369**	–11	33	**12,318**	–8	30
Anglers	14,808	7	38	13,145	–11	32	12,110	–8	30
Hunters	1,720	–1	4	1,741	1	4	1,773	2	4
Total wildlife watchers	**17,449**	**2**	45	**15,066**	–14	37	**13,587**	–10	34
Around the home	15,425	(Z)	40	13,542	–12	33	12,055	–11	30
Away from home	8,314	14	21	6,091	–27	15	5,850	–4	14
	2010								
	Number of participants	Percent change from previous survey	Percent of 6-to-15-year-old population						
Total sportspersons.....................	**11,673**	–5	29						
Anglers	11,379	–6	28						
Hunters	2,026	14	5						
Total wildlife watchers	**12,654**	–7	31						
Around the home	11,130	–8	27						
Away from home	5,287	–11	13						

(NA) Not Available   (Z) Less than 0 5 percent

Appendix C

Appendix C.
Significant Methodological Changes From Previous Surveys and Regional Trends

The 2011 National Survey of Fishing, Hunting, and Wildlife-Associated Recreation (FHWAR) was designed to continue the data collection of the 1955 to 2006 Surveys. While complete comparability between any two Surveys cannot be achieved, this appendix compares major findings of all the Surveys and presents trends for the major categories of wildlife-related recreation where feasible. Differences among the Surveys are discussed in the following two sections.

The principal characteristics of the 1955 to 2011 Surveys are summarized in Table C-1. The table shows the scope and design of all 12 Surveys.

This appendix provides trend information in two sections (1991 to 2011 and 1955 to 1985). A significant change was made in 1991 in the recall period used in the detailed phase of the FHWAR Surveys. The recall period in 1991 was shortened from the 12 months used in previous Surveys to 4 months in order to improve the accuracy of the data collected. As a result of that change, the Surveys conducted since 1991 cannot be compared with those conducted earlier.

The 1955 to 1985 Surveys required respondents to recall their recreation activities for the survey year at the beginning of the following year. The 1991 to 2011 Surveys went to the respondents two or three times during the survey year to get their activity information. The change in the recall period was due to a study[1] of the effect of the respondent recall length

----
[1] Investigation of Possible Recall/Reference Period Bias in National Surveys of Fishing, Hunting and Wildlife-Associated Recreation, December 1989, Westat, Inc

on survey estimates. The study found significant differences in FHWAR Survey results using annual recall periods versus shorter recall periods. Longer recall periods lead to higher estimates. Even when everything else was held constant, such as question-naire content and sample design, increasing the respondent's recall period resulted in significantly higher estimates for the same phenomenon.

The recall study also found that the extent of recall bias varied for different types of fishing and hunting participa-tion and expenditures. For example, annual recall respondents gave an estimate of average annual days of salt-water fishing that was 46 percent higher than the trimester recall estimate, while the annual recall estimate of average annual saltwater fishing trips was 30 percent higher than the trimester recall estimate. This means there is no single correction factor for all survey esti-mates when calculating trends from Surveys using different recall periods.

Reliable trends analysis needs to use data compiled from surveys in which the important elements, such as the sample design and recall period, are not significantly different.

1991 to 2011 Significant Methodological Differences

The most significant design differences in the five Surveys are as follows:

1. The 1991 Survey data was collected by interviewers filling out paper questionnaires. The data entries were keyed in a separate operation after the interview. The 1996, 2001, 2006, and 2011 Survey data were collected by the use of computer-assisted interviews. The

questionnaires were programmed into computers, and the interviewer keyed in the responses at the time of the interview.

2. The 1991 Survey screening phase was conducted in January and February of 1991, when a household member of the sample households was interviewed on behalf of the entire household. The screening interviews for the 1996, 2001, and 2006 Surveys were conducted April through June of their survey years in conjunction with the first wave of the detailed interviews. The 2011 Survey also conducted screening interviews and the first detailed interviews April through June of 2011, but further-more had an additional screening and detailed effort from February 2012 to the end of May 2012. The April–June 2011 screening effort had a high noncontact rate because of poor results using sample tele-phone numbers obtained from a private firm. Census went back to the noncontacted component of the original sample in February-May 2012 and interviewed a subsample, requiring annual recall for those respondents. The Wave 3 screen sample was 12,484 of the total 48,600 household screen sample. A modification of the 2011 sampling scheme was to oversample counties that had relatively high proportions of hunting license purchases.

The screening interviews for all five Surveys consisted primarily of demo-graphic questions and wildlife-related recreation questions concerning activity in the previous year (1990, 1995, etc.) and intentions for recreating in the survey year.

Table C-1. Major Characteristics of Surveys: 1955 to 2011

Characteristic	1955	1960	1965	1970	1975	1980
Survey design: Screening interview mode and population of interest	Combined with detailed phase	Personal interview, 12 years old and older	Personal interview, 9 years old and older	Mail questionnaire, 9 years old and older	Telephone interview, 6 years old and older	Telephone/personal interview, 6 years old and older
Detailed interview mode and population of interest	Personal interview, 12 years old and older	Personal interview, 12 years old and older Substantial participants[1]	Personal interview, 12 years old and older Substantial participants[1]	Personal interview, 12 years old and older Substantial participants[2]	Mail questionnaire, 9 years old and older	Personal interview, 16 years old and older
Respondent's recall period	1 year	1 year	1 year	1 year	1 year	1 year
Sample sizes: Screening phase (households)	20,000	18,000	16,000	24,000	106,294	116,025
Detailed phase (individuals): Fishing and hunting	9,328	10,300	6,400	8,700	20,211	30,291
Wildlife watching[3]	(X)	(X)	(X)	(X)	(X)	5,997
Response rates: Screening phase	(NA)	(NA)	(NA)	(NA)	95 percent	95 percent
Detailed phase: Fishing and hunting	(NA)	93 percent	(NA)	(NA)	37 percent	90 percent
Wildlife watching[3]	(X)	(X)	(X)	(X)	(X)	95 percent
Level of reporting	National	National	National	National	State and National	State and National
Data collection agent	Private contractor	U S Census Bureau	U S Census Bureau	U S Census Bureau	Private contractor	U S Census Bureau

See footnotes at end of table

Table C-1. Major Characteristics of Surveys: 1955 to 2011—Continued

Characteristic	1985	1991	1996	2001	2006	2011
Survey design: Screening interview mode and population of interest	Telephone/personal interview, 6 years old and older	Telephone/personal interview, 6 years old and older	Telephone/personal interview, 6 years old and older	Telephone/personal interview, 6 years old and older	Telephone/personal interview, 6 years old and older	Telephone/personal interview, 6 years old and older
Detailed interview mode and population of interest	Personal interview, 16 years old and older	Telephone/personal interview, 16 years old and older	Telephone/personal interview, 16 years old and older	Telephone/personal interview, 16 years old and older	Telephone/personal interview, 16 years old and older	Telephone/personal interview, 16 years old and older
Respondent's recall period	1 year	4 months	4–8 months	4–8 months	4–8 months	4–12 months
Sample sizes: Screening phase (households)	102,694	102,804	44,000	52,508	66,688	30,400
Detailed phase (individuals): Fishing and hunting Wildlife watching[3]	28,011 26,671	23,179 22,723	13,222 9,802	25,070 15,303	21,938 11,279	11,330 9,329
Response rates: Screening phase	93 percent	95 percent	71 percent	75 percent	90 percent	77 percent
Detailed phase: Fishing and hunting	92 percent	95 percent	80 percent	88 percent	77 percent	67 percent
Wildlife watching[3]	94 percent	95 percent	82 percent	90 percent	78 percent	66 percent
Level of reporting	State and National	State and National	State and National	State and National	State and National	State and National
Data collection agent	U S Census Bureau	U S Census Bureau	U S Census Bureau	U S Census Bureau	U S Census Bureau	U S Census Bureau

(NA) Not available   (X) Not applicable; wildlife-watching (nonconsumptive) interviews were not conducted prior to 1980

[1] Spent $5 00 or more or participated 3 days or more during the year

[2] Spent $7 50 or more or participated 3 days or more during the year

[3] Termed "nonconsumptive" in 1980, 1985, and 1991 Surveys

In the 1991 Survey, an attempt was made to contact every sample person in all three detailed interview waves. In 1996, 2001, 2006, and 2011 respondents who were interviewed in the first detailed interview wave were not contacted again until the third wave (unless they were part of the other subsample, i.e., a respondent in both the sportsperson and wildlife watching subsamples could be in the first and third wave of sportsperson interviewing and the second and third wave of wildlife watching interviewing). Also, all interviews in the second wave were conducted only by telephone. In-person interviews were only conducted in the first and third waves. The 2011 wave 3 screen phase was composed of both telephone and in-person interviews.

Section I. Important Instrument Changes in the 1996 Survey

1. The 1991 Survey collected information on all wildlife-related recreation purchases made by participants without reference to where the purchase was made. The 1996 Survey asked in which state the purchase was made.

2. In 1991, respondents were asked what kind of fishing they did, i.e., Great Lakes, other freshwater, or saltwater, and then were asked in what states they fished. In 1996, respondents were asked in which states they fished and then were asked what kind of fishing they did. This method had the advantage of not asking about, for example, saltwater fishing when they only fished in a noncoastal state.

3. In 1991, respondents were asked how many days they "actually" hunted or fished for a particular type of game or fish and then how many days they "chiefly" hunted or fished for the same type of game or fish rather than another type of game or fish. To get total days of hunting or fishing for a particular type of game or fish, the "actually" day response was used, while to get the sum of all days of hunting or fishing, the "chiefly" days were summed. In 1996, respondents were asked their total days of hunting or fishing in the country and each state, then how

many days they hunted or fished for a particular type of game or fish.

4. Trip-related and equipment expenditure categories were not the same for all Surveys. "Guide fee" and "Pack trip or package fee" were two separate trip-related expenditure items in 1991, while they were combined into one category in the 1996 Survey. "Boating costs" was added to the 1996 hunting and wildlife-watching trip-related expenditure sections. "Heating and cooking fuel" was added to all of the trip-related expenditure sections. "Spearfishing equipment" was moved from a separate category to the "other" list. "Rods" and "Reels" were two separate categories in 1991 but were combined in 1996. "Lines, hooks, sinkers, etc." was one category in 1991 but split into "Lines" and "Hooks, sinkers, etc." in 1996. "Food used to feed other wildlife" was added to the wildlife-watching equipment section, "Boats" and "Cabins" were added to the wildlife-watching special equipment section, and "Land leasing and ownership" was added to the wildlife-watching expenditures section.

5. Questions asking sportspersons if they participated as much as they wanted were added in 1996. If the sportspersons said no, they were asked why not.

6. The 1991 Survey included questions about participation in organized fishing competitions; anglers using bows and arrows, nets or seines, or spearfishing; hunters using pistols or handguns and target shooting in preparation for hunting. These questions were not asked in 1996.

7. The 1996 Survey included questions about catch and release fishing and persons with disabilities participating in wildlife-related recreation. These questions were not part of the 1991 Survey.

8. The 1991 Survey included questions about average distance traveled to recreation sites. These questions were not included in the 1996 Survey.

9. The 1996 Survey included questions about the last trip the respondent took. Included were questions about the type of trip, where the activity took place, and the distance and direction to the site visited. These questions were not asked in 1991.

10. The 1991 Survey collected data on hunting, fishing, and wildlife watching by U.S. residents in Canada. The 1996 Survey collected data on fishing and wildlife-watching by U.S. residents in Canada.

Section II. Important instrument changes in the 2001 Survey

1. The 1991 and 1996 single race category "Asian or Pacific Islander" was changed to two categories "Asian" and "Native Hawaiian or Other Pacific Islander". In 1991 and 1996, the respondent was required to pick only one category, while in 2001 the respondent could pick any combination of categories. The next question stipulated that the respondent could only be identified with one category and then asked what that category was.

2. The 1991 and 1996 land leasing and ownership sections asked the respondent to combine the two types of land use into one and give total acreage and expenditures. In 2001, the two types of land use were explored separately.

3. The 1991 and 1996 wildlife-watching sections included questions on birdwatching for around-the-home participants only. The 2001 Survey added a question on birdwatching for away-from-home participants. Also, questions on the use of birding life lists and how many species the respondent can identify were added.

4. "Recreational vehicles" was added to the sportspersons and wildlife-watchers special equipment section. "House trailer" was added to the sportspersons special equipment section.

5. Total personal income was asked in the detailed phase of the 1996 Survey. This was changed to total

Table C-2. Anglers and Hunters by Census Division: 1991, 1996, 2001, 2006, and 2011

(U.S. population 16 years old and older. Numbers in thousands)

Area and sportsperson	1991		1996		2001		2006		2011	
	Number	Percent	Number	Percent	Number	Percent	Number	Percent	Number	Percent
UNITED STATES										
Total population	189,964	100	201,472	100	212,298	100	229,245	100	239,313	100
Sportspersons	39,979	21	39,694	20	37,805	18	33,916	15	37,397	16
Anglers	35,578	19	35,246	17	34,067	16	29,952	13	33,112	14
Hunters	14,063	7	13,975	7	13,034	6	12,510	5	13,674	6
New England										
Total population	10,180	100	10,306	100	10,575	100	11,233	100	11,593	100
Sportspersons	1,658	16	1,673	16	1,504	14	1,353	12	1,441	12
Anglers	1,545	15	1,520	15	1,402	13	1,246	11	1,355	12
Hunters	444	4	465	5	386	4	374	3	420	4
Middle Atlantic										
Total population	29,216	100	29,371	100	29,806	100	31,518	100	32,392	100
Sportspersons	4,508	15	4,192	14	3,810	13	3,214	10	3,966	12
Anglers	3,871	13	3,627	12	3,250	11	2,550	8	3,496	11
Hunters	1,746	6	1,453	5	1,633	5	1,520	5	1,558	5
East North Central										
Total population	32,188	100	33,121	100	34,082	100	35,609	100	36,199	100
Sportspersons	7,202	22	6,912	21	6,400	19	5,975	17	6,766	19
Anglers	6,264	19	6,006	18	5,655	17	5,190	15	5,861	16
Hunters	2,789	9	2,712	8	2,421	7	2,376	7	2,688	7
West North Central										
Total population	13,504	100	13,875	100	14,430	100	15,458	100	15,860	100
Sportspersons	4,143	31	3,977	29	4,239	29	3,836	25	3,980	25
Anglers	3,647	27	3,416	25	3,836	27	3,284	21	3,591	23
Hunters	1,709	13	1,917	14	1,710	12	1,779	12	1,661	10
South Atlantic										
Total population	33,682	100	36,776	100	39,286	100	43,965	100	46,417	100
Sportspersons	6,996	21	7,282	20	6,957	18	6,633	15	6,749	15
Anglers	6,441	19	6,636	18	6,451	16	6,116	14	6,163	13
Hunters	2,083	6	2,050	6	1,875	5	1,884	4	1,870	4
East South Central										
Total population	11,667	100	12,459	100	12,976	100	13,722	100	14,206	100
Sportspersons	2,984	26	2,907	23	2,865	22	2,689	20	3,010	21
Anglers	2,635	23	2,514	20	2,543	20	2,436	18	2,444	17
Hunters	1,279	11	1,301	10	1,164	9	1,101	8	1,531	11
West South Central										
Total population	19,926	100	21,811	100	23,337	100	25,407	100	27,195	100
Sportspersons	5,125	26	5,093	23	4,924	21	4,499	18	4,855	18
Anglers	4,592	23	4,616	21	4,375	19	3,952	16	4,298	16
Hunters	1,843	9	1,812	8	1,988	9	1,810	7	1,909	7
Mountain										
Total population	10,092	100	11,966	100	13,308	100	15,651	100	17,013	100
Sportspersons	2,488	25	2,761	23	2,757	21	2,372	15	2,976	17
Anglers	2,079	21	2,411	20	2,443	18	2,084	13	2,586	15
Hunters	1,069	11	1,061	9	1,020	8	868	6	1,043	6
Pacific										
Total population	29,508	100	31,787	100	34,498	100	36,681	100	38,438	100
Sportspersons	4,875	17	4,897	15	4,349	13	3,345	9	3,654	10
Anglers	4,505	15	4,501	14	4,111	12	3,094	8	3,319	9
Hunters	1,101	4	1,203	4	837	2	798	2	996	3

Table C-3. Wildlife-Watching Participants by Census Division: 1991, 1996, 2001, 2006, and 2011

(U.S. population 16 years old and older. Numbers in thousands)

Area and wildlife watcher	1991 Number	1991 Percent	1996 Number	1996 Percent	2001 Number	2001 Percent	2006 Number	2006 Percent	2011 Number	2011 Percent
UNITED STATES										
Total population	189,964	100	201,472	100	212,298	100	229,245	100	239,313	100
Total wildlife watchers	76,111	40	62,868	31	66,105	31	71,132	31	71,776	30
Away from home	29,999	16	23,652	12	21,823	10	22,977	10	22,496	9
Around the home	73,904	39	60,751	30	62,928	30	67,756	30	68,598	29
New England										
Total population	10,180	100	10,306	100	10,575	100	11,233	100	11,593	100
Total wildlife watchers	4,598	45	3,710	36	3,875	37	4,489	40	3,954	34
Away from home	1,856	18	1,443	14	1,155	11	1,340	12	1,187	10
Around the home	4,544	45	3,586	35	3,765	36	4,310	38	3,858	33
Middle Atlantic										
Total population	29,216	100	29,371	100	29,806	100	31,518	100	32,392	100
Total wildlife watchers	10,556	36	8,185	28	8,740	29	8,723	28	9,118	28
Away from home	4,166	14	2,960	10	2,849	10	2,729	9	2,561	8
Around the home	10,282	35	8,023	27	8,452	28	8,451	27	8,744	27
East North Central										
Total population	32,188	100	33,121	100	34,082	100	35,609	100	36,199	100
Total wildlife watchers	14,511	45	11,731	35	11,631	34	12,215	34	12,840	35
Away from home	5,572	17	4,501	14	3,571	10	3,792	11	3,168	9
Around the home	14,175	44	11,297	34	11,196	33	11,845	33	12,492	35
West North Central										
Total population	13,504	100	13,875	100	14,430	100	15,458	100	15,860	100
Total wildlife watchers	6,924	51	5,089	37	6,206	43	6,741	44	5,479	35
Away from home	2,654	20	1,927	14	2,059	14	2,163	14	1,783	11
Around the home	6,722	50	4,900	35	5,938	41	6,447	42	5,201	33
South Atlantic										
Total population	33,682	100	36,776	100	39,286	100	43,965	100	46,417	100
Total wildlife watchers	13,047	39	11,252	31	11,395	29	12,862	29	13,315	29
Away from home	4,450	13	3,992	11	3,469	9	3,208	7	4,393	9
Around the home	12,813	38	10,964	30	10,911	28	12,432	28	12,767	28
East South Central										
Total population	11,667	100	12,459	100	12,976	100	13,722	100	14,206	100
Total wildlife watchers	4,864	42	3,904	31	4,514	35	4,931	36	4,663	33
Away from home	1,592	14	1,118	9	1,086	8	1,758	13	1,456	10
Around the home	4,765	41	3,795	30	4,390	34	4,683	34	4,394	31
West South Central										
Total population	19,926	100	21,811	100	23,337	100	25,407	100	27,195	100
Total wildlife watchers	7,035	35	5,933	27	5,747	25	6,764	27	7,164	26
Away from home	2,459	12	2,096	10	1,822	8	2,127	8	1,728	6
Around the home	6,817	34	5,773	26	5,490	24	6,319	25	7,087	26
Mountain										
Total population	10,092	100	11,966	100	13,308	100	15,651	100	17,013	100
Total wildlife watchers	4,437	44	4,099	34	4,619	35	4,968	32	5,189	30
Away from home	2,215	22	1,967	16	2,019	15	2,004	13	2,230	13
Around the home	4,145	41	3,855	32	4,282	32	4,605	29	4,716	28
Pacific										
Total population	29,508	100	31,787	100	34,498	100	36,681	100	38,438	100
Total wildlife watchers	10,139	34	8,966	28	9,377	27	9,439	26	10,054	26
Away from home	5,035	17	3,648	11	3,793	11	3,856	11	3,990	10
Around the home	9,641	33	8,558	27	8,504	25	8,664	24	9,337	24

household income in the 2001 Survey.

6. A question was added to the trip-related expenditures section to ascertain how much of the total was spent in the respondent's state of residence when the respondent participated in hunting, fishing, or wildlife watching out-of-state.

7. Boating questions were added to the fishing section. The respondent was asked about the extent of boat usage for the three types of fishing.

8. The 1996 Survey included questions about the months around-the-home wildlife watchers fed birds. These questions were not repeated in the 2001 Survey.

9. The contingent valuation sections of the three types of wildlife-related recreation were altered, using an open-ended question format instead of 1996's dichotomous choice format.

Section III. Important instrument changes in the 2006 Survey

1. A series of boating questions was added. The new questions dealt with anglers using motorboats and/or nonmotorboats, length of boat used most often, distance to boat launch used most often, needed improvements to facilities at the launch, whether or not the respondent completed a boating safety course, who the boater fished with most often, and the source and type of information the boater used for his or her fishing.

2. Questions regarding catch and release fishing were added. They were whether or not the respondent caught and released fish and, if so, the percent of fish released.

3. The proportion of hunting done with a rifle or shotgun, as contrasted with muzzleloader or archery equipment, was asked.

4. In the contingent valuation section, where the value of wildlife-related recreation was determined, two quality-variable questions were added: the average length of certain fish caught and whether a deer, elk, or moose was killed. Plus the

economic evaluation bid questions were rephrased, from "What is the most your [species] hunting in [State name] could have cost you per trip last year before you would NOT have gone [species] hunting at all in 2001, not even one trip, because it would have been too expensive?", for the hunters, for example, to "What is the cost that would have prevented you from taking even one such trip in 2006? In other words, if the trip cost was below this amount, you would have gone [species] hunting in [State name], but if the trip cost was above this amount, you would not have gone."

5. Questions concerning hunting, fishing, or wildlife watching in other countries were taken out of the Survey.

6. Questions about the reasons for not going hunting or fishing, or not going as much as expected, were deleted.

7. Disability of participants questions were taken out.

8. Determination of the types of sites for wildlife watching was discontinued.

9. The birding questions regarding the use of birding life lists and the ability to identify birds based on their sight or sounds were deleted.

10. Public transportation costs were divided into two sections, "public transportation by airplane" and "other public transportation, including trains, buses, and car rentals, etc.".

Section IV. Important instrument changes in the 2011 Survey

1. The series of boating questions added in 2006 was deleted.

2. Questions about target shooting and the usage of a shooting range in preparation for hunting were added. The types of weapon used at the shooting range were quantified.

3. Questions about plantings expenditures for the purpose of hunting were added.

4. "Feral pig" was recategorized from big game to other animals for all states except Hawaii.

5. "Ptarmigan" was included as its own small game category, instead of lumped in "other."

6. In previous Surveys, "Moose" was included as its own category only for Alaska. For 2011, "Moose" was included as its own big game category, instead of lumped in "other," for all fifty states.

7. In previous Surveys, "Wolf" was included as its own category only for Alaska. For 2011, "Wolf" was included as its own other animal category, instead of lumped in "other," for all fifty states.

8. The household income categories were modified. The top categories were changed from "$100,000 or more" to "$100,000 to $149,999" and "$150,000 or more."

9. The "Steelhead" category was deleted from the saltwater fish species section, with the idea that it would be included in "other."

10. The 2006 around-the-home wildlife-watching category that quantified visitors of "public parks or areas" was rewritten to wildlife watching at "parks or natural areas." This change was to make clear that respondents should include recreating at quasi-governmental and private areas.

11. The 2006 wildlife watching equipment category "Film and developing" was rewritten to "Film and photo processing."

1955 to 1985 Significant Methodological Differences

1955 to 1970 Surveys

The 1955 to 1970 Surveys included only substantial participants. Substantial participants were defined as people who participated at least three days and/or spent at least $5 (the 1955–1965 Surveys) or $7.50 (the 1970 Survey) during the surveyed year. Under most circumstances, the Surveys may be compared for totals, but the effects of differences should be considered when comparing the details of the Surveys.

The 1960, 1965, and 1970 Surveys differed from the 1955 National Survey in classification of expenditures as outlined below:

1. Alaska and Hawaii were not included in the 1955 Survey.

2. Expenditure categories were more detailed in 1970 than in earlier Surveys.

3. The 1960 to 1970 classification of some expenditures differs from the 1955 Survey in the following respects:

   a. "Boats and boat motors" shown under "auxiliary equipment" were included in "equipment, other" in 1955.

   b. "Entrance and other privilege fees" asked separately were included in "trip expenditures, other" in 1955.

   c. "Snacks and refreshments" not included with "food" expenditures in the 1960 to 1970 reports were under "trip expenditures, other" in 1955.

   d. Starting in 1960, expenditures on equipment, magazines, club dues, licenses, and similar items were classified by the one sport activity for which expenditures were chiefly made. In 1955, these expenditures were evenly divided among all the activities in which the sportsperson took part.

   e. Compared with 1955, the 1960 to 1970 Surveys reported fewer expenditures within the "other" category because selected items were transferred to more appropriate categories.

   f. Expenditures on alcoholic beverages were reported separately in the 1970 Survey.

4. The number of waterfowl hunters in the 1970 Survey is not comparable with those reported in the 1960 and 1965 Surveys. In 1960 and 1965, respondent sportspersons were not included in the waterfowl hunter total if they reported that they went waterfowl hunting but did not take the trip chiefly to hunt waterfowl. In 1970, all respondents who reported that they had hunted waterfowl during 1970, regardless of trip purpose, were included in the total. The number of hunters who did not take trips chiefly to hunt waterfowl in 1970 was 1,054,000.

1975 Survey

In contrast to previous Surveys which covered substantial participants 12 years old and older, the 1975 Survey based all the estimates on responses from individuals 9 years of age and older and did not select respondents based upon substantial participation as defined above. As a result, individuals who participated fewer than three days or spent less than $7.50 on hunting or fishing were included in the estimates of participants, days of activity, and expenditures.

Categories of hunting and fishing expenditures differed from the previous four Surveys in that only major categories were reported. For example, hunting equipment expenditures were not further delineated by subcategory. Similarly, no detail was provided within the category of fishing equipment expenditures. Expenses for items such as daily entrance fees, magazines, club dues, and dogs were categorized as "other" in the 1975 report.

In addition to the above differences, the 1975 Survey gathered data on species sought for the favorite hunting and fishing activity. This data replaced the "chiefly" category where hunting or fishing was the primary purpose of the trip or day of activity. Data omitted in the 1975 Survey that were included in previous Surveys include the respondents' population density of residence, occupation, and level of education.

1980 to 1985 Surveys

The 1980 and 1985 Surveys were similar. Each measured participants, rather than substantial participants. Questions were incorporated into the 1980 and 1985 Survey questionnaires to facilitate the construction of categories of data for comparisons with earlier Surveys. The use of "chiefly" to delimit primary purpose appeared in the 1970 and prior Surveys, and its use was continued in the 1980 and 1985 Surveys. The expenditure categories in 1980 and 1985 are similar to the 1970 categories with the addition of fish finders, motor homes, and camper trucks as separate categories. The definition of fishing included the use of nets or seines and spearfishing. An extensive wildlife watching section was added in 1980, necessitating a separate detailed phase subsample.

As in the 1970 and 1975 Surveys, the 1980 and 1985 Surveys used a two-phase process to gather information from households and individuals. In the first phase, household respondents were asked to identify each participant six years of age and older who resided in their household. In comparison, the 1975 and 1970 Surveys screened households for participants who were nine years of age and older. In the second phase, the detailed interview phase, interviews were conducted in person for the 1985, 1980, and 1970 Surveys and were conducted by mail for the 1975 Survey. Participants were included in the detailed phase of the Survey if they were at least 12 years old in 1970, 9 years old in 1975, and 16 years old in 1980 and 1985. As a result, the population of hunters and anglers was more narrowly defined in 1980 and 1985. However, estimates of sportspersons 6 years old and older, 9 years old and older, and 12 years old and older, derived from the screening phase, are available for comparison with past Surveys.

Regional Trends

Section I. Most recent trends

This trends section covers the period from 1991 to 2011. The 1991, 1996, 2001, 2006, and 2011 Surveys used similar methodologies, making all published information for the five Surveys directly comparable.

Section II. Historical trends

This trends section covers the period from 1955 to 1985. The methodology of these Surveys differed (see above), but approximate correction factors were estimated.

Table C-4. Comparison of Major Findings of the National Surveys: 1955 to 1985

(U.S. population 12 years old and older. Numbers in thousands)

Sportspersons	1955	1960	1965	1970	1975	1980	1985
Total sportspersons	24,917	30,435	32,881	36,277	45,773	46,966	49,827
Anglers	20,813	25,323	28,348	33,158	41,299	41,873	45,345
Freshwater	18,420	21,677	23,962	29,363	36,599	35,782	39,122
Saltwater	4,557	6,292	8,305	9,460	13,738	11,972	12,893
Hunters	11,784	14,637	13,583	14,336	17,094	16,758	16,340
Small game	9,822	12,105	10,576	11,671	14,182	12,496	11,130
Big game	4,414	6,277	6,566	7,774	11,037	11,047	12,576
Waterfowl	1,986	1,955	1,650	2,894	4,284	3,177	3,201
Expenditures[1]	11,401,464	13,948,974	14,991,502	19,618,548	33,398,677	34,517,421	42,058,860
Anglers	7,655,522	9,743,971	9,952,411	13,699,311	23,498,506	23,387,469	28,585,686
Freshwater	5,700,187	7,476,454	7,231,851	10,315,966	17,333,212	16,663,239	18,942,060
Saltwater	1,955,336	2,267,512	2,720,574	3,383,345	6,165,294	5,581,976	7,191,387
Hunters	3,745,942	4,204,997	3,814,303	5,919,236	9,900,171	10,812,058	10,256,668
Small game	1,975,707	2,629,360	2,093,137	2,612,390	4,525,942	3,335,852	2,342,860
Big game	1,295,357	1,251,800	1,424,711	2,631,532	4,238,341	5,638,395	5,345,606
Waterfowl	474,878	323,840	296,452	675,315	1,135,889	766,033	783,315
Days	566,870	658,308	708,578	909,876	1,459,551	1,300,983	1,415,379
Fishing	397,447	465,769	522,759	706,187	1,058,075	952,420	1,064,986
Freshwater	338,826	385,167	426,922	592,494	890,576	788,392	895,027
Saltwater	58,621	80,602	95,837	113,694	167,499	164,040	171,055
Hunting	169,423	192,539	185,819	203,689	401,476	348,543	350,393
Small game	118,630	138,192	128,448	124,041	269,653	225,793	214,544
Big game	30,834	39,190	43,845	54,536	100,600	117,406	135,447
Waterfowl	19,959	15,158	13,526	25,113	31,223	26,179	25,933

[1] In 1985 dollars

Note: Methodological differences described in the text make the estimates in this table not comparable with the estimates in Tables C-2 and C-3

Table C-5. Anglers and Hunters by Census Division: 1955 to 1985

(U.S. population 12 years old and older. Numbers in thousands)

Year	Population Number	Population Percent	Sportsperson, fished or hunted Number	Sportsperson, fished or hunted Percent	Anglers Number	Anglers Percent	Hunters Number	Hunters Percent
UNITED STATES								
1955	118,366	100	24,917	21 1	20,813	17 6	11,784	10 0
1960	131,226	100	30,435	23 2	25,323	19 3	14,637	11 2
1965	141,928	100	32,881	23 2	28,348	20 0	13,585	9 6
1970	155,230	100	36,277	23 4	33,158	21 4	14,336	9 2
1975	171,860	100	45,773	26 6	41,299	24 0	17,094	9 9
1980	184,691	100	46,966	25 4	41,873	22 7	16,758	9 1
1985	195,659	100	49,827	25 5	45,345	23 2	16,340	8 4
New England								
1955	7,919	100	1,224	15 4	1,002	12 7	589	7 4
1960	8,349	100	1,368	16 4	1,205	14 4	517	6 2
1965	9,256	100	1,650	17 8	1,488	16 0	583	6 3
1970	8,652	100	1,579	18 3	1,430	16 5	582	6 7
1975	9,910	100	2,004	20 2	1,861	18 8	566	5 7
1980	10,205	100	1,974	19 3	1,788	17 5	572	5 6
1985	10,554	100	2,058	19 5	1,914	18 1	552	5 2
Middle Atlantic								
1955	24,869	100	3,539	14 2	2,811	11 3	1,608	6 5
1960	26,493	100	3,432	13 0	2,569	9 7	1,723	6 5
1965	27,346	100	3,602	13 2	2,760	10 1	1,631	6 0
1970	28,244	100	4,539	16 1	4,504	14 4	1,731	6 1
1975	30,449	100	5,919	19 4	5,097	16 7	2,096	6 9
1980	30,256	100	5,181	17 1	4,332	14 3	2,001	6 6
1985	31,099	100	5,565	17 9	4,820	15 5	1,972	6 3
East North Central								
1955	25,733	100	5,489	21 3	4,583	17 8	2,538	9 9
1960	26,833	100	6,316	32 5	5,317	19 8	2,985	11 1
1965	28,124	100	6,214	22 1	5,336	19 0	2,563	9 1
1970	31,550	100	7,284	23 1	6,699	21 2	2,812	8 9
1975	32,796	100	9,049	27 6	8,181	24 9	3,392	10 3
1980	33,526	100	8,725	26 0	7,891	23 5	2,955	8 8
1985	33,747	100	8,973	26 6	8,270	24 5	2,814	8 3
West North Central								
1955	9,201	100	2,913	31 7	2,346	25 5	1,534	16 7
1960	10,149	100	3,383	33 3	2,855	28 1	1,709	16 8
1965	11,681	100	3,678	31 5	3,226	27 6	1,620	13 9
1970	12,904	100	4,000	31 0	3,579	27 7	1,783	13 8
1975	13,564	100	4,524	33 3	4,089	30 1	1,863	13 7
1980	13,826	100	4,770	34 5	4,220	30 5	1,965	14 2
1985	14,137	100	5,140	36 4	4,681	33 1	1,971	13 9
South Atlantic								
1955	14,336	100	3,223	22 5	2,805	19 6	1,449	10 1
1960	17,798	100	4,423	24 9	3,695	20 8	2,045	11 5
1965	20,593	100	5,626	27 3	5,054	24 5	1,900	9 2
1970	23,539	100	5,461	23 2	5,129	21 8	1,904	8 1
1975	27,127	100	7,110	26 2	6,479	23 9	2,494	9 2
1980	30,512	100	7,769	25 5	7,086	23 2	2,444	8 0
1985	33,636	100	8,721	25 9	8,056	24 0	2,467	7 3
East South Central								
1955	7,959	100	1,963	24 7	1,665	20 9	989	12 4
1960	9,277	100	2,778	29 9	2,207	23 8	1,510	16 3
1965	9,652	100	2,587	26 8	2,201	22 8	1,294	13 4
1970	9,862	100	2,660	27 0	2,464	25 0	1,162	11 8
1975	10,798	100	3,007	27 8	2,689	24 9	1,355	12 5
1980	11,771	100	3,614	30 7	3,173	27 0	1,567	13 3
1985	12,364	100	3,671	29 7	3,308	26 8	1,441	11 7

See footnote at end of table

Table C-5. Anglers and Hunters by Census Division: 1955 to 1985—Continued

(U.S. population 12 years old and older. Numbers in thousands)

Year	Population		Sportsperson, fished or hunted		Anglers		Hunters	
	Number	Percent	Number	Percent	Number	Percent	Number	Percent
West South Central								
1955	10,250	100	2,560	25 0	2,237	21 8	1,165	11 4
1960	11,837	100	3,666	31 0	3,133	26 5	1,750	14 8
1965	12,724	100	3,713	29 2	3,278	25 8	1,571	12 3
1970	14,624	100	4,380	30 0	4,006	27 4	1,918	13 1
1975	16,628	100	5,781	34 8	5,267	31 7	2,563	15 4
1980	19,136	100	5,862	30 6	5,136	26 8	2,456	12 8
1985	21,184	100	6,418	30 3	5,704	26 9	2,572	12 1
Mountain								
1955	4,529	100	1,369	30 2	1,112	24 6	796	17 6
1960	5,222	100	1,646	31 5	1,372	26 3	1,120	21 4
1965	5,029	100	1,565	31 1	1,261	25 1	988	19 6
1970	5,656	100	2,044	36 1	1,769	31 3	980	17 3
1975	7,576	100	2,570	33 9	2,252	29 7	1,159	15 3
1980	9,160	100	2,903	31 7	2,500	27 3	1,268	13 8
1985	10,215	100	3,128	30 6	2,765	27 1	1,241	12 1
Pacific								
1955	13,570	100	2,637	19 4	2,252	16 6	1,116	8 2
1960	15,268	100	3,422	22 4	2,971	19 5	1,279	8 4
1965	17,523	100	4,246	24 2	3,744	21 4	1,433	8 2
1970	20,199	100	4,332	21 4	4,030	20 0	1,466	7 3
1975	23,012	100	5,811	25 2	5,386	23 4	1,607	7 0
1980	26,299	100	6,168	23 5	5,747	21 9	1,531	5 0
1985	38,725	100	6,154	21 4	5,829	20 3	1,310	4 6

Note: Methodological differences described in the text make the estimates in this table not comparable with the estimates in Tables C-2 and C-3

Appendix D

Appendix D.
Sample Design and Statistical Accuracy

This appendix is presented in two parts. The first part is the U.S. Census Bureau Source and Accuracy Statement. This statement describes the sampling design for the 2011 Survey and highlights the steps taken to produce estimates from the completed questionnaires. The statement explains the use of standard errors and confidence intervals. It also provides comprehensive information about errors characteristic of surveys and formulas and parameters to calculate an approximate standard error or confidence interval for each number published in this report. The second part, Tables D-1 through D-11, reports approximate standard errors and 95-percent confidence intervals for selected measures of participation and expenditures for wildlife-related recreation.

Source and Accuracy Statement for the *2011 National Survey of Fishing, Hunting, and Wildlife-Associated Recreation*

SOURCE OF DATA

The estimates in this report are based on data collected in the *2011 National Survey of Fishing, Hunting, and Wildlife-Associated Recreation* (FHWAR) conducted by the Census Bureau and sponsored by the U.S. Fish and Wildlife Service.

The eligible universe for the FHWAR is the civilian noninstitutionalized and nonbarrack military population living in the United States. The institutionalized population, which is excluded from the population universe, is composed primarily of the population in correctional institutions and nursing homes (98 percent of the 4 million institutionalized people in Census 2010).

The 2011 FHWAR was designed to provide state-level estimates of the

number of participants in recreational hunting and fishing and in wildlife watching activities (e.g., wildlife observation). Information was collected on the number of participants, where and how often they participated, the type of wildlife encountered, and the amounts of money spent on wildlife-related recreation.

The FHWAR was conducted in two stages: an initial screening of households to identify likely sportspersons and wildlife-watching participants and a series of follow-up interviews of selected persons to collect detailed data about their wildlife-related recreation during 2011.

SAMPLE DESIGN

The 2011 FHWAR sample was selected from the Census Bureau's master address file (MAF).

The FHWAR is a multistage probability sample, with coverage in all 50 states and the District of Columbia. In the first stage of the sampling process, primary sampling units (PSUs) are selected for sample. The PSUs are defined to correspond to the Office of Management and Budget definitions of Core Based Statistical Area definitions and to improve efficiency in field operations. The United States is divided into 2,025 PSUs. These PSUs are grouped into 824 strata. Within each stratum, a single PSU is chosen for the sample, with its probability of selection proportional to its population as of the 2000 decennial census. This PSU represents the entire stratum from which it was selected. In the case of strata consisting of only one PSU, the PSU is chosen with certainty.

Within the selected PSUs, the FHWAR sample was selected from the MAF.

FHWAR Screening Sample

The total screening sample in the United States consisted of **48,600** households. Interviewing for the screen was conducted during April, May, and June 2011. Due to a high noncontact rate, an additional personal visit screening interview, for a subsample of noncontact cases, occurred again in February, March, April, or May 2012. Of all housing units in sample, about **42,800** were determined to be eligible for interview. Interviewers obtained interviews at **30,400** of these units for a national response rate of **71** percent.[1] The national weighted response rate was **77** percent. The interviewers asked screening questions for all household members 6 years old and older. Noninterviews occur when the occupants are not found at home after repeated calls or are unavailable for some other reason.

Data for the FHWAR sportspersons sample and wildlife-watchers sample were collected in three waves.[2] The first wave started in April 2011, the second in September 2011, and the third in January 2012. In the sportspersons sample, all persons who hunted or fished in 2011 by the time of the screening interview were interviewed in the first wave. The remaining sportspersons in sample were interviewed in the second wave. The reference period was the preceding 4 months for waves 1 and 2. In wave 3, the reference period was either 4, 8, or 12 months depending on when the sample person was first interviewed.

---

[1] Response rates are calculated by using APPOR's RR2 formula

[2] The sample cases selected due to high noncontact rates were only interviewed once They received a screener and, if they had some form of participation, a detailed questionnaire These participants did not get three waves of interviewing The reference period for these sampled cases was between 13 and 16 months

Detailed Samples

Two independent detailed samples were chosen from the FHWAR screening sample. One consisted of sportspersons (people who hunt or fish) and the other of wildlife watchers (people who observe, photograph, or feed wildlife).

A. Sportspersons

The Census Bureau selected the detailed samples based on information reported during the screening phase. Based on information collected from the household respondent, every person 16 years old and older in the FHWAR screening sample was assigned to a sportspersons stratum. The criteria for the strata included time devoted to hunting or fishing in previous years, participation in hunting or fishing in 2011 by the time of the screening interview, and intentions to participate in hunting and fishing activities during the remainder of 2011.[3] The four sportspersons categories were:

1. *Active*—a person who had already participated in hunting or fishing in 2011 at the time of the screener interview.

2. *Likely*—a person who had not participated in 2011 at the time of the screener, but had participated in 2010 OR was likely to participate in 2011.

3. *Inactive*—a person who had not participated in 2010 or 2011 AND was somewhat unlikely to participate in 2011.

4. *Nonparticipant*—a person who had not participated in 2010 or 2011 AND was very unlikely to participate in 2011.

Due to the high noncontact rates in wave 1, all persons in the active, likely, and inactive groups were selected with certainty.

Active sportspersons were given the detailed interview twice—at the time of the screening interview (in April, May, or June 2011) and

again in January or February 2012.[4] Likely sportspersons and inactive sportspersons were also interviewed twice—first in September or October 2011, then in January or February 2012. Persons in the nonparticipant group were not eligible for a detailed interview. About **16,400** persons were designated for interviews in the United States. The detailed sportspersons sample sizes varied by state to get reliable state-level estimates. During each interview period, about **31** percent of the designated persons were not found at home or were unavailable for some other reason. Overall, about **11,300** detailed sportspersons interviews were completed at a response rate of **69** percent.

B. Wildlife Watchers

The wildlife-watching detailed sample was also selected based on information reported during the screening phase. Based on information collected from the household respondent, every person 16 years old and older was assigned to a stratum. The criteria for the strata included time devoted to wildlife-watching activities in previous years, participation in wildlife-watching activities in 2011 by the time of the screening interview, and intentions to participate in wildlife-watching activities during the remainder of 2011. The five wildlife-watching categories were:

1. *Active*—a person who had already participated in 2011 at the time of the screening interview.

2. *Avid*—a person who had not yet participated in 2011, but in 2010 had taken trips to participate in wildlife-watching activities for 21 or more days or had spent $300 or more.

3. *Average*—a person who had not yet participated in 2011, but in 2010 had taken trips to wildlife watch for less than 21 days and had spent less than $300 OR had not participated in wildlife-watching activities but was very

likely to in the remainder of 2011.

4. *Infrequent*—a person who had not participated in 2010 or 2011, but was somewhat likely or somewhat unlikely to participate in the remainder of 2011.

5. *Nonparticipant*—a person who had not participated in 2010 or 2011 AND was very unlikely to participate during the remainder of 2011.

Persons were selected for the detailed sample based on these groupings, but persons in the nonparticipant group were not eligible for a detailed interview.

A subsample of each of the other groups was selected to receive a detailed interview with the chance of selection diminishing as the likelihood of participation diminished. Wildlife-watching participants were given the detailed interview twice.[5] Some received their first detailed interview at the same time as the screening interview (in April, May, or June 2011). The rest received their first detailed interview in September or October 2011. All wildlife-watching participants received their second interview in January or February 2012. Some respondents were given the screener and detailed interview in February, March, April, or May 2012. About **13,900** persons were designated for interviews in the United States. The detailed wildlife-watching sample sizes varied by state to get reliable state-level estimates. During each interview period, about **33** percent of the designated persons were not found at home or were unavailable for some other reason. Overall, about **9,300** detailed wildlife watcher interviews were completed at a response rate of **67** percent.

ESTIMATION PROCEDURE

Several stages of adjustments were used to derive the final 2011 FHWAR person weights. A brief description of the major components of the weights is given below. All statistics for the popu-

---

[3] The sample cases selected due to high noncontact rates were not assigned a sportsperson stratum

[4] The sample cases selected due to high noncontact rates were given the detailed sportsperson interview once

[5] The sample cases selected due to high noncontact rates were given the detailed wildlife-watching interview once

lation 6 to 15 years of age were derived from the screening interview. Statistics for the population 16 years old and older come from both the screening and detailed interviews. Estimates that come from the screening sample are presented in Appendix B.

A. Screening Sample

Every interviewed person in the screening sample received a screening weight that was the product of the following factors:

1. *Base Weight*. The base weight is the inverse of the household's probability of selection.

2. *Household Noninterview Adjustment*. The noninterview adjustment inflates the weight assigned to interviewed households to account for households eligible for interview but for which no interview was obtained.

3. *First-Stage Adjustment*. The 824 areas designated for our samples were selected from 2,025 such areas of the United States. Some sample areas represent only themselves and are referred to as self-representing. The remaining areas represent other areas similar in selected characteristics and are thus designated non-self-representing. The first-stage factor reduces the component of variation arising from sampling the non-self-representing areas.

4. *Second-Stage Adjustment*. This adjustment brings the estimates of the total population into agreement with census-based estimates of the civilian noninstitutionalized and nonbarrack military populations for each state.

B. Sportspersons Sample

Every interviewed person in the sportspersons detailed sample received a weight that was the product of the following factors:

1. *Screening Weight*. This is the person's final weight from the screening sample.

2. *Sportspersons Stratum Adjustment*. This factor inflates the weights of persons selected for the detailed sample to account for the subsampling done within each sportsperson stratum.

3. *Sportspersons Noninterview Adjustment*. This factor adjusts the weights of the interviewed sportspersons to account for sportspersons selected for the detailed sample for whom no interview was obtained. A person was considered a noninterview if he or she was not interviewed in the third wave of interviewing.

4. *Sportspersons Ratio Adjustment Factor*. This is a ratio adjustment of the detailed sample to the screening sample within the sportspersons sampling strata. This adjustment brings the population estimates of persons aged 16 years old and older from the detailed sample into agreement with the same estimates from the screening sample, which was a much larger sample.

C. Wildlife-Watchers Sample

Every interviewed person in the wildlife-watchers detailed sample received a weight that was the product of the following factors:

1. *Screening Weight*. This is the person's final weight from the screening sample.

2. *Wildlife-Watchers Stratum Adjustment*. This factor inflates the weights of persons selected for the detailed sample to account for the subsampling done within each wildlife watcher stratum.

3. *Wildlife-Watchers Noninterview Adjustment*. This factor adjusts the weights of the interviewed wildlife-watching participants to account for wildlife watchers selected for the detailed sample for whom no interview was obtained. A person was considered a noninterview if he or she was not interviewed in the third wave of interviewing.

4. *Wildlife-Watchers Ratio Adjustment Factor*. This is a ratio adjustment of the detailed sample to the screening sample within the wildlife-watchers sampling strata. This adjustment brings the population estimates of persons aged 16 years old and older from the detailed sample into agreement with the same estimates from the screening sample, which was a much larger sample.

ACCURACY OF THE ESTIMATES

A sample survey estimate has two types of error: sampling and nonsampling. The accuracy of an estimate depends on both types of error. The nature of the sampling error is known given the survey design; the full extent of the nonsampling error is unknown.

NONSAMPLING ERROR

For a given estimator, the difference between the estimate that would result if the sample were to include the entire population and the true population value being estimated is known as nonsampling error. There are several sources of nonsampling error that may occur during the development or execution of the survey. It can occur because of circumstances created by the interviewer, the respondent, the survey instrument, or the way the data are collected and processed. For example, errors could occur because:

- The interviewer records the wrong answer, the respondent provides incorrect information, the respondent estimates the requested information, or an unclear survey question is misunderstood by the respondent (measurement error).

- Some individuals who should have been included in the survey frame were missed (coverage error).

- Responses are not collected from all those in the sample or the respondent is unwilling to provide information (nonresponse error).

- Values are estimated imprecisely for missing data (imputation error).

- Forms may be lost; data may be incorrectly keyed, coded, or recoded, etc. (processing error).

The Census Bureau employs quality control procedures throughout the production process, including the overall design of surveys, the wording of questions, and the review of the work of interviewers and coders to minimize these errors. Two types of nonsampling error that can be examined to a limited extent are nonresponse and undercoverage.

Nonresponse. The effect of nonresponse cannot be measured directly, but one indication of its potential effect is the nonresponse rate. For the FHWAR screener interview in the United States, the household-level nonresponse rate was 29 percent. The person-level nonresponse rate for the detailed sportsperson interview in the United States was an additional 31 percent and for the wildlife watchers it was 33 percent. Since the screener nonresponse rate is a household-level rate and the detailed interview nonresponse rate is a person-level rate, we cannot combine these rates to derive an overall nonresponse rate. Since it is unlikely the nonresponding households to the FHWAR have the same number of persons as the households successfully interviewed, combining these rates would result in an overestimate of the "true" person-level overall nonresponse rate for the detailed interviews.

Coverage. Overall screener undercoverage is estimated to be about 13 percent. Ratio estimation to independent population controls, as described previously, partially corrects for the bias due to survey undercoverage. However, biases exist in the estimates to the extent that missed persons in missed households or missed persons in interviewed households have different characteristics from those of interviewed persons in the same age group.

Comparability of Data. Data obtained from the 2011 FHWAR and other sources are not entirely comparable. This results from differences in interviewer training and experience and in differing survey processes. This is an example of nonsampling variability not reflected in the standard errors. Therefore, caution should be used when comparing results from different sources. (See Appendix C.)

A Nonsampling Error Warning. Since the full extent of the nonsampling error is unknown, one should be particularly careful when interpreting results based on small differences between estimates. The Census Bureau recommends that data users incorporate information about nonsampling errors into their analyses, as nonsampling error could impact the conclusions drawn from the results. Caution should also be used when interpreting results based on a relatively small number of cases. Summary measures (such as medians and percentage distributions) probably do not reveal useful information when computed on a subpopulation smaller than 90,000 for screener data, 100,000 for the detailed sportsperson data, and 235,000 for the wildlife-watchers data.

SAMPLING ERROR

Since the FHWAR estimates come from a sample, they may differ from figures from an enumeration of the entire population using the same questionnaires, instructions, and enumerators. For a given estimator, the difference between an estimate based on a sample and the estimate that would result if the sample were to include the entire population is known as sampling error. Standard errors, as calculated by methods described in "Standard Errors and Their Use," are primarily measures of the magnitude of sampling error. However, they may include some nonsampling error.

Standard Errors and Their Use. The sample estimate and its standard error enable one to construct a confidence interval. A confidence interval is a range that has a known probability of including the average result of all possible samples. For example, if all possible samples were surveyed under essentially the same general conditions and using the same sample design, and if an estimate and its standard error were calculated from each sample, then approximately 95 percent of the intervals from 1.96 standard errors below the estimate to 1.96 standard errors above the estimate would include the average result of all possible samples. A particular confidence interval may or may not contain the average estimate derived from all possible samples. However, one can say with specified confidence that the interval includes the average estimate calculated from all possible samples. Standard errors may also be used to perform hypothesis testing, a procedure for distinguishing between population parameters using sample estimates. The most common type of hypothesis is that the population parameters are different. An example would be comparing the proportion of anglers to the proportion of hunters. Tests may be performed at various levels of significance. A significance level is the probability of concluding that the characteristics are different when, in fact, they are the same. For example, to conclude that two characteristics are different at the 0.05 level of significance, the absolute value of the estimated difference between characteristics must be greater than or equal to 1.96 times the standard error of the difference. This report uses 95-percent confidence intervals and 0.05 level of significance to determine statistical validity. Consult standard statistical textbooks for alternative criteria.

Estimating Standard Errors. The Census Bureau uses replication methods to estimate the standard errors of FHWAR estimates. These methods primarily measure the magnitude of sampling error. However, they do measure some effects of nonsampling error as well. They do not measure systematic biases in the data associated with nonsampling error. Bias is the average over all possible samples of the differences between the sample estimates and the true value.

Generalized Variance Parameters. While it is possible to compute and present an estimate of the standard error based on the survey data for each estimate in a report, there are a number of reasons why this is not done. A presentation of the individual standard errors would be of limited use, since one could not possibly predict all of the combinations of results that may be of interest to data users. Additionally, data users have access to FHWAR microdata files, and it is impossible to compute in advance the standard error for every estimate one might obtain from those data sets. Moreover, variance estimates are based on sample data and have variances of their own. Therefore, some methods of stabilizing these estimates of variance, for example, by generalizing or averaging over time, may be used to improve their reliability. Experience has shown that certain groups of estimates have similar relationships between their variances and expected values. Modeling or generalizing may provide more stable variance estimates by taking advantage of these similarities. The generalized variance function is a simple model that expresses the variance as a function of the expected value of the survey estimate. The parameters of the generalized variance function are estimated using direct replicate variances. These generalized variance parameters provide a relatively easy method to obtain approximate standard errors for numerous characteristics. Table D-5 provides the generalized variance parameters for FHWAR data. Methods for using the parameters to calculate standard errors of various estimates are given in the next sections.

Standard Errors of Estimated Numbers The approximate standard error, s_x, of an estimated number shown in this report can be obtained using the following formulas. Formula (1) is used to calculate the standard errors of levels of sportspersons, anglers, and wildlife watchers.

$$s_x = \sqrt{ax^2 + bx} \tag{1}$$

Here, x is the size of the estimate and a and b are the parameters in the tables associated with the particular characteristic.

Formula (2) is used for standard errors of aggregates, i e trips days, and expenditures.

$$s_x = \sqrt{ax^2 + bx + \frac{cx^2}{y}} \tag{2}$$

Here, x is again the size of the estimate; y is the base of the estimate; and a, b, and c are the parameters in the tables associated with the particular characteristic.

Illustration of the Computation of the Standard Error of an Estimated Number

Suppose there were an estimated 37,397,000 persons age 16 years old and older who either fished or hunted in the United States in 2011. Using formula (1) with the parameters $a = -0 000070$ and $b = 16,823$ from table D 5, the approximate standard error of the estimated number of 37,397,000 sportspersons age 16 years old and older is

$$s_x = \sqrt{-0.000070 * 37,397,000^2 + 16,823 * 37,397,000} = 728,857$$

The 95-percent confidence interval for the estimated number of sportspersons 16 years old and older is from 35,968,000 to 38,826,000 i e., 37,397,000 ± 1.96 x 728,857 Therefore, a conclusion that the average estimate derived from all possible samples lies within a range computed in this way would be correct for roughly 95 percent of all possible samples.

Suppose there were an estimated 13,674,000 hunters age 16 years old and older who engaged in 281,884,000 days of participation in 2011. Using formula (2) with the parameters $a = -0.000284$, $b = -127,863$, and $c = 46,699$ from table D-5, the approximate standard error on 281,884,000 estimated days on an estimated base of 13,674,000 hunters is

$$s_x = \sqrt{-0.000284 * 281,884,000^2 - 127,863 * 281,884,000 + \frac{46,699 * 281,884,000^2}{13,674,000}} = 14,586,000$$

The 95-percent confidence interval on the estimate of 281,884,000 days is from 253,295,000 to 310,473,000, i.e., 281,884,000 ± 1.96 x 14,586,000. Again, a conclusion that the average estimate derived from all possible samples lies within a range computed in this way would be correct for roughly 95 percent of all possible samples.

Standard Errors of Estimated Percentages. The reliability of an estimated percentage, computed using sample data for both numerator and denominator, depends on the size of the percentage and its base Estimated percentages are relatively more reliable than the corresponding estimates of the numerators of the percentages, particularly if the percentages are 50 percent or more. When the numerator and the denominator of the percentage are in different categories, use the parameter in the tables indicated by the numerator.

The approximate standard error, $s_{x,p}$, can be obtained by use of the formula

$$s_{x,p} = \sqrt{\frac{bp(100-p)}{x}} \tag{3}$$

Here, x is the total number of sportspersons, hunters, etc., which is the base of the percentage; p is the percentage ; and b is the parameter in the tables associated with the characteristic in the numerator of the percentage.

Illustration of the Computation of the Standard Error of an Estimated Percentage

Suppose there were an estimated 13,674,000 hunters age 16 years old and older of whom 18.9 percent hunted migratory birds. From table D-5, the appropriate b parameter is 15,798. Using formula (3), the approximate standard error on the estimate of 18.9 percent is

$$s_{x,p} = \sqrt{\frac{15,798 * 18.9 * (100 - 18.9)}{13,674,000}} = 1.33$$

Consequently, the 95-percent confidence interval for the estimate percentage of migratory bird hunters 16 years old and older is from 16.3 percent to 21.5 percent, i.e., $18.9 \pm 1.96 \times 1.33$.

Standard Error of a Difference. The standard error of the difference between two sample estimates is approximately equal to

$$s_{x-y} = \sqrt{s_x^2 + s_y^2} \tag{4}$$

where s_x and s_y are the standard errors of the estimates x and y. The estimates can be numbers, percentages, ratios, etc. This will represent the actual standard err r quite accurately for the difference between estimates of the same characteristic in two different areas, or for the difference between separate and uncorrelated characteristics in the same area. However, if there is a high positive (nega ive) c rrelation between the two characteristics, the formula will ove estimate (underestimate) the true standard error.

Illustration of the Computation of the Standard Error of a Difference

Suppose there were an estimated 13,608,000 females in the age range of 18-24 of whom 726,000 or 5.3 percent were sportspersons Similarly, suppo e there were an estimated 12,909,000 males in the same age ange of whom 2,160,000 or 16.7 percent were sportspersons The apparent difference between the pe centage of female and male sportspersons is 11.4 percent. Using formula (3) and the appropriate b parameter from table D-5, the approximate standard errors of 5.3 percent and 16.7 percent are 0.79 and .35, respectively Using formula (4), the approximate standard error of the estimated differ ence of 11 4 percent is

$$s_{x-y} = \sqrt{0.79^2 + 1.35^2} = 1.56$$

The 95-percent confidence interval on the difference be ween 18- to 24 year old female and male sportspersons is from 8 3 to 14.5, i.e., $11.4 \pm 1.96 \times 1.56$ Since the interval does not contain zero, we can conclude with 95 per ent confidence that the percentage of 18- to 24 year old female sportspersons is less than the percentage of 18- to 24-year-old male sportspersons

Standard Errors of Estimated Averages Certain mean values for sportspersons, anglers, etc., shown in the report were calculated as the ratio of two numbers For example, average days per angler is calculated as:

$$\frac{x}{y} = \frac{total\ days}{total\ anglers}$$

Standard errors for these averages may be approximated by the use of formula (5) below.

$$s_{x/y} = \frac{x}{y}\sqrt{\left[\frac{s_x}{x}\right]^2 + \left[\frac{s_y}{y}\right]^2 - 2r\frac{s_x s_y}{xy}} \tag{5}$$

In formula (5), r represents the correlation coefficient between the numerator and the denominator of the estimate In the above formula, use 0.7 as an estimate of r.

Illustration of the Computation of the Standard Error of an Estimated Average

Suppose that the estimated number of the average days per angler age 16 years old and older for all fishing was 16.7 days. Using formulas (1) and (2) above, we compute the standard error on total days, 553,841,000, and total anglers, 33,112,000, to be 20,329,124 and 693,033, respectively. The approximate standard error on the estimated average of 16.7 days is

$$s_{x/y} = \frac{553,841,000}{33,112,000} \sqrt{\left[\frac{20,329,124}{553,841,000}\right]^2 + \left[\frac{693,033}{33,112,000}\right]^2 - 2*0.7\frac{20,329,124*693,033}{553,841,000*33,112,000}} = 0.45$$

Therefore, the 95-percent confidence interval on the estimated average of 16.7 days is from 15.8 to 17.6, i.e., $16.7 \pm 1.96 \times 0.45$.

Table D–1. Approximate Standard Errors and 95-Percent Confidence Intervals for Selected Fishing Estimates: 2011

Anglers, days, and expenditures	Estimate	Standard error	Lower 95 percent	Upper 95 percent
ANGLERS (thousands)				
Total	**33,112**	**693**	**31,754**	**34,470**
Freshwater	27,547	640	26,292	28,802
Freshwater, except Great Lakes	27,060	635	25,815	28,305
Great Lakes	1,665	167	1,338	1,992
Saltwater	8,889	379	8,145	9,633
DAYS OF FISHING (thousands)				
Total	**553,841**	**20,329**	**513,996**	**593,686**
Freshwater	455,862	18,246	420,100	491,624
Freshwater, except Great Lakes	443,223	17,872	408,194	478,252
Great Lakes	19,661	2,989	13,803	25,519
Saltwater	99,474	6,523	86,689	112,259
Average Days Per Angler				
Total	**16.7**	**0.4**	**15 9**	**17.6**
Freshwater	16 5	0 5	15 6	17 5
Freshwater, except Great Lakes	16 4	0 5	15 4	17 3
Great Lakes	11 8	1 3	9 3	14 3
Saltwater	11 2	0 5	10 2	12 2
FISHING EXPENDITURES (thousands of dollars)				
Total	**41,788,936**	**2,152,483**	**37,570,069**	**46,007,803**
Freshwater	25,732,493	1,392,372	23,003,444	28,461,542
Freshwater, except Great Lakes	23,782,678	1,294,461	21,245,535	26,319,821
Great Lakes	1,867,098	321,774	1,236,420	2,497,776
Saltwater	10,266,904	842,314	8,615,969	11,917,839
Average Expenditure Per Angler (dollars)				
Total	**1,262**	**50**	**1,164**	**1,360**
Freshwater	934	39	858	1,010
Freshwater, except Great Lakes	879	36	807	950
Great Lakes	1,121	140	847	1,396
Saltwater	1,155	70	1,018	1,292

Table D–2. Approximate Standard Errors and 95-Percent Confidence Intervals for Selected Hunting Estimates: 2011

Hunters, days, and expenditures	Estimate	Standard error	Lower 95 percent	Upper 95 percent
HUNTERS (thousands)				
Total	**13,674**	**451**	**12,789**	**14,559**
Big game	11,570	417	10,753	12,387
Small game	4,506	264	3,988	5,024
Migratory birds	2,583	201	2,189	2,977
Other animals	2,168	184	1,807	2,529
DAYS OF HUNTING (thousands)				
Total	**281,884**	**14,587**	**253,293**	**310,475**
Big game	212,116	11,905	188,783	235,449
Small game	50,884	4,426	42,208	59,560
Migratory birds	23,263	2,580	18,206	28,320
Other animals	34,434	4,561	25,495	43,373
Average Days Per Hunter				
Total	**20.6**	**0.8**	**19.1**	**22.1**
Big game	18 3	0 7	16 9	19 8
Small game	11 3	0 7	9 9	12 7
Migratory birds	9 0	0 7	7 6	10 4
Other animals	15 9	1 5	12 9	18 8
HUNTING EXPENDITURES (thousands of dollars)				
Total	**33,702,017**	**2,434,362**	**28,930,668**	**38,473,366**
Big game	16,853,654	1,301,699	14,302,324	19,404,984
Small game	2,560,859	294,923	1,982,810	3,138,908
Migratory birds	1,808,030	258,986	1,300,418	2,315,642
Other animals	857,607	145,374	572,674	1,142,540
Average Expenditure Per Hunter (dollars)				
Total	**2,465**	**134**	**2,201**	**2,728**
Big game	1,457	85	1,291	1,622
Small game	568	48	473	663
Migratory birds	700	73	556	844
Other animals	396	50	298	493

Table D–3. Approximate Standard Errors and 95-Percent Confidence Intervals for Selected Fishing and Hunting Expenditure Estimates: 2011

(Thousands of dollars)

Expenditures	Estimate	Standard error	Lower 95 percent	Upper 95 percent
FISHING AND HUNTING EXPENDITURES				
Total	**89,761,524**	**4,417,179**	**81,103,853**	**98,419,195**
Trip-related, total	32,210,653	1,611,890	29,051,348	35,369,958
Food and lodging	11,592,622	600,321	10,415,993	12,769,251
Transportation	11,029,451	567,248	9,917,645	12,141,257
Other trip costs	9,588,580	507,643	8,593,600	10,583,560
Equipment, total	43,227,403	1,973,222	39,359,887	47,094,919
Fishing	6,179,132	346,771	5,499,462	6,858,802
Hunting	8,182,297	580,360	7,044,792	9,319,802
Auxiliary	3,736,648	266,416	3,214,473	4,258,823
Special	25,129,326	2,818,767	19,604,543	30,654,109
Other, total	13,620,867	653,752	12,339,513	14,902,221
Magazines, books, DVDs	319,781	26,571	267,702	371,860
Membership dues and contributions	1,122,787	107,185	912,705	1,332,869
Land leasing and ownership	10,563,362	1,363,654	7,890,601	13,236,123
Licenses, stamps, tags, and permits	1,614,937	83,880	1,450,533	1,779,341
Fishing Expenditures				
Total	**41,788,936**	**2,152,483**	**37,570,069**	**46,007,803**
Trip-related, total	21,789,465	1,130,303	19,574,071	24,004,859
Food and lodging	7,711,318	415,250	6,897,427	8,525,209
Transportation	6,261,536	335,609	5,603,743	6,919,329
Other trip costs	7,816,610	421,072	6,991,309	8,641,911
Equipment, total	15,506,433	811,537	13,915,821	17,097,045
Fishing	6,141,895	346,725	5,462,314	6,821,476
Auxiliary	1,106,865	115,939	879,625	1,334,105
Special	8,257,673	1,196,090	5,913,337	10,602,009
Other, total	4,493,037	249,307	4,004,395	4,981,679
Magazines, books, DVDs	108,308	12,923	82,978	133,638
Membership dues and contributions	321,990	51,720	220,619	423,361
Land leasing and ownership	3,434,097	771,086	1,922,768	4,945,426
Licenses, stamps, tags, and permits	628,642	33,876	562,245	695,039
Hunting Expenditures				
Total	**33,702,017**	**2,434,362**	**28,930,668**	**38,473,366**
Trip-related, total	10,427,189	777,308	8,903,666	11,950,712
Food and lodging	3,881,304	300,335	3,292,647	4,469,961
Transportation	4,767,915	361,834	4,058,720	5,477,110
Other trip costs	1,771,970	212,437	1,355,593	2,188,347
Equipment, total	13,972,490	948,614	12,113,206	15,831,774
Hunting	7,738,324	602,758	6,556,919	8,919,729
Auxiliary	1,844,880	185,407	1,481,483	2,208,277
Special	4,389,286	1,195,275	2,046,546	6,732,026
Other, total	9,308,340	613,476	8,105,927	10,510,753
Magazines, books, DVDs	107,272	13,470	80,871	133,673
Membership dues and contributions	382,817	57,968	269,199	496,435
Land leasing and ownership	7,129,265	1,039,867	5,091,126	9,167,404
Licenses, stamps, tags, and permits	986,385	71,671	845,910	1,126,860

Table D–4. Approximate Standard Errors and 95-Percent Confidence Intervals for Selected Wildlife-Watching Estimates: 2011

Participants and expenditures	Estimate	Standard error	Lower 95 percent	Upper 95 percent
WILDLIFE–WATCHING PARTICIPANTS (thousands)				
Total	**71,776**	**1,196**	**69,431**	**74,121**
Away from home	22,496	762	21,003	23,989
Observe wildlife	19,808	719	18,398	21,218
Photograph wildlife	12,354	578	11,222	13,486
Feed wildlife	5,399	388	4,639	6,159
Around the home	68,598	1,180	66,284	70,912
Observe wildlife	45,046	1,020	43,046	47,046
Photograph wildlife	25,370	804	23,795	26,945
Feed wildlife	52,817	1,083	50,695	54,939
Visit public parks or natural areas	12,311	577	11,181	13,441
Maintain plantings or natural areas	13,399	600	12,223	14,575
DAYS OF PARTICIPATION IN AWAY-FROM-HOME ACTIVITIES (thousands)				
Total	**335,625**	**28,425**	**279,911**	**391,339**
Observe wildlife	268,798	24,209	221,349	316,247
Photograph wildlife	110,459	13,146	84,693	136,225
Feed wildlife	59,255	9,604	40,432	78,078
Average Days of Participation in Away-From-Home Activities				
Total	**14.9**	**0.98**	**13.0**	**16.8**
Observe wildlife	13 6	0 95	11 7	15 4
Photograph wildlife	8 9	0 83	7 3	10 6
Feed wildlife	11 0	1 35	8 3	13 6
EXPENDITURES (thousands)				
Total	**54,890,272**	**3,146,979**	**48,722,193**	**61,058,351**
Trip–related, total	17,274,675	1,431,121	14,469,677	20,079,673
Food and lodging	9,349,439	822,822	7,736,707	10,962,171
Transportation	6,006,860	505,292	5,016,488	6,997,232
Other trip costs	1,918,376	214,540	1,497,879	2,338,873
Equipment and other, total	37,615,597	2,194,526	33,314,326	41,916,868
Equipment, total	27,150,921	1,544,420	24,123,857	30,177,985
Wildlife watching equipment	11,323,179	671,280	10,007,471	12,638,887
Auxiliary equipment	1,555,374	207,202	1,149,258	1,961,490
Special equipment	14,272,368	3,249,460	7,903,427	20,641,309
Other, total	10,464,677	739,717	9,014,832	11,914,522
Magazines, books, DVDs	420,395	43,842	334,465	506,325
Membership dues and contributions	2,163,568	227,318	1,718,024	2,609,112
Land leasing and ownership	5,676,794	1,723,393	2,298,943	9,054,645
Plantings	2,203,920	254,626	1,704,853	2,702,987

Table D–5. Approximate Standard Errors and 95-Percent Confidence Interval for Participants in Wildlife-Related Recreation by Participant's State of Residence: 2011

(Numbers in thousands)

Participant's state of residence	Total participants	Standard error	Lower 95 percent	Upper 95 percent
United States, total	**90,108**	**1,310**	**87,541**	**92,675**
Alabama	1,490	174	1,149	1,831
Alaska	337	23	292	382
Arizona	1,660	113	1,438	1,882
Arkansas	1,119	91	941	1,297
California	7,360	378	6,620	8,100
Colorado	1,854	118	1,622	2,086
Connecticut	1,204	73	1,062	1,346
Delaware	260	18	225	295
Florida	4,652	274	4,115	5,189
Georgia	2,752	310	2,145	3,359
Hawaii	222	18	188	256
Idaho	638	68	505	771
Illinois	3,493	226	3,050	3,936
Indiana	2,131	204	1,732	2,530
Iowa	1,097	73	954	1,240
Kansas	1,011	69	875	1,147
Kentucky	1,470	130	1,216	1,724
Louisiana	1,380	164	1,059	1,701
Maine	520	45	431	609
Maryland	1,396	93	1,213	1,579
Massachusetts	1,779	106	1,571	1,987
Michigan	3,709	245	3,228	4,190
Minnesota	2,107	186	1,742	2,472
Mississippi	1,017	101	819	1,215
Missouri	2,105	135	1,841	2,369
Montana	334	31	272	396
Nebraska	499	42	416	582
Nevada	594	58	481	707
New Hampshire	470	30	412	528
New Jersey	2,057	113	1,835	2,279
New Mexico	592	53	487	697
New York	5,143	390	4,378	5,908
North Carolina	2,717	223	2,280	3,154
North Dakota	(NA)	(NA)	(NA)	(NA)
Ohio	4,078	261	3,567	4,589
Oklahoma	1,549	119	1,317	1,781
Oregon	1,396	106	1,187	1,605
Pennsylvania	4,063	348	3,381	4,745
Rhode Island	309	18	274	344
South Carolina	1,299	123	1,059	1,539
South Dakota	371	43	287	455
Tennessee	2,121	162	1,803	2,439
Texas	5,888	404	5,097	6,679
Utah	784	52	682	886
Vermont	316	22	273	359
Virginia	2,580	161	2,265	2,895
Washington	2,311	156	2,005	2,617
West Virginia	868	95	683	1,053
Wisconsin	2,499	172	2,161	2,837
Wyoming	250	18	215	285

(NA) Not available

Table D–6. Parameters a and b for Calculating Approximate Standard Errors of Sportspersons, Anglers, Hunters, and Wildlife-Watching Participants

(These parameters are to be used only to calculate estimates of standard error s for characteristics developed from the screening sample)

State	6 years old and older		6 to 15 years old only	
	a	b	a	b
United States, total	**–0.000043**	**12,272**	**–0.000387**	**15,783**
Alabama	–0 001517	6,503	–0 009621	5,974
Alaska	–0 001275	795	–0 010120	986
Arizona	–0 000765	4,622	–0 003646	3,484
Arkansas	–0 001766	4,647	–0 014655	5,761
California	–0 000236	7,936	–0 002632	13,492
Colorado	–0 000805	3,719	–0 006685	4,508
Connecticut	–0 000429	1,384	–0 004817	2,149
Delaware	–0 000758	614	–0 009410	1,051
Florida	–0 000354	6,040	–0 004700	10,400
Georgia	–0 000756	6,717	–0 003496	4,981
Hawaii	–0 000603	694	–0 007618	1,184
Idaho	–0 001708	2,389	–0 017208	3,904
Illinois	–0 000633	7,425	–0 005382	9,348
Indiana	–0 000849	4,951	–0 012557	10,925
Iowa	–0 000988	2,714	–0 008723	3,356
Kansas	–0 001014	2,584	–0 009102	3,499
Kentucky	–0 001476	5,802	–0 009316	5,165
Louisiana	–0 000840	3,418	–0 014093	8,744
Maine	–0 001824	2,210	–0 016808	2,441
Maryland	–0 000570	2,976	–0 008290	6,120
Massachusetts	–0 000394	2,406	–0 003000	2,365
Michigan	–0 001153	10,458	–0 009872	12,626
Minnesota	–0 001905	9,166	–0 015878	10,749
Mississippi	–0 001191	3,137	–0 012208	5,053
Missouri	–0 000858	4,672	–0 004859	3,768
Montana	–0 001690	1,418	–0 015626	1,816
Nebraska	–0 001546	2,519	–0 015670	3,805
Nevada	–0 000431	1,029	–0 007455	2,739
New Hampshire	–0 000920	1,125	–0 015100	2,356
New Jersey	–0 000359	2,868	–0 003386	3,831
New Mexico	–0 000706	1,294	–0 006025	1,703
New York	–0 000416	7,444	–0 005818	13,956
North Carolina	–0 000905	7,706	–0 008882	11,091
North Dakota	(NA)	(NA)	(NA)	(NA)
Ohio	–0 000807	8,454	–0 006870	10,159
Oklahoma	–0 001132	3,772	–0 008501	4,297
Oregon	–0 001359	4,806	–0 010991	5,226
Pennsylvania	–0 000593	6,843	–0 005995	9,017
Rhode Island	–0 000308	300	–0 003287	405
South Carolina	–0 000739	3,060	–0 005611	3,303
South Dakota	–0 001620	1,194	–0 034414	3,643
Tennessee	–0 000730	4,204	–0 003532	2,887
Texas	–0 000807	18,178	–0 004712	18,120
Utah	–0 001050	2,638	–0 008515	4,056
Vermont	–0 001401	811	–0 014942	1,003
Virginia	–0 000533	3,805	–0 004771	4,816
Washington	–0 000640	3,938	–0 006644	5,691
West Virginia	–0 001618	2,714	–0 015297	3,266
Wisconsin	–0 002449	12,656	–0 016762	11,855
Wyoming	–0 002057	1,013	–0 029622	2,038

(NA) Not available

Table D–7. Parameters a and b for Calculating Approximate Standard Errors for Levels for the Detailed Sportspersons Sample

State	Sportspersons and anglers 16 years old and older		Hunters 16 years old and older	
	a	b	a	b
United States, total	**–0.000070**	**16,823**	**–0.000066**	**15,798**
Alabama	–0 002013	7,375	–0 001789	6,556
Alaska	–0 003854	2,028	–0 002828	1,488
Arizona	–0 001928	9,801	–0 001483	7,539
Arkansas	–0 006403	14,328	–0 008765	19,615
California	–0 000352	10,066	–0 000199	5,673
Colorado	–0 001432	5,651	–0 000959	3,784
Connecticut	–0 001549	4,309	–0 000814	2,264
Delaware	–0 001485	1,038	–0 000692	484
Florida	–0 000737	10,943	–0 000364	5,407
Georgia	–0 001334	9,948	–0 000897	6,692
Hawaii	–0 001157	1,151	–0 000846	842
Idaho	–0 010247	12,009	–0 004564	5,348
Illinois	–0 001679	16,769	–0 002058	20,557
Indiana	–0 002038	10,118	–0 002294	11,391
Iowa	–0 002068	4,887	–0 002076	4,905
Kansas	–0 002932	6,342	–0 002590	5,602
Kentucky	–0 003245	10,954	–0 002763	9,328
Louisiana	–0 003723	12,838	–0 001421	4,899
Maine	–0 003040	3,241	–0 003340	3,561
Maryland	–0 001084	4,855	–0 000949	4,252
Massachusetts	–0 000437	2,325	–0 000367	1,950
Michigan	–0 002590	20,167	–0 001899	14,792
Minnesota	–0 004611	19,060	–0 001598	6,606
Mississippi	–0 006731	14,944	–0 006339	14,075
Missouri	–0 001315	6,139	–0 001437	6,706
Montana	–0 006507	5,056	–0 005775	4,488
Nebraska	–0 001667	2,313	–0 001801	2,498
Nevada	–0 001056	2,136	–0 001108	2,241
New Hampshire	–0 002879	3,070	–0 000896	956
New Jersey	–0 000704	4,827	–0 000287	1,967
New Mexico	–0 002617	4,059	–0 000648	1,006
New York	–0 001079	16,730	–0 000725	11,247
North Carolina	–0 001281	9,305	–0 001279	9,290
North Dakota	(NA)	(NA)	(NA)	(NA)
Ohio	–0 001605	14,444	–0 001351	12,159
Oklahoma	–0 005114	14,461	–0 002771	7,836
Oregon	–0 002276	6,968	–0 001995	6,108
Pennsylvania	–0 001820	18,266	–0 001269	12,740
Rhode Island	–0 000764	649	–0 000291	247
South Carolina	–0 002655	9,438	–0 001677	5,961
South Dakota	–0 009550	6,028	–0 011761	7,424
Tennessee	–0 002018	9,981	–0 000754	3,728
Texas	–0 001644	30,704	–0 001150	21,490
Utah	–0 001969	4,009	–0 002043	4,159
Vermont	–0 003247	1,662	–0 003046	1,559
Virginia	–0 000965	5,920	–0 001933	11,864
Washington	–0 001320	6,986	–0 000561	2,971
West Virginia	–0 002455	3,594	–0 001928	2,822
Wisconsin	–0 002985	13,311	–0 003141	14,006
Wyoming	–0 004945	2,095	–0 005055	2,141

(NA) Not available

Table D–8. Parameters a, b, and c for Calculating Approximate Standard Errors for Expenditures for the Detailed Sportspersons Sample

State	Sportspersons and anglers 16 years old and older			Hunters 16 years old and older		
	a	b	c	a	b	c
United States, total	**0.001159**	**–575,615**	**45,670**	**0.001923**	**–978,460**	**44,416**
Alabama	0 021918	–163,227	21,197	0 026237	–310,700	20,618
Alaska	0 068721	–3,823	2,765	0 086885	–80,157	2,587
Arizona	0 072204	–64,996	7,713	0 112668	32,711	4,512
Arkansas	0 190512	–51,366	5,554	0 208269	3,305	4,958
California	0 041958	323,332	11,979	0 056429	1,177,647	6,717
Colorado	0 038767	15,704	8,931	0 080446	–49,174	5,370
Connecticut	0 062963	–54,211	6,250	0 156423	–403,680	4,065
Delaware	0 138101	–7,091	1,280	0 206480	–291	823
Florida	0 031125	129,668	13,980	0 044416	–273,423	13,786
Georgia	0 133758	–35,054	10,761	0 180457	–30,025	9,196
Hawaii	0 099271	–1,810	905	0 154210	–1,865	677
Idaho	0 197816	–5,230	3,806	0 216778	170,971	2,339
Illinois	0 016086	–95,430	23,661	0 059422	–369,151	14,496
Indiana	0 084408	56,304	7,293	0 113115	42,035	5,378
Iowa	0 110741	–6,756	5,107	0 110417	–42,038	6,849
Kansas	0 119262	–8,287	3,770	0 130458	–38,144	4,212
Kentucky	0 032291	–262,907	19,693	0 050336	–549,944	21,014
Louisiana	0 125543	72,794	4,657	0 123353	–129,712	6,086
Maine	0 073133	–64,912	4,685	0 133009	–24,957	2,602
Maryland	0 069557	–8,036	7,163	0 119862	–92,688	6,155
Massachusetts	0 041124	13,503	3,733	0 092555	–231	2,727
Michigan	0 071988	–130,103	28,404	0 026267	–153,883	33,794
Minnesota	0 056048	–43,079	17,112	0 064508	–189,054	15,975
Mississippi	0 143495	–50,131	8,984	0 146486	14,053	8,097
Missouri	0 027623	–7,268	10,503	0 066759	–24,068	8,944
Montana	0 178611	–16,817	2,622	0 105263	–209,610	3,801
Nebraska	0 100459	–1,618	2,551	0 119872	–19,296	2,785
Nevada	0 040428	–34,210	2,962	0 141457	–114,260	1,968
New Hampshire	0 127497	6,106	2,383	0 176749	14,447	1,443
New Jersey	0 027546	11,544	6,195	0 036515	–45,032	6,045
New Mexico	0 036052	–17,835	4,123	0 147509	–35,750	2,313
New York	0 152342	–343,859	17,854	0 209665	–176,671	10,911
North Carolina	0 029116	–209,241	18,945	0 064157	–163,564	13,190
North Dakota	(NA)	(NA)	(NA)	(NA)	(NA)	(NA)
Ohio	0 128010	–37,131	20,232	0 216544	–1,019,186	18,675
Oklahoma	0 098427	–170,608	14,307	0 276027	126,332	2,101
Oregon	0 010568	7,416	9,002	0 011236	96,792	7,900
Pennsylvania	0 039841	–43,889	24,057	0 037830	–316,859	27,692
Rhode Island	0 077596	–203 9579	657	0 110230	–39,344	696
South Carolina	0 180012	–120,717	6,857	0 181351	–87,421	5,445
South Dakota	0 114248	–43,160	4,683	0 102506	–203,831	6,355
Tennessee	0 051884	–61,213	15,306	0 073335	–522,076	17,760
Texas	0 049244	–64,415	42,177	0 077228	–819,919	50,873
Utah	0 063366	–20,537	4,266	0 066238	–2,994	4,293
Vermont	0 271264	–10,725	1,629	0 339375	–128,675	1,810
Virginia	0 034590	–93,405	11,648	0 037134	–222,277	13,083
Washington	0 067952	22,119	7,169	0 080042	–119,224	6,687
West Virginia	0 173583	–44,746	4,014	0 117366	–52,107	4,868
Wisconsin	0 045614	–215,022	29,192	0 057107	164,685	22,483
Wyoming	0 037366	–31,308	2,986	0 032006	–10,196	3,038

(NA) Not available

Table D–9. Parameters a, b, and c for Calculating Approximate Standard Errors for Days or Trips for the Detailed Sportspersons Sample

State	Sportspersons and anglers 16 years old and older			Hunters 16 years old and older		
	a	b	c	a	b	c
United States, total	**0.000068**	**−160,414**	**51,951**	**−0.000284**	**−127,863**	**46,699**
Alabama	−0 006409	−33,141	16,434	−0 001309	−24,163	13,815
Alaska	0 040044	−1,378	2,306	0 014819	−3,686	3,262
Arizona	0 010858	−12,760	16,639	0 094988	−10,415	13,604
Arkansas	0 029081	−47,335	22,178	−0 069327	−298,461	51,645
California	0 018455	62,656	11,126	0 002617	35,822	14,331
Colorado	0 012264	−4,831	7,675	0 057492	−4,094	6,123
Connecticut	0 010321	−20,427	7,687	0 178663	1,319	1,609
Delaware	0 202009	−718	940	0 322859	−120	316
Florida	0 030335	−13,138	12,228	0 050279	−17,145	11,045
Georgia	−0 016400	−22,749	29,830	0 034924	−19,534	26,050
Hawaii	0 011790	−1,565	1,950	0 134936	−560	912
Idaho	0 044270	113	10,482	0 221214	−2,323	5,468
Illinois	−0 005565	−7,990	21,553	−0 015684	−60,913	34,960
Indiana	0 079426	−2,044	8,077	0 088709	7,770	5,819
Iowa	0 012302	−22,937	13,314	0 074986	−46,595	14,146
Kansas	0 061820	−2,259	4,674	0 158439	10,639	277
Kentucky	0 023655	−6,641	17,832	0 015712	−15,751	21,050
Louisiana	0 105459	53,216	2,251	0 124945	55,464	167
Maine	0 026901	−3,659	4,612	−0 011197	−41,449	8,337
Maryland	0 023534	−8,872	6,975	0 039987	−4,806	5,572
Massachusetts	0 032450	−2,312	3,371	0 038816	−2,548	3,080
Michigan	0 006455	−21,327	31,990	−0 023017	−23,908	33,169
Minnesota	0 000310	−20,823	26,365	0 008351	−106,597	30,823
Mississippi	0 001714	−39,317	19,444	0 020445	−27,887	17,239
Missouri	0 004697	−8,884	10,776	−0 002402	9,637	8,938
Montana	0 055324	−1,581	4,356	−0 059715	−48,367	13,442
Nebraska	0 037329	−2,510	3,593	0 034127	−72	2,640
Nevada	0 005007	−8,090	4,055	0 008052	600	2,787
New Hampshire	0 112057	177	1,530	0 259509	1,299	402
New Jersey	0 030384	−392	4,901	0 103886	9	2,432
New Mexico	−0 011244	−8,297	9,568	0 230217	−2,553	3,300
New York	0 046461	−16,384	18,549	0 060195	14,380	6,931
North Carolina	0 013151	−7,442	16,655	−0 007341	−5,733	18,773
North Dakota	(NA)	(NA)	(NA)	(NA)	(NA)	(NA)
Ohio	0 008805	44,579	17,178	−0 000533	−55,316	25,603
Oklahoma	0 010053	17,862	15,896	0 135080	27,988	6,568
Oregon	0 017087	−5,837	8,095	0 009877	−8,838	8,179
Pennsylvania	0 050758	−16,535	18,668	0 056836	−15,548	18,131
Rhode Island	0 046582	−1,416	914	0 102558	−994	499
South Carolina	0 039217	−3,630	7,815	0 020949	−8,305	10,720
South Dakota	−0 000329	−9,205	11,194	0 070309	−4,221	7,158
Tennessee	0 084448	−9,998	12,576	0 203468	−3,342	5,689
Texas	0 114686	−85,855	44,518	0 128279	−71,291	38,430
Utah	0 009602	−5,402	7,922	0 007556	−7,585	7,951
Vermont	0 042093	−2,395	2,132	0 067655	−2,349	1,435
Virginia	0 079698	778	4,363	0 112100	9,122	1,340
Washington	0 095993	−3,056	4,652	0 084185	−13,640	6,129
West Virginia	0 042905	−11,238	6,458	0 012519	−13,442	7,608
Wisconsin	0 014256	−12,514	22,081	0 021117	−19,455	18,855
Wyoming	−0 003362	−3,606	4,480	−0 030790	−4,007	4,809

(NA) Not available

Table D–10. Parameters a and b for Calculating Approximate Standard Errors for Levels of Wildlife-Watching Participants for the Detailed Wildlife-Watching Sample

State	Away–from–home participants		Wildlife–watching participants[1]	
	a	b	a	b
United States, total	**–0.000134**	**32,078**	**–0.000119**	**28,477**
Alabama	–0 003523	12,908	–0 009869	36,163
Alaska	–0 004221	2,221	–0 005350	2,815
Arizona	–0 001319	6,703	–0 001925	9,787
Arkansas	–0 003939	8,814	–0 003938	8,814
California	–0 000739	21,116	–0 000937	26,764
Colorado	–0 003019	11,913	–0 003309	13,057
Connecticut	–0 002392	6,653	–0 002609	7,256
Delaware	–0 001438	1,005	–0 002547	1,780
Florida	–0 001411	20,956	–0 001591	23,634
Georgia	–0 003335	24,875	–0 007832	58,421
Hawaii	–0 002051	2,041	–0 001805	1,797
Idaho	–0 007948	9,315	–0 008539	10,006
Illinois	–0 001219	12,172	–0 001994	19,916
Indiana	–0 002020	10,030	–0 006775	33,637
Iowa	–0 003386	8,000	–0 003220	7,607
Kansas	–0 003728	8,064	–0 003222	6,969
Kentucky	–0 002201	7,431	–0 005428	18,327
Louisiana	–0 001619	5,582	–0 009544	32,914
Maine	–0 003739	3,986	–0 006455	6,881
Maryland	–0 000762	3,414	–0 001982	8,879
Massachusetts	–0 001036	5,512	–0 001839	9,783
Michigan	–0 003032	23,610	–0 003331	25,940
Minnesota	–0 005468	22,603	–0 006274	25,934
Mississippi	–0 005131	11,393	–0 005454	12,110
Missouri	–0 002842	13,264	–0 003139	14,653
Montana	–0 004110	3,194	–0 004772	3,708
Nebraska	–0 003608	5,004	–0 004078	5,656
Nevada	–0 005369	10,865	–0 004111	8,319
New Hampshire	–0 002275	2,425	–0 002428	2,589
New Jersey	–0 000795	5,449	–0 001272	8,715
New Mexico	–0 003021	4,686	–0 004748	7,364
New York	–0 002450	37,975	–0 002910	45,114
North Carolina	–0 003857	28,014	–0 004098	29,769
North Dakota	(NA)	(NA)	(NA)	(NA)
Ohio	–0 001006	9,055	–0 003043	27,382
Oklahoma	–0 001850	5,230	–0 005081	14,367
Oregon	–0 002304	7,055	–0 004554	13,942
Pennsylvania	–0 003639	36,519	–0 004874	48,914
Rhode Island	–0 001580	1,340	–0 001829	1,552
South Carolina	–0 004536	16,126	–0 004877	17,337
South Dakota	–0 002833	1,788	–0 013684	8,638
Tennessee	–0 007450	36,840	–0 004097	20,260
Texas	–0 001436	26,817	–0 001909	35,657
Utah	–0 002560	5,211	–0 002329	4,741
Vermont	–0 007044	3,605	–0 006399	3,275
Virginia	–0 002247	13,787	–0 002743	16,828
Washington	–0 004645	24,585	–0 003371	17,846
West Virginia	–0 019113	27,981	–0 015998	23,421
Wisconsin	–0 004020	17,926	–0 005124	22,851
Wyoming	–0 003576	1,515	–0 004694	1,988

(NA) Not available

[1] Use these parameters for total wildlife-watching participants and around-the-home participants

Table D–11. Parameters a, b, and c for Calculating Approximate Standard Errors for Expenditures and Days or Trips for Wildlife-Watching Sample

State	Expenditures			Days or trips		
	a	b	c	a	b	c
United States, total	**0.001308**	**−1,548,024**	**112,362**	**0.002307**	**826,023**	**54,100**
Alabama	0 292431	−9,893	10,505	−0 079778	174,629	61,748
Alaska	0 108738	−34,916	4,682	0 016446	−58,833	12,421
Arizona	0 077675	−4,716	7,536	−0 027772	286,426	30,687
Arkansas	0 313406	−11,247	9,078	0 062790	−194,867	34,370
California	0 048430	−43,155	28,990	0 006079	−38,139	52,624
Colorado	0 124349	−14,729	9,702	0 026976	183,987	10,254
Connecticut	0 007486	−436,089	16,607	−0 024420	125,914	23,606
Delaware	0 061895	−18,947	3,005	−0 074027	13,351	10,785
Florida	0 083730	104,408	21,053	0 007541	−194,343	57,112
Georgia	0 249488	−25,092	26,678	0 050793	−3,332,773	479,805
Hawaii	0 120445	−32,991	1,567	0 083382	−9,149	3,825
Idaho	0 223371	−147,314	10,203	−0 062345	−258,027	89,698
Illinois	0 107605	−13,356	18,919	0 044699	−354,008	68,862
Indiana	0 193872	−322,885	13,396	−0 040883	−166,121	69,136
Iowa	0 021305	94,648	4,636	0 079467	−75,095	20,869
Kansas	0 072491	6,025	5,519	−0 013518	−72,502	27,154
Kentucky	0 157856	−96,510	5,459	0 029898	−95,012	43,749
Louisiana	0 362140	107,638	6,464	0 246426	368,942	−24,469
Maine	0 094142	−35,394	5,069	0 150679	−50,401	9,088
Maryland	0 095353	39,360	3,760	−0 020442	−46,263	37,328
Massachusetts	0 014009	−163,624	14,762	−0 020104	−59,530	32,483
Michigan	0 072396	489	41,625	0 046186	1,002,661	−40,953
Minnesota	0 096860	−27,052	22,699	0 018847	−405,415	80,062
Mississippi	0 040018	23,616	8,811	−0 060202	−43,904	39,904
Missouri	0 077023	−29,229	11,649	0 021741	−290,522	62,546
Montana	0 102248	27,322	3,406	−0 004215	−16,717	12,349
Nebraska	0 250670	−146,886	4,935	0 027770	347,687	3,046
Nevada	0 100312	−90,487	4,723	−0 038534	−44,832	21,999
New Hampshire	0 024368	−13,607	3,264	0 043269	9,164	578
New Jersey	0 089631	−120,587	9,071	−0 020528	−231,435	57,548
New Mexico	0 110251	1,905	3,130	0 021449	197,267	5,813
New York	0 122911	−1,425,885	68,948	0 006340	−44,103	93,311
North Carolina	0 017031	−326,265	56,212	−0 058093	−593,772	133,445
North Dakota	(NA)	(NA)	(NA)	(NA)	(NA)	(NA)
Ohio	0 080684	−39,489	26,461	0 001012	−1,543	45,574
Oklahoma	0 235454	57,625	3,593	0 014729	−152,377	38,659
Oregon	0 099298	−158,238	13,407	0 010117	−157,164	46,869
Pennsylvania	0 084612	−12,972	30,509	−0 007189	−465,695	137,527
Rhode Island	0 097369	−15,709	1,525	−0 006225	65,378	2,641
South Carolina	0 063035	−24,816	15,855	0 022948	−180,925	43,937
South Dakota	0 071413	123,949	5,679	0 089793	−8,087	10,884
Tennessee	0 031635	−32,698	21,276	0 086824	−18,925	12,703
Texas	0 072728	−140,319	44,225	0 058100	−1,079,923	206,159
Utah	0 085970	−75,950	8,631	−0 041299	−141,530	33,231
Vermont	0 038545	−10,496	2,590	−0 014657	6,845	6,875
Virginia	0 077984	46,506	9,684	−0 013749	−12,650	34,877
Washington	0 046435	−44,547	25,839	−0 074088	−88,929	109,017
West Virginia	0 369202	18,732	2,180	0 243904	−8,874	7,939
Wisconsin	0 256246	−223,513	26,643	−0 019357	−228,892	138,515
Wyoming	0 098137	502	2,339	0 039285	−9,043	7,534

(NA) Not available